Mosemans' Illustrated Guide

FOR PURCHASERS OF

Horse Furnishing Goods

Novelties and Stable Appointments

IMPORTED AND DOMESTIC.

WAREROOMS:

126 & 128 Chambers Street,
New York.

**ARCO PUBLISHING, INC.
NEW YORK**

To my father, Bernard Kauffman,
and to my grandfather and great grandfather
for their craftsmanship, knowledge
and dedication to horsemen

First published by C. M. Moseman and Brother, New York City in 1892.
This edition published 1976 by Arco Publishing, Inc.
215 Park Avenue South, New York, NY 10003

Second Printing, 1985

Foreword copyright © 1985, 1976 by Charles F. Kauffman
Introduction copyright © 1985 by James S. Hutchins

Printed in the United States of America

Library of Congress Cataloging in Publication Data

Moseman (C.M.) and Brother.
Moseman's illustrated guide for purchasers of horse fur-
nishing goods, novelties, and stable appointments, imported
and domestic.
Reprint of the 1982 ed. published by Moseman, New
York; with new introd.
1. Horses—Equipment and supplies—Catalogs.
2. Moseman (C.M.) and Brother. I. Title.
SF309.9.M67 1976   636.1′08′3   76-854
ISBN 0-668-06449-8 (Cloth Edition)
ISBN 0-668-06450-1 (Paper Edition)

FOREWORD

LIKE THE TOMBS of the Pharoahs, the attic of the former horse auction gallery which now houses a famous saddlery company in New York City withheld its secrets for many years. The owners decided to celebrate the company's 100th anniversary by exploring the accumulation which had been stored for over fifty years in its huge arched loft. Day after day articles of horse memorabilia would emerge: carriage jacks, a 10-inch draught horse bit, footwarmers for carriages, ancient harness brackets of wood and iron, side saddles and more. The most precious discovery and the "Rosetta Stone" of the collection was the finding in perfect condition of *Moseman's Illustrated Guide for Purchasers of Horse Furnishing Goods, Novelties and Stable Appointments*. Here was the most profusely and copiously illustrated compilation of articles for the horse ever made.

In his superb introduction to this facsimile edition, James S. Hutchins, noted author and historian in the Smithsonian Institution's National Museum of American History, has filled out the flesh and bones of the history of C.M. Moseman & Brother. He points, as well, to the mystery of the missing Moseman price list which had been published periodically to accompany this catalogue. It is his hope and mine that one of our readers will discover a copy.

The original book, which sold for only one dollar, is huge in size, 15 inches x 19 inches, printed on heavy coated stock and bound in vellum. Each of its 3000 illustrations was a hand engraving. No wonder that book repeatedly admonishes the consumer or dealer in harness and saddlery, "Do Not Cut This Book. . . . It will surely serve as a lamp to light the way through the many perplexities which are incidental to the Harness Industry."

Among the oddities catalogued are a parasol driving whip for ladies, a sun bonnet for a horse, Wallace's Most Wonderful Oil ("crooked legs made straight") and such amenities as colored sands for floor monograms and crests, metal bit burnishers, sleighing plumes and chimes and French flowers for horses' heads.

On the final page of this superb work, the Mosemans, who had a worldwide empire (New York, London, Paris, Berlin and Moscow) and who had just produced the most definitive book in their industry, prophetically note "PROGRESS is the watchword of the present era . . . new ideas and new inventions for increasing the speed of the horse and promoting the comfort of the driver are patented daily . . . consequently there will continue to be many useful appliances introduced to the public long after this book has found its place among the lovers of the horse in all parts of the world." Ironically, "progress" transformed the horse's purpose from that of basic transportation to the ever growing love and nostalgic status of the pleasure horse which it currently enjoys. Perhaps Moseman's catalogue will carry us back to that earlier, more elegant era.

CHARLES F. KAUFFMAN

INTRODUCTION

In New York City in 1866, immense quantities of army goods remaining from the Civil War were going for a song at auction. One of the buyers was a canny twenty-nine year old feed store clerk named Charles M. Moseman. In 1868 young Moseman's profits from reselling war surplus enabled him to open, in partnership with his father, William C. Moseman, a feed concern at 89 Avenue D. A year later, while continuing in the feed business, the firm of W. C. & C. M. Moseman ventured into the saddlery and harness business at 148 Chambers Street. In 1871, when Charles persuaded a brother, Edgar W., to join him in the harness business, the feed store was closed up and W. C. & C. M. Moseman gave way to C. M. Moseman & Brother, a firm name destined to survive for forty-four years and to become renowned in the saddlery and harness business.

By the late 1890s, when the catalogue before us appeared (I have not been able to determine the exact date of issue), C. M. Moseman & Brother was thriving, occupying all of a five-story building at 128 Chambers Street, amidst the area west of Broadway where nearly all New York's leading saddlery and harness wholesalers were concentrated. The firm's showrooms were among the largest and handsomest of their sort in the city. Even the basement featured an elegant 110-foot long room where some 275 different styles of harness were displayed. In 1901 the concern opened an uptown store at 571 Fifth Avenue, of which one familiar with such places commented, "There is not a finer nor more swell establishment of the kind in this city or any other."

The general trade of C. M. Moseman & Brother was in the finer grade of goods. Probably few other saddlery and harness houses in the United States offered so varied a line and for such unusual purposes. The concern furnished, for example, a great deal of the fanciful, showy parade harness used by Barnum & Bailey and other circuses. From time to time, as the import and export sides of its business grew, the firm opened branch offices in Paris, Berlin, Moscow, Vienna, and Walsall, England. As a result, while Moseman & Brother could not be called strictly a jobbing house, there were many things that the jobbing trade could not obtain elsewhere on account of this concern being the American agent for such articles.

The flourishing of C. M. Moseman & Brother was, without doubt, largely a product of the business acumen and enterprising spirit of Charles M. Moseman. As characterized by a business associate, "Mr. Moseman was a far-sighted man. Nothing was too large for him to handle. He had the experience of many years trading and the nerve to enter into large transactions if, by so doing, he could control the output of an article." Charles M. Moseman was a firm believer in advertising and was one of the first to have large signs erected along the railroad lines entering New York. After his death in 1907 the concern lost ground steadily and closed its doors in 1915.

To the contemporary trade, *Moseman's Illustrated Guide* was a convenient, highly useful reference tool. As one of his colleagues observed at Moseman's passing: "Who among the jobbers and dealers has not one of the handsome 'Moseman' illustrated catalogues? If anything odd was needed, all one had to do was to turn to it and either order direct or describe it as Moseman's Number so and so." Note that in no instance does the book mention the cost of an article. That was handled in a separate price list, much less expensive to update than a volume such as this.

The crowded pages of this superb catalogue evoke an era that most of us in the late twentieth century can scarcely imagine—an age when life moved at the pace of the horse (wherever the railroad and the steamboat did not run); when a modishly attired horse was thought next in importance to a fashionably dressed person; and when changes of style in equine furnishings were almost as frequent as in women's hats. That long age was drawing to its close even as this fifth edition of "Moseman's book" appeared. A few crude automobiles were already sputtering over the roads, much to the consternation of horses, but not to the great majority of men who dealt in horse goods. To them it was unthinkable that these mechanical monstrosities could be more than a passing fancy, a "rich man's toy."

There was, however, at least one seasoned saddlery and harness merchant with vision enough to grasp something of the portent of the horseless carriage. Sailing for Europe in 1903, Charles M. Moseman did so with four objects in mind. He wished to be named sole American agent for an improved saddle and also for a certain make of horse-measuring cane. He desired to arrange for the manufacture of non-rusting riding and driving bits to be sold under the Moseman name. His other objective? To "gain control of brass clocks for use on automobiles." No wonder Charles M. Moseman was called a far-sighted man.

James S. Hutchins

SHOULD BE CAREFULLY READ.

IN presenting this, the Fifth Edition of our "Illustrated," to the Horse owners of this country and the world at large, we have spared neither expense, time nor trouble to produce a much needed, very useful and unique work—in which we show, by many expensive and truthful drawings, numerous articles used in connection with Horses to develop their speed, to dress for show or comfort, to harness for business or pleasure, or to decorate according to the tastes of their owners or drivers.

We ask a careful and not too hasty an examination of the many illustrations of the various articles of Horse Furnishing Goods herein shown and described, and hope by such inspection both the readers and publishers may be benefited—the readers by finding something that would be useful to them, and the publishers by receiving an order for the same.

In ordering goods at any time, please be careful to give your **name, post office address,** (also Express office), **County** and **State,** in **plain, bold letters,** so that we may make no mistake in shipping. All orders will be filled by us with a desire to please the party ordering, and where goods are not particularly specified, but left partly or fully to our discretion, we will do the best in our judgment to satisfy the purchaser—but would at all times prefer the buyer to state plainly what is wanted.

If you do not buy of us this book will help you to buy of others.

Where goods are sent C. O. D. a deposit of at least $2.00 will be required to assure us that the goods will be taken from the Express office upon arrival.

Reliable parties cannot object to this reasonable request.

CORRESPONDENCE BUREAU.

IF YOU DO BUSINESS IN

Egypt, India, Africa, Turkey, China, Japan, Russia, Prussia, Austria, France, Italy, Spain, Germany, Switzerland, Norway, Sweden, Denmark, Holland, Belgium, England, Ireland, Scotland, Australia, North or South America, the United States, or any other part of the World the sun shines on ; and are

MANUFACTURERS OF HIGH CLASS GOODS,

Which would apply in any way to our line of business, you might do yourself a favor by **communicating with us,** either by mail or personally explaining your line of production, which might lead to business connections that would be to our mutual advantage.

Samples of your production, or circulars refering to them, might be sent us by mail if not too bulky.

Information respecting the introduction to the trade of new goods freely given.

All questions promptly and properly answered so far as we are able.

An invitation is extended to all to visit our place of business when in New York City.

If from a distance, when in this city have your mail sent to our care.

Correspondence Solicited on any Business Subject.

Yours for business,

C. M. MOSEMAN & BROTHER,

Nos. 126 & 128 Chambers Street,

NEW YORK, U. S. A.

STABLE REQUISITES

SECTION.

STABLE REQUISITES.

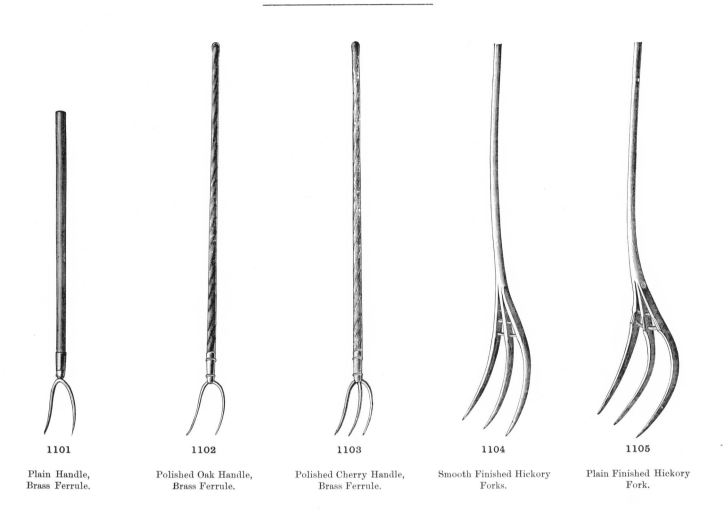

1101	1102	1103	1104	1105
Plain Handle, Brass Ferrule.	Polished Oak Handle, Brass Ferrule.	Polished Cherry Handle, Brass Ferrule.	Smooth Finished Hickory Forks.	Plain Finished Hickory Fork.

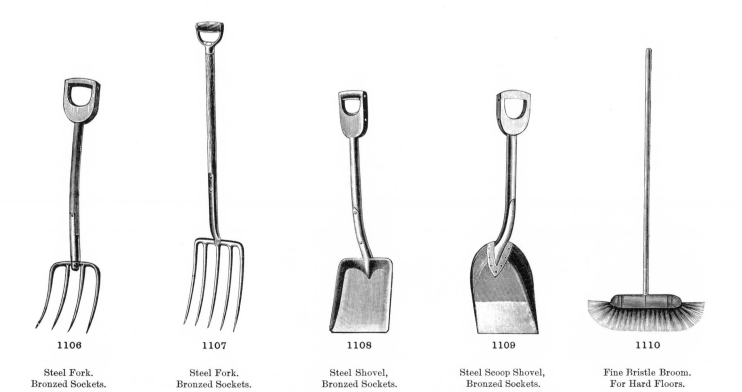

1106	1107	1108	1109	1110
Steel Fork. Bronzed Sockets.	Steel Fork. Bronzed Sockets.	Steel Shovel, Bronzed Sockets.	Steel Scoop Shovel, Bronzed Sockets.	Fine Bristle Broom. For Hard Floors.

Forks and Shovels finished in Brass if desired.

STABLE REQUISITES.

1111

Specially made Corn Broom,
for Carriage House Floors.

1112

Corn and Splint Mixed Broom,
for Stable and Yard.

1113

Strong all Rattan Broom.

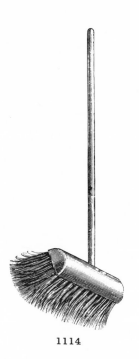

1114

Brown Bass Stable Broom.
Fine and Soft.

1115

Stable Mop.

1116

Rattan Street and Stable Broom.
16 inch Back, 5 Row Splints.

1117

Broom with Scraper
on Back.

1118

Rubber Squegee for Drying
Stable Floor.

1119

Manure Basket,
1 to 2 Bushel.

1120

Manure Basket,
Holding 6 Bushels.

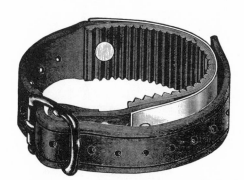

1121

Horse Tail Tie.

1122

Handy Stall Basket, Zinc Lined.

1123

Basket Seive for Cleaning Grain.

STABLE REQUISITES.

1124—Extra Quality Pure White Bristle.

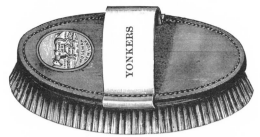

1125—Good Quality Brown Bristles.

1126—Extra Quality Pure Brown Okatka Bristles.

1127—Good Quality Brown Bristles.

1128—Extra Quality Pure Black Bristles.

1129—Old Paint Stubs Mixed.

1130—Extra Quality Pure Grey Bristles.

1131—Fair Quality Mixed Bristles.

1132—Pure Grey Bristles.

1133—Fair Quality Mixed Bristles.

1134—Pure White Bristles, long and soft, for Runners.

1135—Mixture of Bristles and Tampico.

STABLE REQUISITES.

1136—Small Size Root Brush.

1137—Medium Size Root Brush.

1138—Full Size Root Brush.

All High Grade Goods.

1139—Large Size Root Brush.

1140—2 Row Bristle Spoke Brush for Washing Carriage Wheels.

1141—Bristle Mane Brush.

1142—3 Row Bristle Spoke Brush for Washing Carriage Wheels.

1143—Extra Quality Bristle Mane Brush.

1144—Half Round French Bristle Spoke Brush for Washing
Carriage Wheels.

1145—Fine all Bristle Water Brush for Washing
Horses' Hoofs.

1146—Two-thirds Round French Bristle Spoke Brush.

1147—Good Bristle Water Brush for Washing Horses' Hoofs.

STABLE REQUISITES.

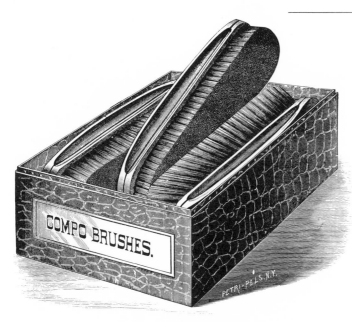

1148—Harness Cleaning Brushes in sets of three, for Cleaning, Blacking and Polishing.

1149—Harness Cleaning Brushes in sets of two, For Cleaning, Blacking and Polishing.

1150—Boot Top Brushes, Hard and Soft, with Square Corners.

1151—Button Brush for Carriage Cushions.

1152—Boot Top Brushes, Hard and Soft, with Round Corners.

1153—High Class, all Black Bristle Cloth Brush.

1154—All Bristle Cloth Cushion and Button Brush.

1155—High Class Cloth Brush.

1156—Glove Brush.

1157—Curved Bristle Cloth Brush.

1158—5 Row Crest or Ornament Brush, Hard and Soft, Oak Finished.

1159—Button Stick on which to Polish Metal Buttons on the Coat.

STABLE REQUISITES.

1160—Feather Duster with 10, 12, 14, 16, 18 and 20 inch Feathers. Turkey or Ostrich.

1161—Window Brush for the Carriage House. With Extension Handle.

1162—Whisk Broom. Specially made for Carriage House purposes.

1163—Long Coarse Bristle Cobweb Brush, for the Carriage House.

THE OLD WAY   THE NEW WAY

1164—Bonner's Horse Cleaner.

Removes Dandruff and Dirt. Leaves the skin soft, white and clean. No Mange. $100 for any case it will not cure.

Keeps the hair fine, soft and silky. Stops all irritation and rubbing. **A preventitive against flies.** Finest mane and tail cleaner in the world; no matting. **A tonic**—keeps skin in healthful condition. Strengthens the muscles. **Aids in shedding.** Sure preventitive against scratches. **Destruction to lice.** Horse cleaned in one-half the time with its use. A well groomed horse requires less feed than the poorly groomed horse. Takes stains out of white horse. Keeps black horse from fading out. By its use your horse will have a coat like velvet. Takes so little to clean a horse, that the expense is but a trifle.

STABLE REQUISITES.

1165—8 Bar Shingle Back Curry Comb.   A good article.

1166—Plain Steel Curry Comb.

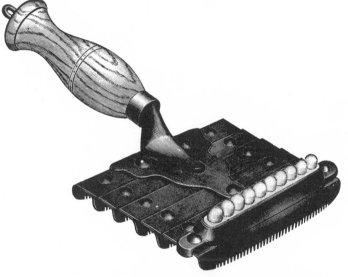

1167—6 Bar Shingle Back Curry Comb with Rubber Hair Shedder.

1168—6 Bar Shingle Back Curry Comb with Mane Comb.

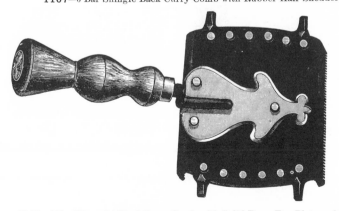

1169—8 Bar Wrought Steel Curry Comb with Solid Brass Top Plate and Rivets.

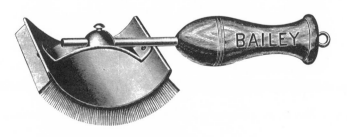

1170—Wire Curry Card, for fine skinned animals.

1171—Fenton's Patent Hair Shedder, for cleaning out loose hair.

1172—Wire Curry Card, for Mane and Tail.   Also good for Cattle.

STABLE REQUISITES.

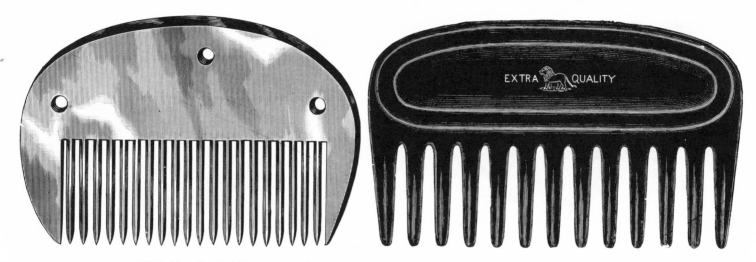

1173—Mane Comb of Horn.   1174—Mane Comb of Rubber.

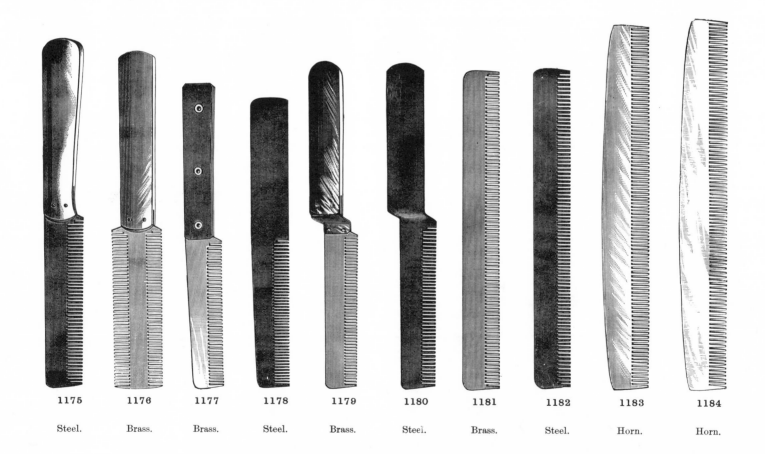

1175	1176	1177	1178	1179	1180	1181	1182	1183	1184
Steel.	Brass.	Brass.	Steel.	Brass.	Steel.	Brass.	Steel.	Horn.	Horn.

1185—Clipping Comb of Rubber.

STABLE REQUISITES.

1186—Large Heavy Shears for Trimming Manes and Tails.
10, 11, 12, 14 and 15 inches long, with Leather Covered Bows.

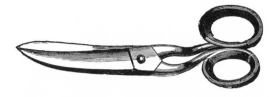

1187—Bent Heel Trimming and Clipping Shears with Leather Covered Bows.
For Trimming Fetlocks, Legs, &c.

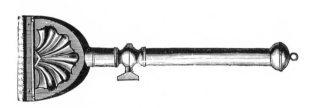

1188—Singeing Lamps of Brass and Copper.
For burning Alcohol or Oil.

1189—Singeing Lamps, Brass Top and Wood Handles, for burning Gas.
Complete with large and small burner.

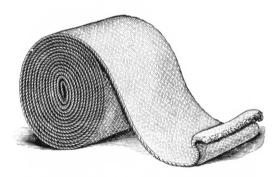

1190—Cotton Wick for use in Oil Singeing Lamps.

1191—Steel Mane Drag with Buckhorn Handle.
For Trimming out the Mane.

1192—Salt Brick and Feeder.   For convenience of the Horse in Stable.

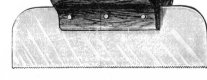

1193—Brass Sweat Scraper.

STABLE REQUISITES.

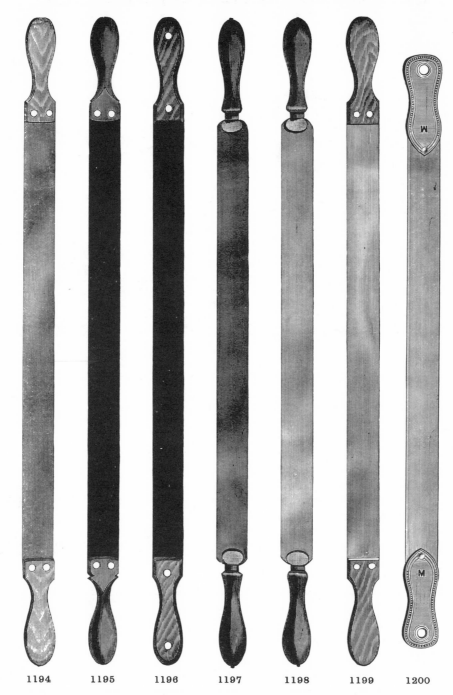

1194   1195   1196   1197   1198   1199   1200

Steel and Brass Sweat Scrapers with Leather and Wooden Handles.

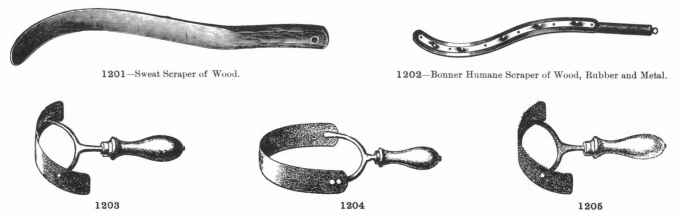

1201—Sweat Scraper of Wood.   1202—Bonner Humane Scraper of Wood, Rubber and Metal.

1203   1204   1205

One Hand Brass Sweat Scrapers.

STABLE REQUISITES.

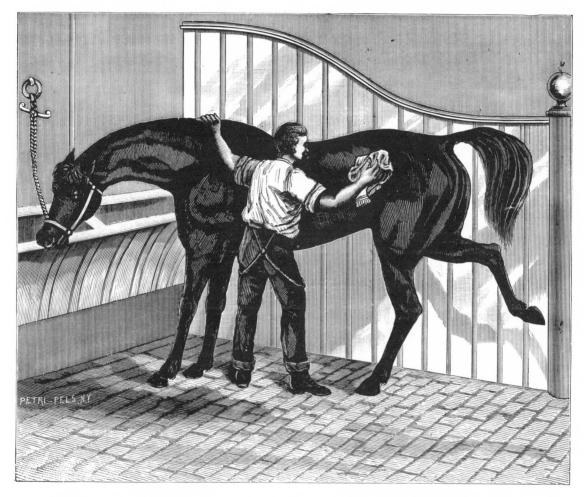

1206

Using the Rubbing Cloth makes the Horse's Coat shine and promotes health.

1207	1208
Linen Stable Rubbers.	Turkish Stable Rubbers.
To be used on the Horse as above.	To be used on the Horse as above.

STABLE REQUISITES.

1209—Moseman's American Jerome Bandages, White or Colored.
Warranted 3 yards long.

1210—Moseman's Red Label American Turf Bandages.
Extra heavy, 5½ inches wide, 2½ yards long.

1211—Rubber Bandage for Veterinary use.

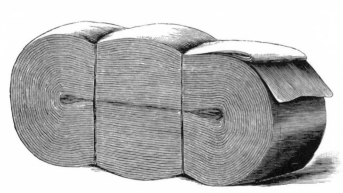

1212—English Bandage Serge, Scarlet, White, Fawn and other colors.

1213—Woolen Bandages made from Serge in Red, White, Blue, Grey and Fawn.

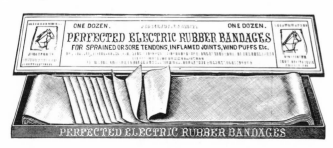

1214

1215—Linen Bandages.

STABLE REQUISITES.

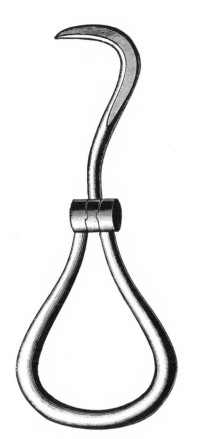

1216—Folding Hoof Pick for the Pocket.

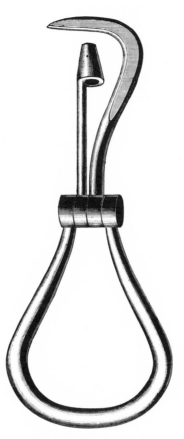

1217—Folding Hoof Pick and Punch.

1218—Folding Hoof Pick, Punch and Cork Screw.

1219—Common Iron Hoof Pick and Hammer.

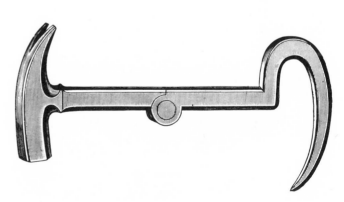

1220—Folding Hoof Pick and Hammer, Nickel-plated.

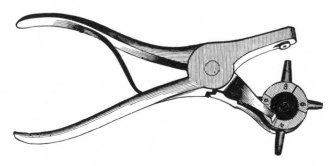

1221—4 Tube Harness Punch.

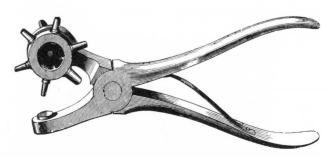

1222—6 Tube Harness Punch.

All different sized holes.

STABLE REQUISITES.

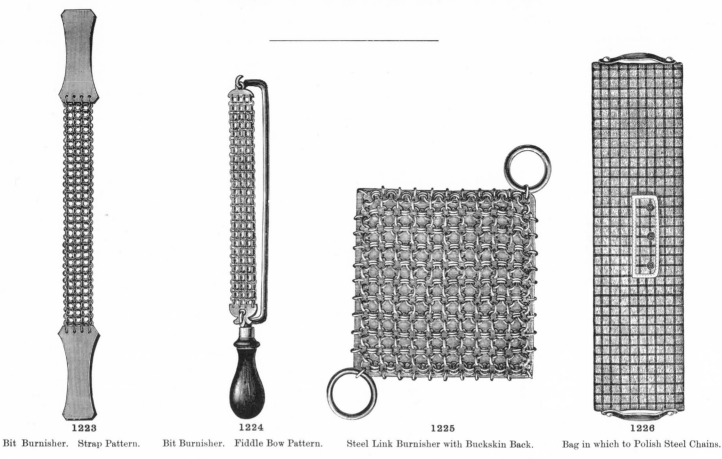

1223	1224	1225	1226
Bit Burnisher. Strap Pattern.	Bit Burnisher. Fiddle Bow Pattern.	Steel Link Burnisher with Buckskin Back.	Bag in which to Polish Steel Chains.

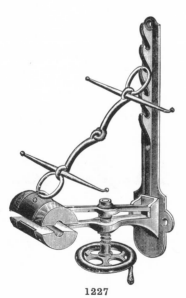

1227

Bit Holder, for Cleaning and Polishing.

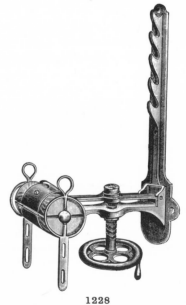

1228

Holder, for Cleaning and Polishing Bit Chains.

1229

Silver Sand, for Polishing Steel Chains and Decorating Floors.

DIFFERENT COLORED SANDS

FOR

FLOOR MONOGRAMS, CRESTS, ETC.

STEEL POLISHING CLOTHS.

STABLE REQUISITES.

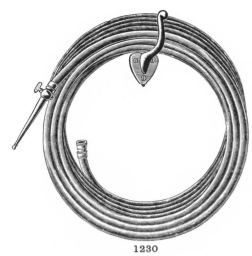

1230
Hose for washing Carriages, etc.

1231
Plain Flush Bottom Cedar or Oak Stable Pail.

1232
Cedar or Oak Flush bottom Soaking Tubs.
Plain, Brass, and other Finishes.

1233
Fine Wire Seives, for Grain.

1234—Rubber Boots for Coachmen and others.

1239—Best Sheepwool Sponges
for all purposes.

PETRI & PELS. N.Y.

1237—Live Chamois.

1240—Fine French and English Chamois Leathers for Washing and Polishing Purposes.

1235—Stable Pails of fine finished Oak, Cherry or other
Woods, Brass Hoops and Handle. On hand and to order.

1236
2, 3, 4 and 8 Quart Measures.

1238
Patent Folding Pails.

1241
Folding Pail, Closed-up.

STABLE REQUISITES.

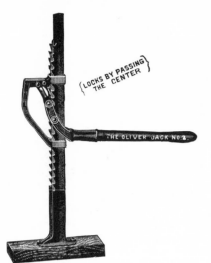

1242
Carriage Jack.

1243
Carriage Jack.

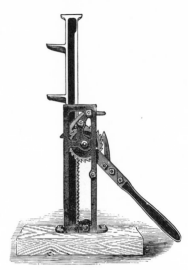

1244
Carriage Jack.

1245
Carriage Jack.

1246
Boston Coach Oil.

1247

1248
Carriage Jack.

1249
Carriage Jack.

1250—Patent Shaft Holder from
Dash to Cross Bar.

1251—Boot Cleaning Rack, for Wall
and for Table.   New way.

1252
Old way.

STABLE REQUISITES.

Stable and Carriage Lamps.

1253—Lamp for Post or Bracket as below.

1254—Candles for Carriage Lamps in sizes to suit all.

1255—Stable Lamp, with Reflector.

1256—Iron Bracket, 14 inches to 20 inches long.

1257

1258—Dash Lamp Holder.

1259—Dietz Tubular Driving Lamp. Japanned No. 0 Burner. For Kerosene.

1260

1261

1262

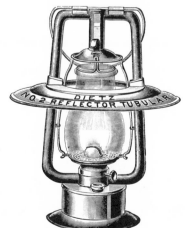

1263

1264

1265

STABLE REQUISITES.

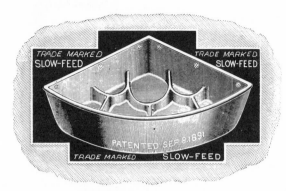

1266—Slow Feed Corner Manger.

1267—Slow Feed Corner Manger.

1268—National Feed Box and Bracket.

Compels slow feeding.   Saves oats.   Prevents waste.   Tempts dainty feeders.
Is portable and easy to carry.   Can be thoroughly cleansed after wet food.

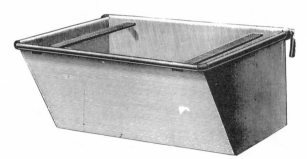

1269—Portable Galvanized Iron Manger.
For use in Racing Stables.

1270—Wooden Harness Pin with Iron Socket.

1271—Portable Telephone.   Can be purchased and put up anywhere
and will carry clear and strong for one mile.

1272—Moseman's Latest Pattern Red Enameled Harness Bracket.

1273—Moseman's Latest Pattern Red Enameled Rein Bracket.

STABLE REQUISITES.

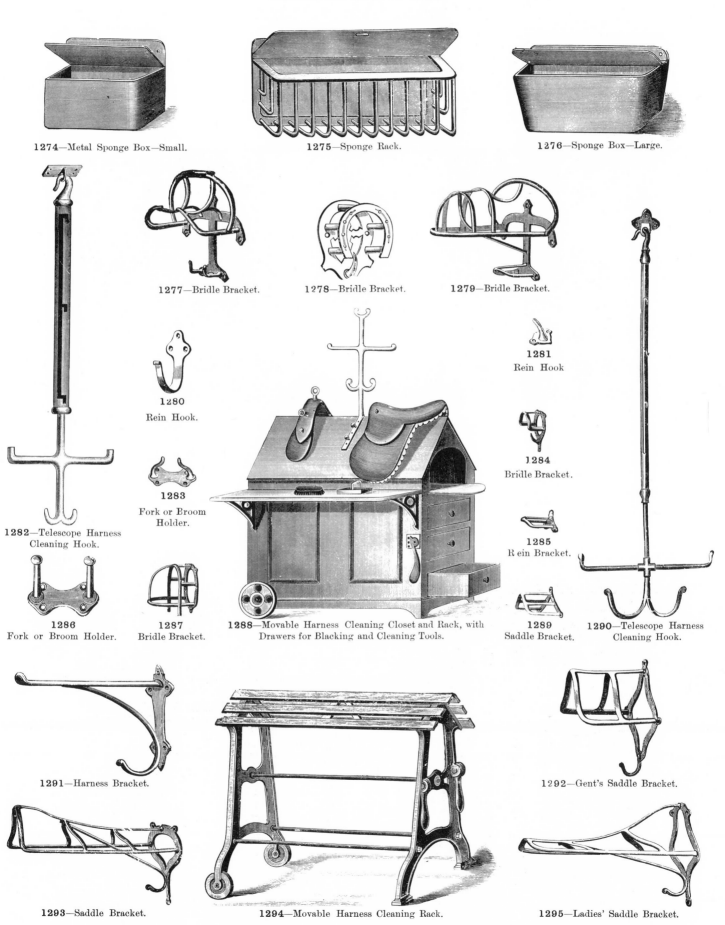

1274—Metal Sponge Box—Small.

1275—Sponge Rack.

1276—Sponge Box—Large.

1277—Bridle Bracket.

1278—Bridle Bracket.

1279—Bridle Bracket.

1280
Rein Hook.

1281
Rein Hook

1282—Telescope Harness
Cleaning Hook.

1283
Fork or Broom
Holder.

1284
Bridle Bracket.

1285
Rein Bracket.

1286
Fork or Broom Holder.

1287
Bridle Bracket.

1288—Movable Harness Cleaning Closet and Rack, with
Drawers for Blacking and Cleaning Tools.

1289
Saddle Bracket.

1290—Telescope Harness
Cleaning Hook.

1291—Harness Bracket.

1292—Gent's Saddle Bracket.

1293—Saddle Bracket.

1294—Movable Harness Cleaning Rack.

1295—Ladies' Saddle Bracket.

These Brackets, Hooks, etc., can be furnished in Plain Black, Galvanized, Enameled in different Colors or of Solid Brass.

STABLE REQUISITES.

1296

1297

Decorating Straw Matting for Floors, Posts and Ceilings.

1298

1299

Showing Section of Mat and Pilican for Stall Post.

Stable Dressings made to order of any Length, Color of Braid and Cord.

STABLE REQUISITES.

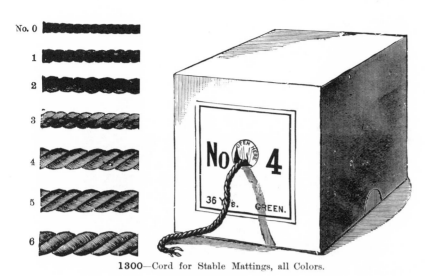

BRAID FOR STABLE MATTINGS,

ALL COLORS.

In Rolls of 18 Yards each.

1300—Cord for Stable Mattings, all Colors.

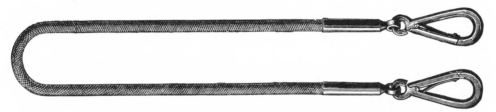

1301—White Whip Cord Pillar Rein, with Brass or Nickel Snaps.

1302—This Cut shows a Stable Partly Dressed, with Braided Straw Matting for Ceilings, Floors and Posts. Matting, Pilicans, Crowns, Rosettes, Flies, etc., furnished to order in Colored Braids to suit all tastes.

STABLE REQUISITES.

Clark's Patent Tail Squarer.   In the act of Squaring Tail.

1304—Showing Horse's Tail Squared.

1303
Tail Squarer.

STABLE REQUISITES.

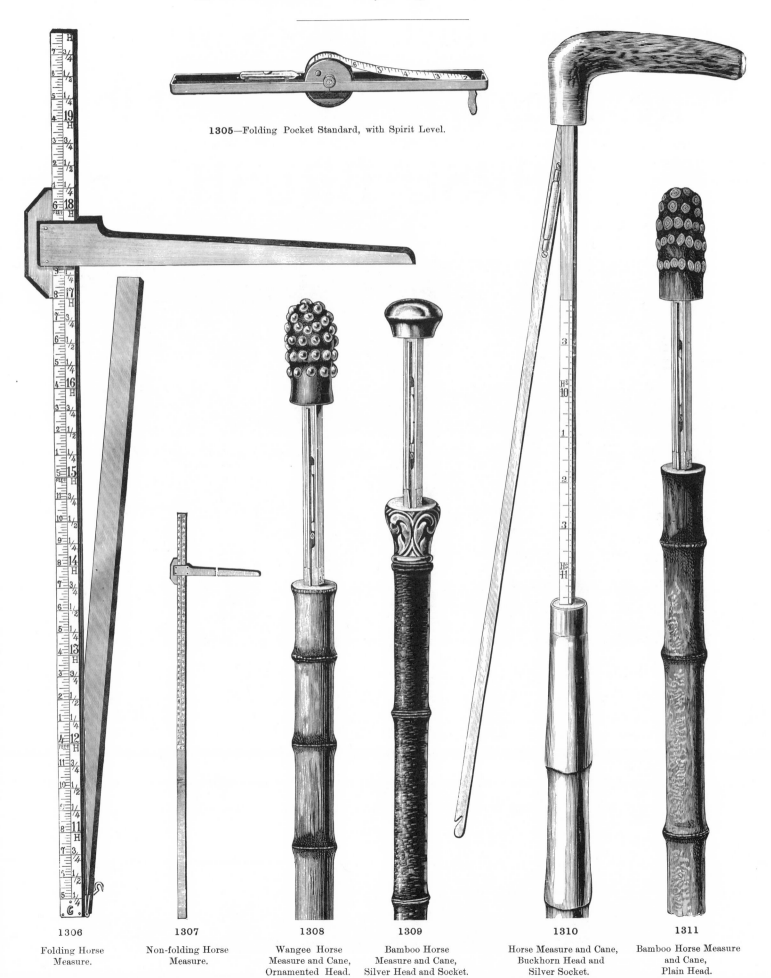

1305—Folding Pocket Standard, with Spirit Level.

1306
Folding Horse Measure.

1307
Non-folding Horse Measure.

1308
Wangee Horse Measure and Cane, Ornamented Head.

1309
Bamboo Horse Measure and Cane, Silver Head and Socket.

1310
Horse Measure and Cane, Buckhorn Head and Silver Socket.

1311
Bamboo Horse Measure and Cane, Plain Head.

 HORSEMEN,

CLEAN YOUR HORSES WITH

The Magoris Cactus Fibre

HORSE BRUSH.

PATENTED.

Made from the fibre of the long leaved Cactus of Yucutan. It lasts longer than your horse. A good rub once or twice a day with the Cactus Fibre Horse Brush stimulates the hair glands and follicles, producing a healthy circulation which results in a fine coated animal in a few weeks.

Fits into, around and upon every surface. The only Brush in the world that can be washed and boiled without harm. It is impossible for your horse to chill if rubbed with the Cactus Fibre Brush.

The Cactus Fibre Brushes are not a new experiment; they are used by some of the best Veterinary Surgeons, Horse Breeders, Trainers and Drivers in the country. If you have the time and inclination to read, we can furnish you with testimonials by the hundreds and thousands.

Halters, Muzzles, Halter Ties and Hitching Weights SECTION.

"DO NOT CUT THIS BOOK."

Every consumer or dealer in Harness and Saddlery, no matter in what part of the world he does business, will promote his own interests by sending us **ONE DOLLAR** and receiving in return a copy of this complete Illustrated Guide Book. It is the key to success in the prosecution of business. He cannot afford to be without the knowledge it contains of every department of the trade. It will surely serve as a lamp to light him through the many perplexities which are incidental to the Harness Industry.

With this Book in your possession you are at liberty to write to us, or to any manufacturer or dealer in Harness or Saddlery Goods with whom you do business, asking questions or sending orders, and either will know just what you want if you will mention "Moseman's Book" and give the "Number" under the article you wish to know about, or mention the picture of the article you may have under consideration at the time.

In any event, **DO NOT CUT THIS BOOK!** but simply give "Number" of the article you wish to obtain.

We are, yours for business,

C. M. MOSEMAN & BROTHER,

126 & 128 Chambers Street,

New York, U. S. A.

HALTERS.

1312—Best quality, Queens Pattern, 1¼ inch Russet Leather, Sewed 3 Rows, with Brass Furniture, White Buff Leather Brow Band.

1313—Best quality, Queens Pattern, 1¼ inch all White Buff Leather, Sewed 3 Rows, with Brass or Nickel Furniture.

1314—Best quality, 1¼ inch Russet Leather, Sewed 3 Rows, Buckles both side of Head, White Buff Front, Brass Furniture.

1315—Best quality, 1¼ inch Russet Leather, Sewed 3 Rows, Buckles both side of Head and Throat, Brass Furniture.

1316—Best quality, 1¼ inch White Buff Leather, Sewed 3 Rows, Buckle one side of Head, Brass or Nickel Furniture.

1317—Extra quality, ¾ and ⅞ inch Raised Beaded Centres of Colored or Plain Leather, Silver Furniture Specially made, Buckles both side of Head and Throat.

Several Styles of these fine Halters always in Stock. Exhibition Halters made to order.

HALTERS.

1318—White Buff, Queens Pattern, 3 Row, 1¼ inch Round Throat Halter, with Brass Furniture. Showing Portable Head Protector. To be used in Shipping Horses.

1319—Neat, Light Leather Box Stall Halter, with Leather Tie.

1320—New Style, Extra Chin Brace, Full Lined and Stitched, Round Throat Halter, with Brass Buckles each side of Head and Loose Chin Strap to take up.

1321—Plain Lined Cheek, Round Throat, Russet Leather Halter, Tinned Furniture.

1322—Plain Single Strap Colt Halter.

Several Sizes.

1323—6 Ring Halter, Strong and Heavy, in any quality.

1324—Plain Strap, Flat Throat, Russet or Black Leather Halter, with Rope Tie.

1325—Caveson Head Halter, with Double Chin Strap.

1326—Caveson Head Halter, with Single Chin Strap and Stitched Nose Band.

HALTERS.

1327—Tubular Web, with Colored Leather Nose and Brow Band, Russet Leather Throat and Chin Strap, Leather Tie.

Good Exhibition Pattern.

An assortment of colors kept in stock or made to order.

1328—Fine Light Linen Tubular Web, with Leather Tie.

1329—Cotton Tubular Web, in Red, Blue, Fawn and White, best Russet Leather Fittings, Well and Neatly Made.

1330—Heavy Corded Cotton Web, finished in a Plain and Strong Manner.

1331—Cotton Tubular Web, with or without Brow Band, finished in a Plain Manner.

1332—Cotton Tubular Web, in Fancy Colors, with or without Brow Band, finished in a Plain Manner.

HALTERS.

1333—Heavy Strong Adjustable Corded Web Halter.

1334—Strong Jute Worked Eye Shipping Halter.

1335—Leather Cow Halter.　On hand or made to order.　For General and Exhibition Purposes.

1336—Best White Jute Worked Eye Shipping Halter,

1337—Bridle Halter and Fine Linen Nose Net for Muzzle Purposes.

MUZZLES.

1338—Slow Feed Muzzle.

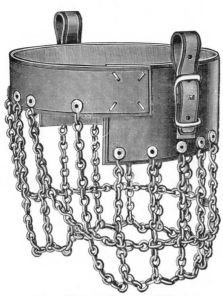

1339—Gillespie's Patent Anti-Blanket Tearing Muzzle.

1340—Nose Net of fine Linen Cord to prevent Pulling. Colors to match Color of Horse.

1341—Sheet Iron Muzzle, Copper Nose.

1342—Wire Muzzle with Stiffening Bars. Wool Skin bound.

1343—Light Wire Muzzle. Wool Skin bound.

1344—Strong Wire Muzzle. Leather bound.

1345—The Gedney Pat. Wire Muzzle. Best quality made.

1346—Solid Leather Box Muzzle, zinc-lined bottom, brow band and loose throat. **Head sewed on Muzzle.**

1347—Solid Leather Box Muzzle, zinc-lined bottom, riveted head and throat.

1348—Patent Detachable Bottom Box Muzzle. Bottom can be taken out to feed horse.

1349—Solid Light Leather Racing Muzzle.

1350—Anti-biting Muzzle.

HALTER TIES AND HITCHING WEIGHTS.

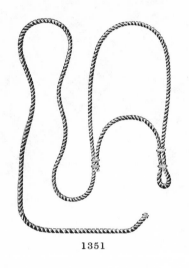

1351

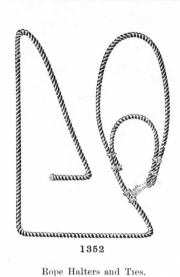

1352

Rope Halters and Ties.

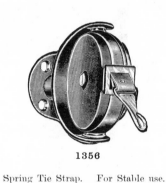

1353

1354

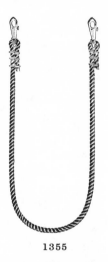

1355

Rope Halters and Ties.

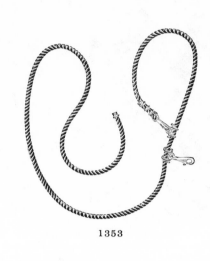

1356

Spring Tie Strap.   For Stable use.

1357—Worthley's Patent Overhead Safety Hitcher, for
Carriage House.   Adjustable for Single or Team use.

1358—Coil Spring Tie.
For Stable use.

1359

Spring Tie Weight.   For Street use.

Russet Leather Halter Ties with Brass Swedged Buckles.

OILS AND DRESSINGS

SECTION.

All Goods shown in this Section furnished at Lowest Wholesale Prices.

"DO NOT CUT THIS BOOK."

Every consumer or dealer in Harness and Saddlery, no matter in what part of the world he does business, will promote his own interests by sending us **ONE DOLLAR** and receiving in return a copy of this complete Illustrated Guide Book. It is the key to success in the prosecution of business. He cannot afford to be without the knowledge it contains of every department of the trade. It will surely serve as a lamp to light him through the many perplexities which are incidental to the Harness Industry.

With this Book in your possession you are at liberty to write to us, or to any manufacturer or dealer in Harness or Saddlery Goods with whom you do business, asking questions or sending orders, and either will know just what you want if you will mention "MOSEMAN'S BOOK" and give the "NUMBER" under the article you wish to know about, or mention the picture of the article you may have under consideration at the time.

In any event, **DO NOT CUT THIS BOOK!** but simply give "Number" of the article you wish to obtain.

We are, yours for business,

C. M. MOSEMAN & BROTHER,

126 & 128 CHAMBERS STREET,

NEW YORK, U. S. A.

OILS AND DRESSINGS.

1360

1361

1362

1363

1364

1365

1366

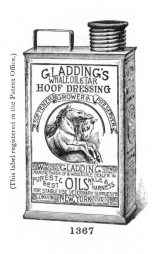

1367

1368

1369

1370

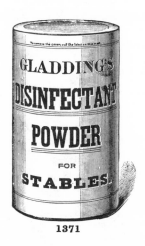

1371

OILS AND DRESSINGS.

FRANK MILLER'S CELEBRATED HARNESS DRESSING.

A superior article for the use of both manufacturer and owner of harness. Unequaled for use in livery, express and private stables. Gives a beautiful jet black finish that does not peel, crack, smut or harden the leather. With it a harness can be dressed as quickly as the sponge can be passed over the surface and in five minutes is ready for use. It is the "Standard of the World."

One Gallon.   Half Gallon.   One Quart.   One Pint.   **1372**

PREPARED HARNESS OIL BLACKING.

For harness that has become hard and dry this preparation is invaluable as it penetrates the leather and keeps it permanently soft and pliable. It adds life to the leather and consequently strength to the harness. "A chain is only as strong as its weakest link" and your harness is only as strong as its weakest part. Buy a good harness and keep it in perfect order.

1373—Half Pint.   One Pint.   One Quart.   Half Gallon.   One Gallon.

AXLE OIL.

Superior to Castor Oil. Wears longer and will not gum. Gives perfect satisfaction and works equally well in either warm or cold climate.

One Gallon.   Half Gallon.   One Quart.   One Pint.   **1374**

HARNESS SOAP.

Unrivalled for cleaning, softening and blacking harness, carriage tops, etc., imparting a beautiful finish, which will not soil the hands or gloves. Made under an improved patent process This Soap is absolutely pure; consequently free from rosin and an excess of alkali.

1375—2½ lbs.   **1376**—¾ lb.

1377

1380

1378

1379

1381

OILS AND DRESSINGS.

1382—Pint Jar.

1383

1384—Quart Jar.

1385—Imported Pure Castile
Soap, White and Mottled.

In Cases or Bars.

1386—Imported in Casks containing either 6 dozen Quart or Pint Jars.

1387

1388

1389

OILS AND DRESSINGS.

The Richmond Metal Polish known all over the World by the Familiar Trade Mark as S. P. S.

1390

1391

1392

Liquid Polish, known as S. P. S., for giving a beautiful lustre to any kind of metal.

Glass bottles, put up in 3 sizes, large, medium and small.

1393—Putz Metal Polishing Liquid.
A good Brass Polish, put up in various sizes.

1394—Putz Metal Polishing Paste.
Put up in various sizes.

1395—Electro-Silicon.
A Soft White Powder for Polishing Silver

OILS AND DRESSINGS.

1396   1397   1398   1399

Everett's Brilliant Blacking for plain Leather of any kind.   French Harness Dressing.
Put up in Stone Jars or Bottles.   3 sizes as above.

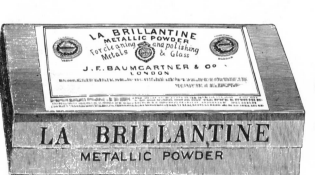

1400—Brilliant Soft Metal Polishing Powder.   1401—La Brillantine.   1402—Brecknell's Saddle Soap.
Square Boxes.   Round Boxes.   For Brown Leather.

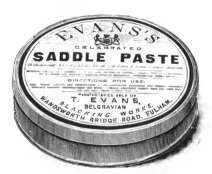

1403   1404   1405—Goddard's Plate Powder.   1406—Evans' Saddle Paste.
For Silver or Brass.   For removing stains on Brown Leather.

OILS AND DRESSINGS.

S. & H. Harris' Preparations.

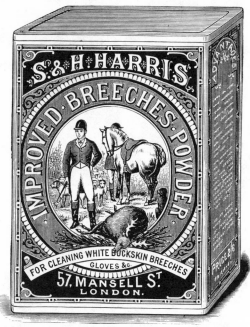

1407

1408

1409

1410

1411

1414

1415

1412

1413

1416

1417

1418

1419

1420

1421

1424

1425

1422

1423

OILS AND DRESSINGS.

E. Brown & Son's Preparations.

1426

1427

1428

1429

1430

1431

1432

1433

1434

OILS AND DRESSINGS.

1435

1436

1437

1438

1439

1440

1441

1442

1443

1444

OILS AND DRESSINGS.

E. Brown & Son's High Class Patent Leather Polish, put up in Stone Bottles of 5 sizes.

1445

1446

1447

1448

E. Brown & Son's Waterproof Varnish in Stone Bottles of 3 sizes.

1449

1450

1451

1452

OILS AND DRESSINGS.

J. Propert's Preparations.

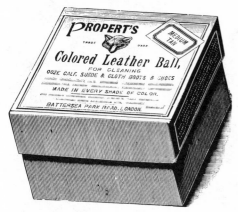

1453—Colored Balls for Cleaning Leather as on Label of Box.

Balls of any color may be had.

1454—Prepared Pipe Clay and Chalk for Cleaning White Cloth.

1455

1456—Pipe Clay for Whitening and Cleaning White Leather Goods.

1457

1458

1459—For Cleaning White Gloves and Breeches, White Horse Collars, Halters and Military Leather.

OILS AND DRESSINGS.

J. Propert's Preparations.

1460

1461

1462

1463

1466

1464

1465

1467

1468

OILS AND DRESSINGS.

J. Propert's Preparations.

1469

1470

1471

1472

1473

1474

1475

1476

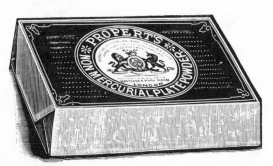

1477

1478

OILS AND DRESSINGS.

J. Propert's Preparations.

1479

1480

1481

1482

1483

1484

1485

1486

1487

OILS AND DRESSINGS.

J. Propert's Preparations.

1488

1489

1490

1491

1492

1493

1494

1495

1496

OILS AND DRESSINGS.

J. Propert's Preparations.

1497

1498

1499

1500

1501

1502

OILS AND DRESSINGS.

Clark's Preparations.

1503

1504

1505

1506

1507

1508

1509

1510

OILS AND DRESSINGS.

Clark's Preparations.

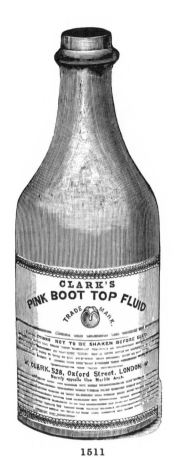

1511

1512

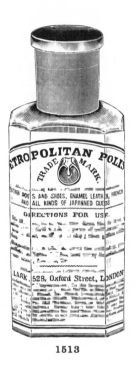

1513

1514

1515

1516

1517

1518

Veterinary Preparations

SECTION.

All Goods shown in this Section furnished at Lowest Wholesale Prices.

"DO NOT CUT THIS BOOK."

Every consumer or dealer in Harness and Saddlery, no matter in what part of the world he does business, will promote his own interests by sending us **ONE DOLLAR** and receiving in return a copy of this complete Illustrated Guide Book. It is the key to success in the prosecution of business. He cannot afford to be without the knowledge it contains of every department of the trade. It will surely serve as a lamp to light him through the many perplexities which are incidental to the Harness Industry.

With this Book in your possession you are at liberty to write to us, or to any manufacturer or dealer in Harness or Saddlery Goods with whom you do business, asking questions or sending orders, and either will know just what you want if you will mention "MOSEMAN's BOOK" and give the "NUMBER" under the article you wish to know about, or mention the picture of the article you may have under consideration at the time.

In any event, **DO NOT CUT THIS BOOK !** but simply give "Number" of the article you wish to obtain.

We are, yours for business,

C. M. MOSEMAN & BROTHER,

126 & 128 CHAMBERS STREET,

NEW YORK, U. S. A.

VETERINARY PREPARATIONS.

Put up by W. Clark.

1519

1520

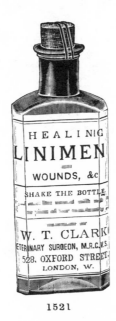

1521

1522

1523

1524

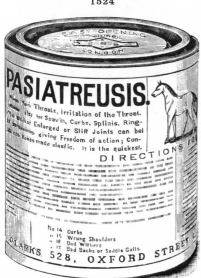

1525

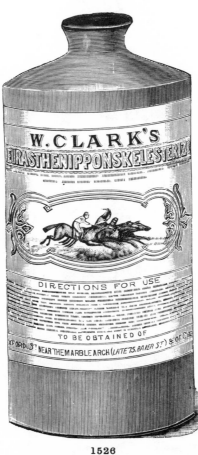

1526

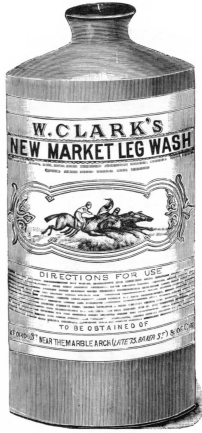

1527

VETERINARY PREPARATIONS.

Put up by W. Clark.

1528

1529

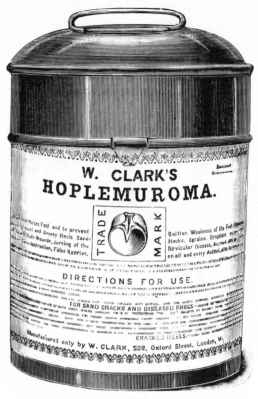

1530

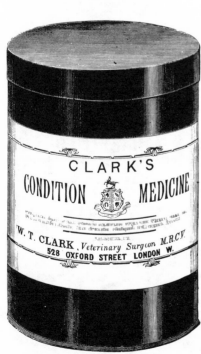

1531

1532

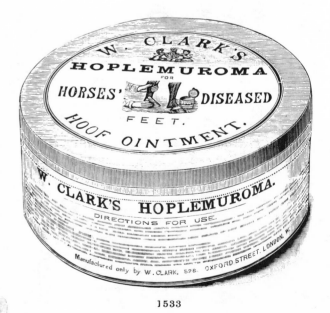

1533

VETERINARY PREPARATIONS.

Prepared by W. T. Clark, London.

Member of the Royal College of Veterinary Surgeons.

CATHARTIC BALLS.

In boxes containing one dozen each, prepared with four, five or six drachms of the principal ingredient, as required.

FEVER BALLS.

In boxes containing one dozen.

COUGH BALLS.

In boxes containing one dozen.

DIURETIC BALLS.

In boxes containing one dozen.

ASTRINGENT BALLS.

For Diarrhœa. In boxes containing one dozen.

CONDITION BALLS.

For loss of condition in Hunters. In packets of one dozen.

ALTERATIVE BALLS.

In boxes containing one dozen.

COLIC DRAUGHTS.

For Flatulent and Spasmodic Colic. In bottles containing six doses.

FEVER DRAUGHTS.

For Shivering, Dullness, Fever, etc. Six doses in in each bottle.

CRACKED HEEL LINIMENT.

For Horses.

HEALING LINIMENT.

For Scratches, Cuts, Wounds, etc.

BLISTERING OINTMENT.

For Splints, Spavins, Ring Bone, etc., etc.

CONDITION MEDICINE.

In 1-lb packets.

ALTERATIVE POWDER.

In 1-lb packets.

FEVER POWDERS.

In packets containing one dozen.

VERMIFUGE PILLS.

For Dogs. Three sizes of pills in each box to suit all Dogs.

LAXATIVE MIXTURE.

For Dogs. A safe experiment.

MANGE OINTMENT.

For Mange and other Skin Diseases in Dogs.

CANKER LINIMENT.

For Canker in the ear of the Dog.

CATHARTIC DRINKS.

For Cattle.

DIARRHOEA MIXTURE.

For Sheep and Calves.

AND EVERY DESCRIPTION OF MEDICINE FOR DOMESTICATED ANIMALS.

W. CLARK'S HOPLEMUROMA.

1534

For the Cure of Horses' Brittle Feet, Shelly Feet, Sand Cracks, Seedy Toes, Diseased Frogs and Quitter in Horses' Feet. For the Cure of Fever in Horses' Feet.

This preparation is invaluable during and after frosty weather, when the horn of the hoof has become broken away by the frequent removal of the shoes. It causes a rapid growth of the horn, and renders it elastic.

VETERINARY PREPARATIONS.

1535

1536—3 lb. Box.   **1537**—10 lb. Pail.   **1538**—20 lb. Pail.   **1539**—50 lb. Tub.

VETERINARY PREPARATIONS.

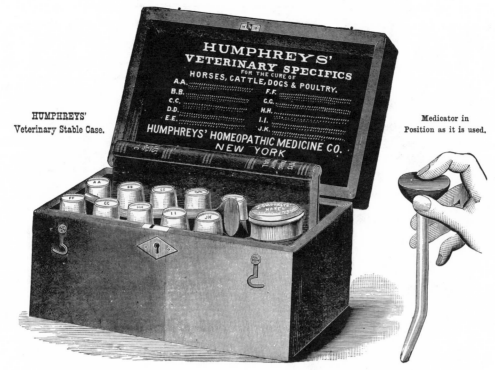

HUMPHREYS'
Veterinary Stable Case.

Medicator in
Position as it is used.

1540

HUMPHREYS' VETERINARY SPECIFICS,

For the Cure of Horses, Cattle, Sheep, Dogs, Hogs and Poultry.

Millions of Dollars' worth of Domestic Animals and Poultry are every year lost or sacrificed, because owners are not acquainted with their diseases, and do no know how to treat them. Yet sick animals, under DR. HUMPHREYS' SPECIFIC SYSTEM, are more readily treated and cured than people. The greatest blessing of modern times for Domestic Animals is their treatment, when sick, by this system. That they are daily so cured in thousands of instances, is as true as that the people ride on railroads, sew with sewing machines, or send messages by telegraph.

A.A.}
CURES} CONGESTIONS, FEVERS, INFLAMMATIONS, Etc.

This Specific is curative for all *Congestions, Inflammations, Fevers* and *febrile conditions;* and hence for all conditions attended with *quick, full and strong pulse, heat or excitement* of the system; and for the coldness, shaking or panting, which precede inflammation.

B.B.}
CURES} STRAINS, LAMENESS, INJURIES, RHEUMATISM.

This Specific is especially curative for all diseases or affections of the *Muscles, Sinews, Tendons and Joints.*

C.C.}
CURES} SORE THROAT, QUINSY, FARCY, NASAL GLEET INFLUENZA, Etc.

This Specific is especially curative for all diseases of the *Mucous Membrane and Glands.*

D.D.}
CURES} BOTS, GRUBS, WORMS.

This Specific is curative for all diseases arising from the various kinds of *Bots, Grubs, or Worms* in animals, as well as the morbid cause which produces them.

E.E.}
CURES} Coughs, Bronchitis, Broken Wind, Inflamed Lungs, Pleuro-Pneumonia.

This Specific is curative for all diseased conditions of the *Air Passages and Lungs,* especially after the more acute symptons have been removed by the Specific *A.A.*

F.F.}
CURES} COLIC, BELLY-ACHE, WIND-BLOWN, DIARRHEA, DYSENTERY.

This Specific is especially curative for the various forms of *Colic or Enteralgia,* and derangements arising from *improper food, deranged digestion or over-feeding.*

G.G.}
CURES} HEMORRHAGE, MISCARRIAGE, IMPERFECT CLEANSING, Etc.

This Specific is more especially curative for all diseases of the reproductive system. Hence *prevents Miscarriage or Abortion and Sterility.*

H.H.}
CURES} URINARY AND KIDNEY DISEASES AND DROPSY.

Especially curative for all diseases of the urinary apparatus, the *Kidneys, Bladder, and Appendages.*

I.I.}
CURES} Eruptions, Ulcers, Mange, Grease, Farcy, Abscesses, Fistulas, Unhealthy Skin.

This Specific is especially curative for all diseases of the *Skin and underlying Tissues,* and for all *Abscesses and Ulcerations,* and the diseased conditions preceding or attending them.

J.K.}
CURES} Bad Condition, Indigestion, Costiveness, Stomach Staggers, Paralysis.

This Specific is especially curative for all *Morbid Conditions or Derangements of the Digestive System,* or diseased conditions of the *cerebro-spinal system* connected therewith.

CASES AND SINGLE BOTTLES.

SINGLE BOTTLES, 50 doses.
SINGLE BOTTLES, Medium Size, four times as much as small bottles.
SINGLE BOTTLES, Large Size, eight times as much as small bottles.
SMALL STABLE CASE, Black Walnut, Handle, Lock and Key, containing Manual (450 pages), ten Bottles Specifics, Jar Veterinary Cure Oil, and Medicator.

MEDIUM STABLE CASE, Black Walnut, Handle, Lock and Key, containing Manual (450 pages), ten medium size Bottles Specifics, Jar Veterinary Cure Oil, and Medicator.
LARGE STABLE CASE, Black Walnut, Handle, Lock and Key, containing Manual (450 pages), ten large size Bottle Specifics, Jar Veterinary Cure Oil, and Medicator.

HUMPHREYS' VETERINARY CURE OIL has now become the STANDARD REMEDY among the thousands of stable and stockmen acquainted with its use. Nothing has ever been produced so simple in application, so promptly and widely and wonderfully curative in its action, as HUMPHREYS' VETERINARY CURE OIL. It has more than justified the highest expectation of its sponsors, and justly stands at the head of ALL CURATIVE APPLICATIONS.

It is the Best possible Application and Cure for;—Injuries from Kick, Nails, Thorns, Spikes, Barbed Wire, Stakes, or any Lacerated, Torn or Cut Wounds; Burns or Scalds; Sores or Indolent Ulcers, Sore, Scabby, Itching Patches or Bare Places on the Skin, Harness, Collar or Saddle Galls or Chafing; Sore Teats; Fistulas or Deep-seated Ulcers; Broken Knees or Open Joints; Old Sores; Horny Places or Warts; Hot Swellings; Boils or Tumors; Scratches, Greased or Cracked Heels; Broken Hoof: Sand or Quarter-Crack; Corns; Tender or Bruised Soles; Dry, Shaly or Ill-Growing Hoofs.

Apply the "CURE OIL" with the end of the finger along the upper edge of the hoof after cleaning at night.

VETERINARY PREPARATIONS.

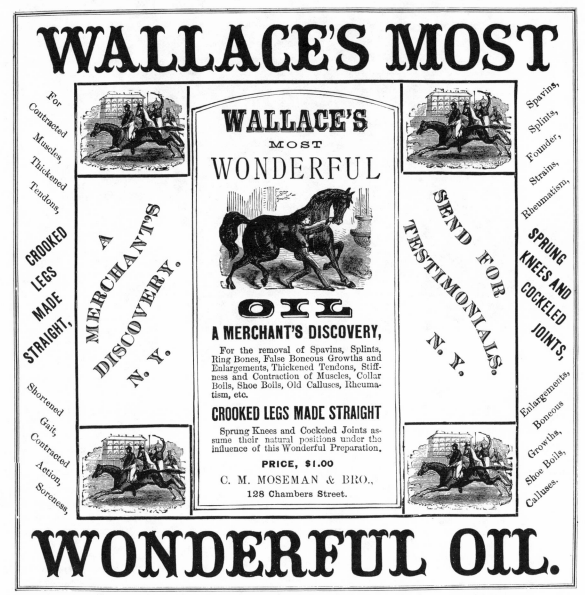

WALLACE'S MOST

For Contracted Muscles, Thickened Tendons, CROOKED LEGS MADE STRAIGHT, Shortened Gait, Contracted Action, Soreness,

A MERCHANT'S DISCOVERY. N.Y.

SEND FOR TESTIMONIALS. N. Y.

Spavins, Splints, Founder, Strains, Rheumatism, SPRUNG KNEES AND COCKELED JOINTS, Enlargements, Boneous Growths, Shoe Boils, Calluses.

WALLACE'S MOST WONDERFUL OIL

A MERCHANT'S DISCOVERY,

For the removal of Spavins, Splints, Ring Bones, False Boneous Growths and Enlargements, Thickened Tendons, Stiffness and Contraction of Muscles, Collar Boils, Shoe Boils, Old Calluses, Rheumatism, etc.

CROOKED LEGS MADE STRAIGHT

Sprung Knees and Cockeled Joints assume their natural positions under the influence of this Wonderful Preparation.

PRICE, $1.00

C. M. MOSEMAN & BRO.,
128 Chambers Street.

WONDERFUL OIL.

1541

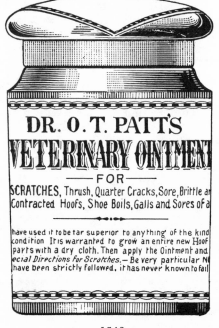

DR. O. T. PATT'S
VETERINARY OINTMENT
— FOR —
SCRATCHES, Thrush, Quarter Cracks, Sore, Brittle and Contracted Hoofs, Shoe Boils, Galls and Sores of all

have used it to be far superior to anything of the kind condition It is warranted to grow an entire new Hoof parts with a dry cloth. Then apply the Ointment and ecial Directions for Scratches.— Be very particular N have been strictly followed, it has never known to fail

1542

ESTABLISHED 1844.
BAKER'S
HOOF LINIMENT
FOR
Quarter or Sand Cracks, Corns, Thru Contracted, Hard and Brittle Hoof, &

MADE ONLY BY
E. F. BAKER
NEW YORK.

1543

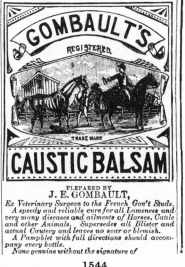

GOMBAULT'S
REGISTERED
TRADE MARK
CAUSTIC BALSAM

PREPARED BY
J. E. GOMBAULT,
Ex Veterinary Surgeon to the French Gov't Studs.
A speedy and reliable cure for all Lameness and very many diseases and ailments of Horses, Cattle and other Animals. Supersedes all Blister and actual Cautery and leaves no scar or blemish.
A Pamphlet with full directions should accompany every bottle.
None genuine without the signature of

1544

VETERINARY PREPARATIONS.

SAVE AND IMPROVE YOUR STOCK BY USING

Recommended by Thousands

Recommended by Thousands

One application will instantly and positively protect your horses and cattle from any annoyance from Flies, Gnats, and Insects of every kind. improves the appearance of the coat.

1545—Put up in quart, one gallon and five gallon cans.

1546

NAVICULINE.—To cure lameness, no matter how caused quicker than any other preparation in the market. It is the most powerful paint that has ever been used for Splints, Spavins, Curbs, Bowed Tendons, Knuckling, Weak Kidneys, Shoulder Lameness, Buckshins, Quittor, Navicular Disease, Sprung Legs, Ringbone, Saddle Galls, Shoe Boils, Farcy, Windgalls, Founder, Scratches, Greased Heels, Overreach, Thoroughpin and all bony enlargements, etc. This paint has been used at Newmarket, England, G. B., with immense success. It penetrates muscle, membrane and tissue to the very bone itself.

1547

I WILL GUARANTEE MY CURINE to be the most powerful paint that medical science can formulate. It will reach deeper seated troubles and produce better effects for lameness and unhealthy sores than any other preparation in the world, for which local medication is indicated, such as Spavins, Curbs, Ringbones, Sprung Knees, Capped Hocks and Knees, Saddle Galls, Rheumatism, shoulder Lameness, Wind Puffs, Navicular Disease, Joint Lameness, Fistulae, Shoe Boils, Quittor, Tumors, Muscle Soreness, Splints, Thoroughpins, Sprung Tendons, Enlarged and Suppurated Glands, Soft Bunches, Bony Growths, Etc., Etc.

W. A. W. TURNBULL, V. M. D.,
Formerly Resident Surgeon in charge of the Veterinary Hospital, University of Pennsylvania.

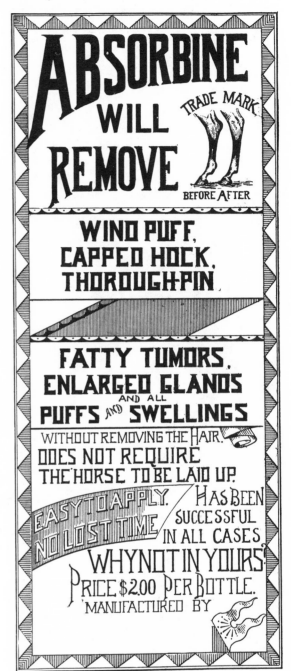

1548

1549

1550—Kitchell's Liniment for Rubbing Down after a race.
Sold in Pint and Quart Bottles.

CALORIC VITA OIL.

The Wonderful California Remedy. Is Indispensable in Racing Stables. Endorsed by the Best Trainers in the Land.

SAN FRANCISCO, March 6, 1893.

DR. B. J. SMITH—Dear Sir: I am pleased to state that I have used your **"Caloric Vita Oil"** for several years past, and have found it a safe and valuable remedy for horses in case of strained muscles and tendons, sore throat and distemper of young stock, and in reducing calloused enlargements; and especially in relieving soreness from a hard or postponed race, and in many other ailments to which the racing-horse is subject. I keep it constantly on hand at my stock farm and training stables in Pleasanton, and through the circuit races at the East; and I feel warranted in saying that I think it a remedy that no one, breeding or handling valuable stock, can afford to dispense with.

Respectfully,
MONROE SALISBURY.

VETERINARY PREPARATIONS.

1551—Drenching Bit, Patented December 20th, 1888.

Showing the Bit taken to pieces for
cleansing purposes.

1552—Horse Cradles, to prevent
tearing blankets, gnawing
blisters, etc.

1553—Horse Medicine Bottle, made of Rubber.

1554—Medicine Horn.

1555—Medicine Horn.

1556—Showing File and manner of fastening.

1557—Stiff.

1558—Jointed.

1559—Old Style.

This is not a *rasp* but a *Smooth File*, and is endorsed by a host of gentlemen of preputation in horse matters.   The advantages of its adjustable feature will at once be seen.   The file is cut on both sides, and held in the holder by a screw, and when one side becomes worn, simply by reversing it you have a new file.   With the instructions which accompany each instrument, any one can use it with perfect success.

VETERINARY PREPARATIONS.

1560—Device for Preventing Horses from Cribbing.
J. Meyer, Patentee.

1561

BE SURE AND WORK THE HORSE.

1562—Bickmore Gall Cure. For Horses and Cattle.

Sure cure for Galls, Scratches, Cuts, Sore Shoulders,
Necks, Backs, Mudscalds, Corns, etc.
Also all Skin Troubles of Horses and Cattle.
It gives immediate relief and quick cure for Sore
Teats on Cows.

1563—Rubber Syringes. All sizes.

1564—Sling to Hoist or Hold up Sick or Lame Horses.

1565—Balling Iron.

1566

1567—One Gallon Can.

1568—Half Gallon Can.

1569—Quart Can.

1570—Oil of Witch Hazel.
Good for all sores.

VETERINARY PREPARATIONS.

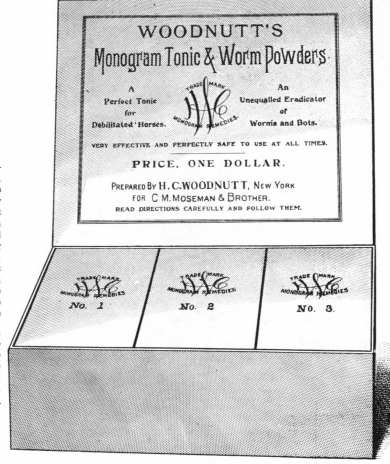

THE WOODNUTT
MONOGRAM REMEDIES

Are put up by one of the most experienced horsemen in the United States, who has used them extensively in his capacity of both breeder and trainer for the past twenty years with the most satisfactory results. They have been on the market several months, and already command a strong lead among the most Valuable Horse Remedies. They are used by all of the prominent Stock Farms in the United States from Vermont to Florida, and are a valuable contingent in the stables of all of the noted Trainers and Drivers, whose testimonials attest their excellence. These Remedies have been adopted by the Fire Department of the City of Brooklyn, the Police Department of the City of New York, and several of the largest Express Companies. All the large Boarding, Sale and Livery establishments both use and recommend them to their patrons.

1571

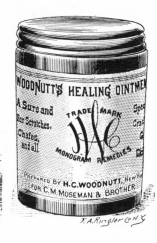

1572

1573

DR. A. H. DIXON'S
ALTERATIVE AND CONDITION POWDERS.

These Powders prove an invaluable remedy in all cases of inflammatory action, Coughs, Colds, Epidemic Influenza, Bronchitis, Pneumonia, Heaves and the like, removing all Urinary Derangements, Œdema, or Swelling of the Legs, Cracked Heels and all Impurities of the Blood. An unfailing Specific for all Diseases of the Skin; they quickly produce a beautiful and blooming coat, and in the first stages of Acute Laminitis or Founder their administration is guaranteed to effect a speedy and lasting cure. They readily correct all Derangements of the Appetite and Digestion, arising either from Overwork, General Debility or Worms; requiring neither change of food nor cessation from work, and showing, both in coat and condition, perfect health restored and preserved.

Recommended by Robert Bonner, Wm. L. Simmons, Edwin Thorne, Chas. Backman, Chas. Marvin, John Splan and others.

1574

1575

HARVELL'S CONDITION POWDER.

1576

THE BEST REMEDY EVER DISCOVERED FOR HORSES AND CATTLE

THESE POWDERS may be given with great advantage in all cases of worms, loss of appetite, roughness of the hair or coat, stoppage of water and bowels, all coughs and colds, inflammation of the lungs and bowels, recent founders, swelling of the glands of the throat, horse distemper, hide bound, botts, scurvy, loss of cud, horn distemper, black tongue, etc., and also will backen the heaves, and in recent cases, effect a cure. In fact, there is no case of disease among Horses and Cattle where these valuable Powders are not called for, and by their timely administration will save the lives of many valuable animals.

VETERINARY PREPARATIONS.

Cope's Condition Balls.
Hopkins' Healing Powder, large.
"   "   "   small.
Going's Tonic Powders.
"   Cough   "
"   Colic   "
"   Worm   "
Continental Hoof Ointment, large.
"   "   "   small.
Hippona Healing Powders, large.
"   "   "   small.
"   "   Salve, large.
"   "   "   small.
Kendall's Spavin Cure.
"   Blister Ointment.
Veazies' Bege Wind Puff Cure.
"   "   Blistering Ointment.
"   "   Condition Powders.
Campbell's Hoof Remedy, 5 gallons.
"   "   "   1   "
"   "   "   ½   "
"   "   "   quarts.
"   Shampoo, quarts.
Kitchell's Liniment, quarts.
"   "   pints.
"   Wind Puff Cure.
"   Spavin Cure.
Tuttle's Elixir.
"   Worm Powders.
"   Hoof Dressing.
Baker's Hoof Liniment, cans.
"   "   "   bottles.
Heard's Hoof Liniment.
"   Condition Powders.
"   Embrocation.
Baum's Condition Powders, 10 lb. pkgs.
"   "   "   2   "   "
"   Hoof Dressing.
Bonner's Horse Cleaner, 1 gallon.
"   "   "   ½   "
"   "   "   quarts.
"   "   "   pints.
"   Barn Dust.
Boyce's Tablets, large.
"   "   small.
Powers' Hoof Dressing.

Dr. Daniels' Hoof Grower.
"   "   Worm Killer.
"   "   Oster Crocus.
"   "   Liniment.
"   "   Wonder Worker.
"   "   Fever Drops.
"   "   Colic Cure.
"   "   Renovator.
"   "   Blister.
Dr. Patt's Veterinary Ointment.
Tough on Flies, 5 gallon cans.
"   "   1   "   "
"   "   ½   "   "
"   "   quart
Tweed's Liniment, small botttles.
"   "   medium   "
"   "   large   "
"   "   1 gallon cans.
"   "   5   "   "
Dr. Turnbull's Curine.
"   "   Procatine.
"   "   Ovarine.
"   "   Hoofine.
"   "   Worm Powders.
"   "   Tonic   "
Cooper's Horse Powders.
"   Worm   "
"   Colic Cure.
"   Stimulating Liniment.
"   Blistering Ointment.
"   Healing Salve.
"   "   Lotion.
Quinn's Ointment.
Dally's Salve.
Gombault's Caustic Balsam.
Dixon's Condition Powders.
Evans' White Liniment.
"   Prussian Febrifuge.
Ellis' Hoof Ointment.
Herrick's Liniment, large.
"   "   small.
Smith's Hoof Liniment.
Eureka Hoof Ointment.
Lathrop's Hoof Ointment.
Scott's Gall Paste.
Bickmore's Gall Cure.

Houghton's Cosmoline.
Goodenough's Salve.
Electric Healing Liniment.
Peabody's Condition Powders.
Cattnacht's   "   "
Clark's   "   "
Harvell's   "   "
Gladdings' Witch Hazel.
O'Shea's Hoof Liniment.
Gladdings' Hoof Dressing.
Scott's Arabian Hoof Paste.
Absorbine.
Naviculine.
Cuticline.
McNally's Liniment.
Parker's Titan Salve.
Perrins' Liniment Leg Wash.
"   Knuckling Liniment.
"   Mange Cure.
"   Spavin   "
"   Tonic.
"   Foot Expander.
Macauley's Lotion.
Bennett's Liniment.
Barry's   "
Martin's   "
McHenry's   "
Cole's Ossidine.
Sparkhall's Specific.
Dr. Fuller's Leg Wash.
Wallace's Wonderful Oil.
Tobias' Liniment.
Newton's Heave Cure.
Marvin's Food.
Peat Moss Hoof Stuffing, boxes.
"   "   "   "   pails.
Brokaw's Remedy, 1 gallon.
"   "   "   ½   "
"   "   "   quarts.
Union Liniment, large.
"   "   small.
Caloric Vita Oil.
Veterinary Hoof Liniment.
"   "   Ointment.
Foote's Invigorating Food.
Searle's Horse and Cattle Powder.

OILS AND DRESSINGS.

Day & Martin's Blacking, large
"   "   "   medium.
"   "   "   small.
Everett's Blacking, large.
"   "   medium.
"   "   small.
Birk's Metalic Lustre.
Pipe Clay.
Blakemore's Brass Polish.
"   Paris Paste.
"   Sponge Composition.
"   Harness Composition.
Hearst's Plate Powder.
Kiley's Harness Composition.
American Soap Polish.
Sullivan's Silver Dawn Polish.
Nubian Harness Composition.
Crystal Patent Leather Polish, large.
"   "   "   "   small.
Electro Silicon.
Prestoline.
Wolfe's Acme Blacking.
Crosby's Axle Oil.
Billing's Harness Dressing.
Frazer's Axle Grease, boxes.
"   "   "   pails.

Synovial Axle Grease.
Prussian Army Oil.
Coachman's Lazy Polish.
Hauthaway's Harness Dressing, gallons.
"   "   "   "   quarts.
"   "   "   "   pints.
"   "   Edge Blacking.
Vacuum Harness Oil, quarts.
"   "   "   pints.
"   "   "   ½ pints.
Borsum's Brilliantine.
"   American Liquid Polish, cans.
"   Pomade, boxes.
Powers' Harness Dressing.
"   Patent Leather Polish.
Miller's Harness Dressing, 5 gallons.
"   "   "   1 gallon.
"   "   "   quarts.
"   "   "   pints.
"   "   Oil, 1 gallon.
"   "   "   quarts.
"   "   "   pints.
"   "   "   ½ pints.
West's Enamel Carriage Top Dressing, 1
"   "   "   "   "   2
"   "   "   "   "   3
"   "   "   "   "   4

Gladding's Castor Oil, in 1 gallon or quarts.
"   Neatsfoot Oil   "   "
"   Sperm   "   "   "
"   Sweet   "   "   "
Lamp Black.
Champion Harness Oil, large.
"   "   "   small.
"   Axle   "
"   Oil Paste, large.
"   "   "   small.
Baum's Axle Oil, quarts.
"   "   "   pints.
"   Harness Oil, quarts.
"   "   "   pints.
"   "   Dressing, quarts.
"   "   "   pints.
Boston Coach Oil, gallons.
"   "   "   quarts.
"   "   "   pints.
Richmond's S. P. S. Polish, large.
"   "   "   "   medium.
"   "   "   "   small.
Brokaw's Leather Renovator, large.
"   "   "   "   medium.
"   "   "   "   small.
James' Harness Composition.

And hundreds of other articles of Home and Foreign make not mentioned here.

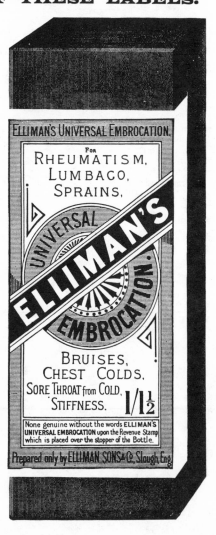
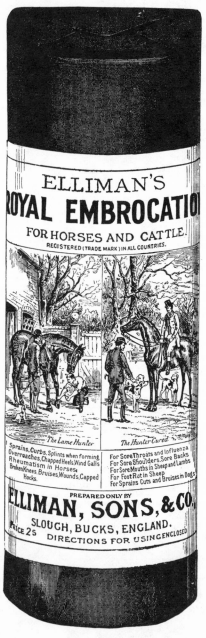

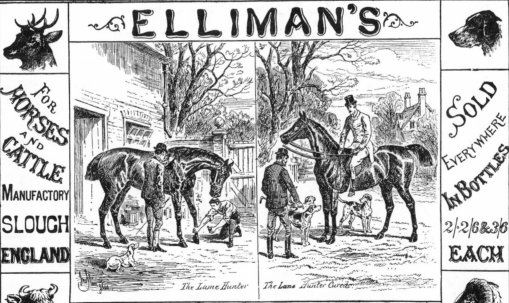

Stallion Shields, Boots, Toe Weights, &c. SECTION.

All Goods shown in this Section furnished at Lowest Wholesale Prices.

STALLION SHIELDS.

1577—Keller's Patent Stallion Shield, with Fine Wire Protection.

1578—Patent Quick Detaching Serving Hopple for Mares, to prevent kicking the Stallion.

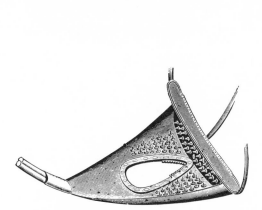

1579—Fenton Shield, detached.

1580—Fenton's Patent Stallion Shield.

1581—Tenny's Patent Stallion Shield.   For yearlings, two and three year old and aged stallions.

1582—Stallion Truss or Support, with Rubber Pouch.

1583—The Mascot Shield of Straps, with Prickers and Lead Weights to hold it in place.

TROTTING APPLIANCES.

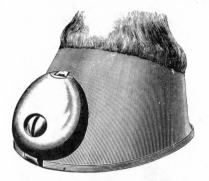

On the foot.

The Chicago Toe Weight.

1584   Off the foot.

Spur to be welded on shoe.

1585—The Hartford Toe Weight. Interchangeable Weights
can be made into 2, 3 and 4 ounce, with one set of Clips.

On the foot.

Security Toe Weight.

1586   Off the foot.

Spur to be screwed on foot.

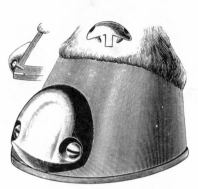

1587

Stick Fast Toe Weight, to be screwed on foot.

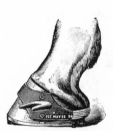

1588—The Temple Patent Two Prong Boot.

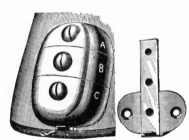

1589—The New York Toe Weight. Interchangeable, making any weight required.

1590—Leather Pocket Toe Weight, showing the sheets of Lead out of Pocket.

1591—Leather Pocket Toe Weight, ready for use.

HORSE BOOTS.

1592—Elbow Boot of Leather and Fine Felt.

1593—Large Elbow Boot of Wool and Fine Felt.

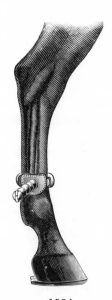

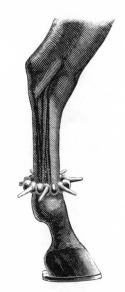

1594	1595	1596	1597	1598
Keystone Spreader.	Meyer's Paris Pat. Rubber Tickler.	Bristle Ankle Boot.	Bolles' Patent Spreader.	Yorkshire Boot of Wool.

HORSE BOOTS.

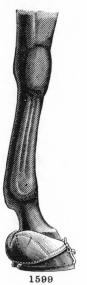

1599
Quarter Boot.

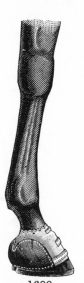

1600
Quarter Boot.

1601
Pacing Quarter Boot.

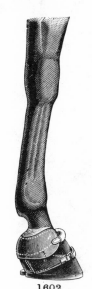

1602
Strap Hinged Quarter Boot.

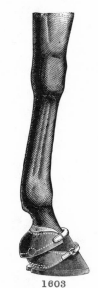

1603
Rivet Hinged Quarter Boot.

1604
Rivet Hinged Quarter Boot, with Steel Lining.

1605
Rivet Quarter Boot.

1606
Quarter Boot.

1607
Quarter Boot.

1608
Quarter Boot, Buckskin Top and Leather Bottom.

1609
Quarter Boot, made of Elk Skin. Light and Soft.

1610
Felt Top Quarter Boot.

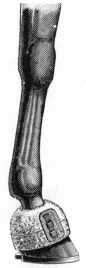

1611
Wool Quarter Boot.

1612
Wool and Leather Quarter Boot.

HORSE BOOTS.

1613
Side Hitting Scalper.

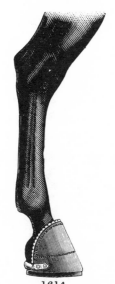
1614
Half Front Hitting Scalper.

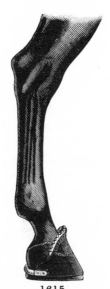
1615
Front Hitting Scalper.

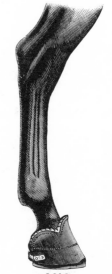
1616
Front and Side Hitting Scalper.

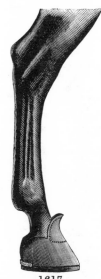
1617
Front and Side Hitting Scalper.

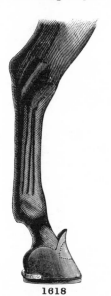
1618
Front and Side Hitting Scalper.

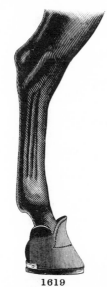
1619
Front and High Side Hitting Scalper.

1620
Front Hoof and Speedy Cut Boot.

1621
Front Hoof and Speedy Cut Boot.

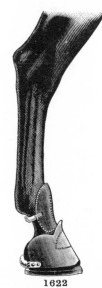
1622
Front and Side Hoof and Speedy Cut Boot.

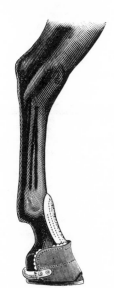
1623
Hoof and Speedy Cut Boot of Leather and White Felt Cloth.

1624
Ankle and Speedy Cut Boot.

1625
Fine Felt Cloth Ankle Boot.

1626
Fine Calf Leather Ankle Boot.

1627
Fine Calf Leather Ankle Boot, with Heel Extension.

HORSE BOOTS.

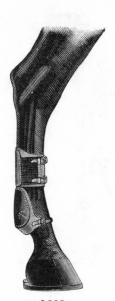

1628

Heel and Back Cord.

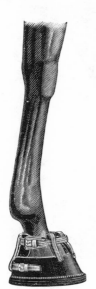

1629

Lawn Boot.

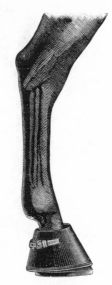

1630

Zinc Caulking Boot.

1631

Leather Caulking Boot.

1632

White Felt Soaking Boot.

1633

White Felt Soaking Boot, with Bottom.

1634

Leather Poultice Boot.

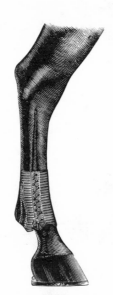

1635

Short Elastic Stocking and Heel Boot.

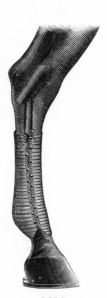

1636

Elastic Stocking.

1637

Haughey Patent Dangler.

1638

Knee Cap.

1639

Shoe Boil Boot.

1640

Rubber Ball and Spur Boot.

1641

Hopples.

1642

Hopples Kersey Lined.

1643

Rubber Ball Spur Boot.

HORSE BOOTS.

1644

Plain Shin with Elastic.

1645

Buckskin Shin Rolls, with
from 3 to 8 Rolls.

1646

Wide Shin and Ankle, with
Elastic.

1617

Narrow Shin and Ankle, with
Elastic.

1648

Shin and Ankle, with Cord
Extension and Elastic.

1649

Hinged Shin and Ankle,
Elastic.

1650

Shin, Ankle and Cord, with
Elastic.

1651

Half Knee, Shin and Ankle,
with Cord and Elastic.

1652

Half Knee, Shin and Ankle,
Elastic.

1653

Shin, Ankle and Speedy Cut,
Elastic.

1654

Shin, Ankle and Front Cord,
with Speedy Cut.

1655

Hinged Shin, Ankle and Front
Cord, with Speedy Cut.

1656

Shin and Ankle, with Speedy
Cut.

1657

Shin and Ankle, with Speedy
Cut, no Elastic.

1658

Hock, Shin, Ankle and
Speedy Cut.

HORSE BOOTS.

1659

Double Hock, Shin,
Ankle and Speedy Cut

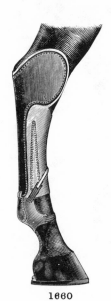

1660

Hock, Back Cord and
Heel.

1661

Back Cord or Tendon.

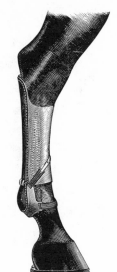

1662

Back Cord and Heel, or
Cutting down Boot.

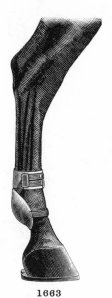

1663

Elastic Heel Boot.

1664

Hock and Shin.

1665

Hock for Stable use.

1666

Hock for Stable use.

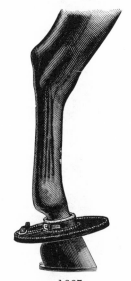

1667

To prevent one foot standing
on the other in the stall.

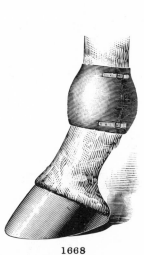

1668

Rubber Ankle Boot.

1669

Bog Spavin Truss.

1670—Roberge's Patent Hoof
Expander, in several sizes.

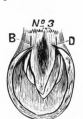

1671

Mackey's Spiral Spring Hoof Expander

For the Cure and Prevention of all foot
trouble. With the Spiral Spring, any
foot that has never been maltreated, or
is at all curable, can be put in perfect
order.

Made in all sizes to fit any foot.

Last from eight to twelve months,
constant use. Never gets too small for
foot; each remove gives the desired
pressure.

Full directions for applying with each pair.

In ordering, send exact width of heel from B to D.

1672

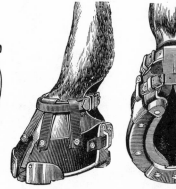

1673—Improved Patent Self-Adjusting Portable Hinge Horse Sandals, 5 sizes.

HORSE BOOTS.

1674
Knee and Arm Boot.

1675
Knee and Full Arm Boot.

1676
Hinged Knee and Arm Boot..

1677
Hinged Knee, Arm and Back Arm Boot.

1678
Felt and Leather Knee Boot.

1679
Knee and Arm Boot.

1680
Knee and Short Arm Boot.

1681
Hinged Knee Boot.

1682
Felt Knee Boot.

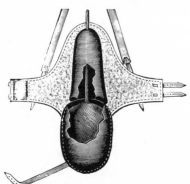

1683—Pneumatic Knee Boot.

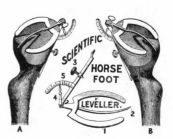

1684—Level Feet Promote Speed as well as prevent Hoof Ailments.   Keep your Horses' Feet Level and save Veterinary Fees.

RUBBER FROG PADS.

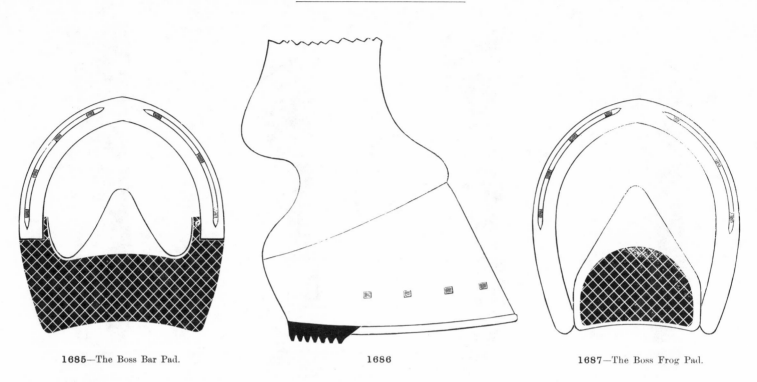

1685—The Boss Bar Pad.　　　　　**1686**　　　　　**1687**—The Boss Frog Pad.

The Boss Pads retain all the good qualities of the Pads now in the market without any of their defects. The rubber is keyed to the backing and will stay until worn off. The backing used is not affected by heat or moisture, will retain its shape, and is cooling to the foot.

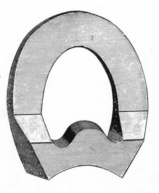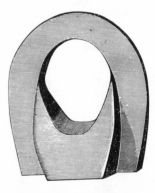

1688—Leather and Rubber Frog Pad.　　**1689**—Leather and Rubber Frog Pad.　　**1690**—All Rubber Frog Pad.　　**1691**—All Rubber Frog Pad.

1692　　　　　　　　**1693**　　　　　　　　**1694**

Bitting Harness, Hopples

and Spreaders

SECTION.

All Goods shown in this Section furnished at Lowest Wholesale Prices.

"DO NOT CUT THIS BOOK."

Every consumer or dealer in Harness and Saddlery, no matter in what part of the world he does business, will promote his own interests by sending us **ONE DOLLAR** and receiving in return a copy of this complete Illustrated Guide Book. It is the key to success in the prosecution of business. He cannot afford to be without the knowledge it contains of every department of the trade. It will surely serve as a lamp to light him through the many perplexities which are incidental to the Harness Industry.

With this Book in your possession you are at liberty to write to us, or to any manufacturer or dealer in Harness or Saddlery Goods with whom you do business, asking questions or sending orders, and either will know just what you want if you will mention "MOSEMAN'S BOOK" and give the "NUMBER" under the article you wish to know about, or mention the picture of the article you may have under consideration at the time.

In any event, **DO NOT CUT THIS BOOK!** but simply give "Number" of the article you wish to obtain.

We are, yours for business,

C. M. MOSEMAN & BROTHER,

126 & 128 CHAMBERS STREET,

NEW YORK, U. S. A.

DUMB JOCKEY.

1695—Blackwell's Patent Whalebone and Rubber Dumb Jockey and Breaking Cavesson.

COLTS AND UNTRACTABLE HORSES broken by kind and gentle Treatment, Temperate and Easy Mouthed by using **Blackwell's Patent Whalebone and Gutta Percha Jockeys,** with Rubber Springs (of any length by tieing the inside cord), and for exercising in frost, in boxes, and in stalls; on Led Horses to prevent falling and broken knees. They yield easily if a Colt rolls over on his back, and he is not injured as with the old Wood or Iron Jockey. Used by the first Breeders and Owners of Horses. Above 10,000 in use. The Dumb Jockey should not be kept on the Colt more than half an hour at a time, as he is apt to turn sulky, and it can be put on several half hours in a day. With two dees on the side, the lunge reins are passed to the bit, and the horse may be driven or lunged round. This plan is adopted by most of the large breakers, and very little lungeing is done.

Breaking tackle of all kinds; Cavessons, Lunge-reins, Improved Straight Mouth Slide Cheek Breaking Bits with Players from 1 to 4 lbs. By placing two bags of shot weighing about 1 lb. each on the rings of the bit, the weight is increased to 3 lbs. or 4 lbs. When this bit is used, the Colt will not allow the weight to rest upon the lower jaw, but puts his nose in, until the weight is thrown entirely on the head, by which means he forms a fine crest, without pulling at his mouth and spoiling it.

Double Spring Hooks to attach the bits to the Cavesson or Head-collar in the stable; they save the Colt's ears being pulled about, as the Head-collar forms the bridle head.

BLACKWELL, Patent Saddlery and Harness Manufacturer to Her Majesty and the Prince of Wales.

PARIS: M. P. GERMAIN, Sellier, Harnacheur, 18 Rue Louis Le Grand, and to be had of all Saddlers.

PRIZE MEDALS (1851, 1862) London; Dublin, 1865; and the only First-class Medal, Paris, 1855, for Saddlery, and Cologne, 1865.

C. M. MOSEMAN & BRO. Selling Agents for United States and Canadas, 126 & 128 Chambers St. N. Y.

1696

1697

DUMB JOCKEY.

1698—Green's Patent Dumb Jockey, for Breaking and Training Colts to Saddle.

The reins from the Cavesson or bridle work around springs in the arms of the Dumb Jockey, and give and take with the motion of the colt's head, the same as if a boy was sitting on his back driving him.

WRIGHT'S PATENT DEVELOPER.

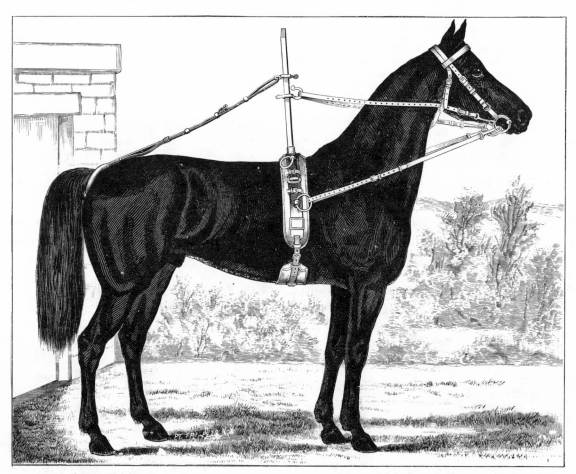

1699—Wright's Patent Developer, for Bitting the Horse and developing style to Neck and Head.

Crupper and Reins adjustable on Steel Standard of Saddle.

BITTING HARNESS.

1700—Bitting Harness, fitted for the Field.

1701—Bitting Harness, fitted for the Stable or Field.

1702—Elastic Rein Safes, for the Ends of Shafts.

1703—McKenny's Patent Horse Controller. The Rein working through Pulleys.

HARNESS SPECIALTIES.

1704—The Iowa Gaiter.   (Patented October 13, 1891.)

Consists of light weight bent sticks, fastened to the shafts. Pads around legs, adjustable elastic cords, connecting pads and sticks, and a strap fastened to ends of shafts and to the saddle.   It will lengthen the stride, steady and quicken motion, prevents striking elbows, and by turning ends of sticks outward will cause horse to travel wider in front, or by turning them in will draw legs together. For one that goes to one side in shafts, turn points of sticks both in one direction, and to give more knee action draw the sticks back about one foot so as to lift the knees instead of drawing legs forward. Is used for both slow and fast work.

1705—Noyes' Patent Gait Spreader.

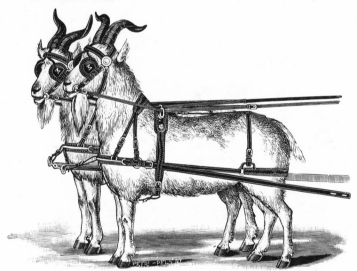

1706—Double Goat Harness, in various qualities.

1707—Single Goat Harness, in various qualities.

1708—Triple Power Anti-Kicking Strap has two swivels and rollers on each shaft, and is designed for horses that cannot travel when checked high and for the worst kickers.

1709—Pneumatic Hopples, to make a horse trot or pace.

SINGLE HARNESS

SECTION.

All Goods shown in this Section furnished at Lowest Wholesale Prices.

RIDING & DRIVING

CAPS,
JACKETS

BREECHES
& BOOTS.

SPECIAL
COLORS

MADE
TO ORDER

1710—Light, Fast and Reliable Trotting Harness of every Pattern and Patent.

Adapted for use with Bicycle Sulkies.

JOCKEYS' TRACK GOODS.

Drivers Caps in Cotton, Worsted, Satin or Silk.

1711

1712

1713

1714

1715—Drivers Boot Shield, to prevent Boot from damage on Sulky Shaft Stirrup.

1716—Arm Plate Numbers for Track Drivers.

1717—Winker Hood, to use on the track to make horse see straight ahead only.

1718—Sulky Seat Cushion, with Pocket for carrying Weight.

TWO MINUTE TRACK HARNESS.

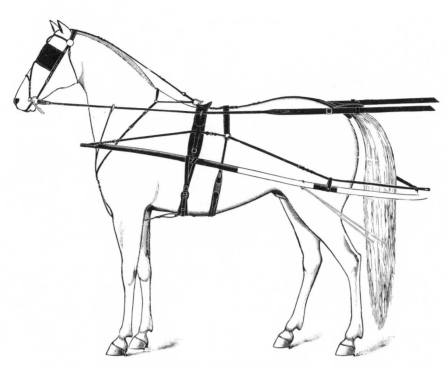

1719—The Two Minute Track Harness.

The Two Minute and 1:58 Track Harness. THEIR USES AND ADVANTAGES. One of the principal objects of this harness is to give the horse a rigid hitch without tieing him up so as to impede his action in the smallest degree. It is a harness that trotting and pacing horsemen have been looking for for many years and some attempts have been made to produce a harness that would bring these desired results, but it has never been done for there is no harness in existence in which the valuable principles are used which go into this harness. The principle seems a plain one, yet some may not fully have studied or adequately comprehended the great speed producing qualities of the harness. It took years of careful study, close observation and repeated trials to bring this harness to the high point of excellence to which it has attained. However, it is the testimony of the greatest drivers and trainers all over the world that a horse can trot faster hitched with this harness than with any other, and for this reason we flatter ourselves that it will be the only method used to hitch a horse. The harness has unquestioned merit and practical utility in many other ways than we can mention, many of which will be obvious on trial. In general, we know that a horse can be trained easier, brought to his speed quicker, trot or pace squarer and make faster time than with any other harness in existence.

1720—Rahn's New Pattern 1:58 Harness.

SINGLE HARNESS.

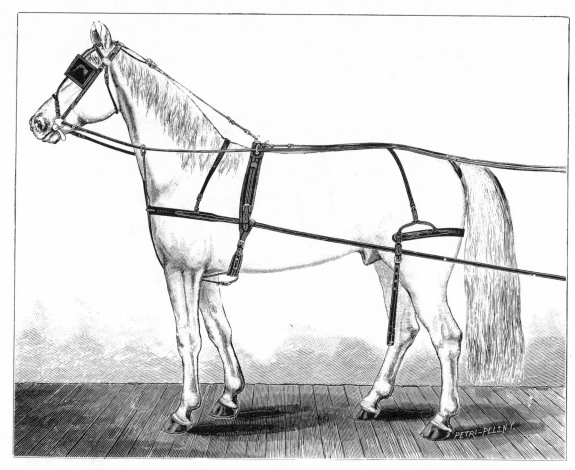

1721—First Quality, Single Strap Light Driving or Speeding Harness, Traces Sewed on.

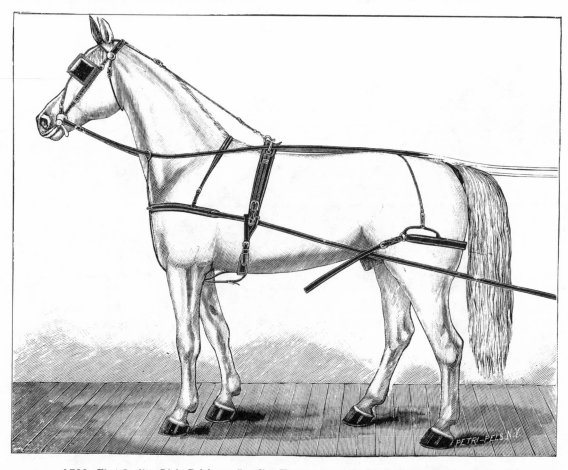

1722—First Quality, Light Driving or Speeding Harness, Enameled Leather Folds, Traces Sewed on.

SINGLE HARNESS.

1723—First Quality, Stout, Plain Single Strap Exercising Harness, adapted to practice work and hard usage.

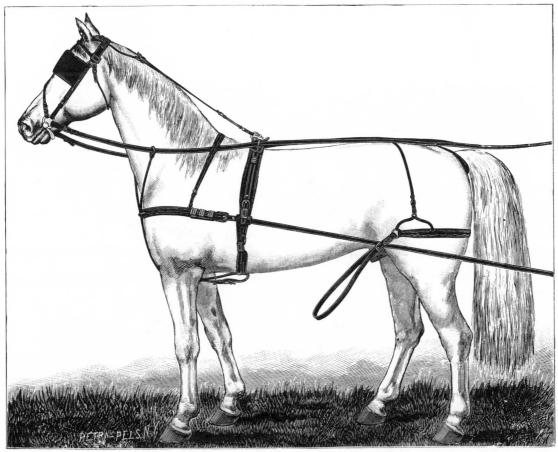

1724—First Quality, Light Harness, with $\frac{3}{4}$, $\frac{7}{8}$ or 1 inch Traces.   Rubber, Gold or Silver Terretts, Buckles, etc.

SINGLE HARNESS.

1725—First Quality Light Harness, with 1 or 1⅛ inch Traces.   Rubber, Gold or Silver Terretts, Buckles, etc.

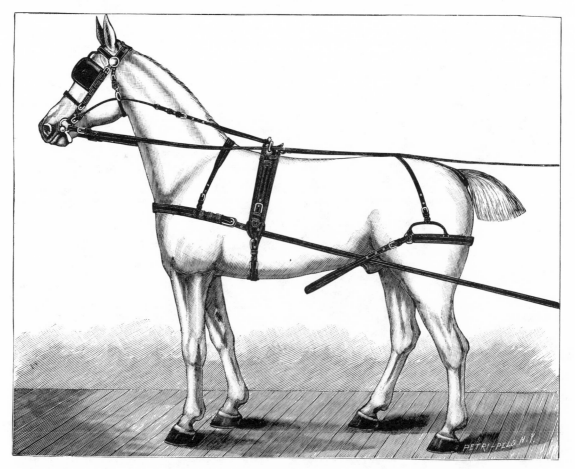

1726—First Quality, Stout Light Surrey or 4 Passenger Harness.

SINGLE HARNESS.

1727—First Quality, Full Plated, Hame Collar Harness, adapted for Light Surrey or Runabout use.

1728—First Quality, Full Plate Hame Collar Harness, adapted for Buckboard or Carryall use.

SINGLE HARNESS.

1729—First Quality, Full Plate Cart or Trap Harness.

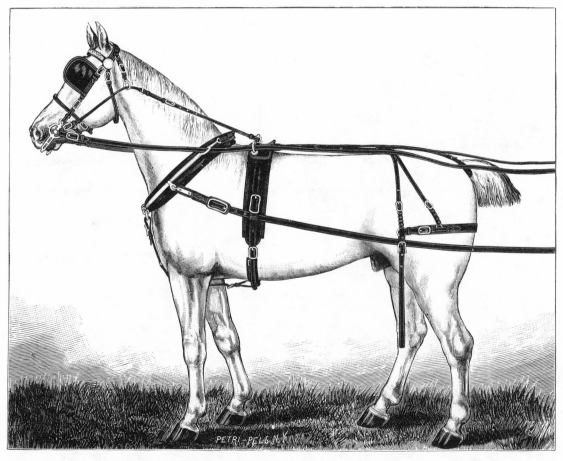

1730—First Quality, Full Plate Light Brougham, Cart or Trap Harness, with Extension Breeching.

WOOL HARNESS COVERINGS.

1731

An easier and better way of putting Coverings on Harness, than when they are sewed on permanently. Then they become soiled, and when wet it is impossible to dry, and therefore very injurious. To obviate this, we are manufacturing a Wool Covering in rolls of 25, 50, and 100 feet lengths for the trade, so that consumers can purchase the exact length and width they require for any part of the Harness. The edges are furnished with hooks so that they can be put on and taken off at pleasure.

FOLDING SEAT.

1732

It is the only practical third seat for a vehicle.

It is the cleanest, best and most artistic bassock on the market.

It is a foot rest that will not slip away from the user.

It is a child's chair which can be recklessly handled without injury to itself or the children, and forms an excellent substitute for a high chair at the table.

It is a strong, light, and portable seat for fishermen either on shore or in a boat.

BELL ODOMETER, FOR CARRIAGES.

1733—Engraving shows method of attaching to Axle with Pin in Hub. A Polished Nickel Shield protects the Instrument from mud.

Registers the distance travelled, rings a small bell as each mile is passed, keeps a record for 1,600 miles, and repeats.

SINGLE HARNESS.

1734 - Stylish Trap Harness, with French Hame Tug Eye.

1735 — First Quality, Heavy Single Coupe Harness, furnished in all styles of Furniture.

1736—Dress Soiled.—No Wheel Cover.

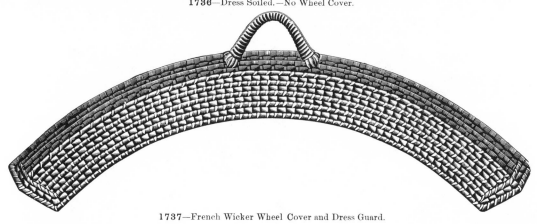

1737—French Wicker Wheel Cover and Dress Guard.

1738—Dress Clean.—With Wheel Cover.

VILLAGE CART HARNESS.

1739

We make VILLAGE CART HARNESS in the Latest Style, in Russet or Black Leather for Large and for Small Horses or Ponies, and trim with Solid Nickel, Silver or Brass, with English Rush, White Canvas, Colored or Black Leather Collars, and grade the price according to amount of work and quality of trimmings.

We continue the above illustration from a former book published by us in 1884, for the reason that it shows seated in the cart, the Father of those who founded and still carry on the business, and whose form, face and name, WM. C. MOSEMAN (who died October 5th, 1890, aged 76 years) we delight to honor.

SINGLE HARNESS.

1740—Extra Quality, White Buff Leather Trap or Cart Harness, with French Tilbury Shaft Tugs and Extension Breeching.　Tandem and Four-in-Hand Harness also made in White Buff, Brown, Red or other Colored Leathers for Private, Exhibition or Advertising Purposes.

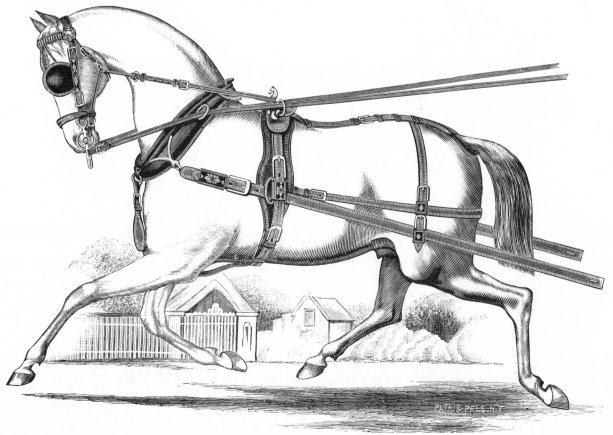

1741—First Quality, Heavy Strong Cab Harness, with Breeching suitable for use where Stop Plates are put an Shafts, particularly for Bent Shafts.

SINGLE HARNESS.

1742—First Quality, Heavy Stylish Brougham, Cart or Trap Harness, French Tilbury Tugs, Metal Hame Tug Loops.   Used with or without Breeching.

1743—Duplicate of above, with Leather Loops instead of Metal on Hame Tug.

RULE 1
THAT EACH MEMBER SHALL BE PROVIDED WITH TWO HORSES, A VEHICLE, AND MAN.

RULE 2
THE VEHICLE MUST BE A TWO-WHEELER, WHATEVER THE DESCRIPTION.

RULE 3
THE MAIN IDEA OF THE TANDEM CLUB, NOT BEING ONE OF FASHION BUT ONE OF UTILITY, FOR THE PROMOTION OF THE NOBLE ART, ANY MEMBER MAY TURN OUT AS HE PLEASES, AS LONG AS THE TWO FOREGOING RULES ARE OBSERVED.

RULE 4
TANDEM DRIVING TENDING TO ENGENDER QUITE A NUMBER OF DIFFICULTIES ON THE ROAD, ALL MEMBERS MUST PRACTICE THE MANLY ART.

RULE 5
THE CLAIMS TO ARISTOCRATIC LINEAGE BEING SOMEWHAT UNCERTAIN IN THIS COUNTRY; NO APPLICANT FOR MEMBERSHIP SHALL BE ASKED WHO HIS GRANDFATHER WAS; BUT SHALL BE ADMITTED ON HIS RESPECTABILITY AND DECENT APPEARANCE.

RULE 6
ANY MEMBER COMING UP OR STOPPING IN THE ABOVE MANNER, TWO-HORSE FASHION, SHALL BE SUBJECT TO A FINE OF NO LESS THAN $5.

RULE 7
ANY MEMBER ALLOWING HIS LEADER THE LIBERTY OF REFRESHING HIMSELF AT HIS LEISURE ON THE ROAD, SHALL BE CONSIDERED AS GUILTY OF A MISDEMEANOR.

RULE 8
NO MEMBER SHOULD ALLOW HIS SHAFT HORSE TO PLAY LEAP FROG WITH HIS LEADER.

RULE 9
ELEGANCE AND CORRECTNESS BEING, HOWEVER, MOST DESIRABLE POINTS, IT SHALL, IN CONSEQUENCE, BE OBLIGATORY WITH THE PRESIDENT AND VICE-PRESIDENT OF THE CLUB THAT THEY TURN OUT IN THE MOST APPROVED AND WORKMANLIKE FORM, THEREBY PLACING THEMSELVES AS EXAMPLES BEFORE THE EYES OF THE OTHER MEMBERS.

RULE 10
NO LEADER MUST BE ALLOWED, WHILST ON THE ROAD, TO SIT DOWN AND REST; THE STABLE IS THE PROPER PLACE FOR THIS.

RULE 11
THE ATTEMPT, BY ANY MEMBER, TO KNOCK DOWN THE TREES IN CENTRAL PARK, OR THE COMMITTAL OF ANY DAMAGE OF A KINDRED NATURE, SHALL CAUSE HIS APPEARANCE BEFORE A SPECIAL COMMITTEE WHOSE DUTY IT SHALL BE TO CENSURE AND INFLICT A HEAVY FINE ON THE SAME.

RULE 12
ANY MEMBER TOLERATING SUCH EXTRAVAGANCIES, IN A LEADER, AS THE ABOVE, SHALL BE LIABLE TO A FINE OF $25.

RULE 13
IT SHALL NOT BE PERMISSIBLE TO INFLICT ANY SUCH INDIGNITY AS THE ABOVE ON PARK POLICEMEN BECAUSE THEY HAPPEN TO INTERFERE WITH THE PACE.

RULE 14
ANY MEMBER AUTHORIZING SUCH PLAYFUL BEHAVIOR IN HIS HORSES, SHALL BE ADMONISHED AND CENSURED THE FIRST TIME. A REPETITION OF THE SAME SHALL BE FOLLOWED BY DISMISSAL, AS SUCH CONDUCT REFLECTS ON THE DIGNITY OF THE CLUB.

RULE 15
NO MEMBER SHALL ALLOW HIS HORSES TO ENTER ANY STORE OF WHATSOEVER KIND.

Gray-Parker

REVISED RULES OF THE AMERICAN TANDEM CLUB.

TANDEM HARNESS.

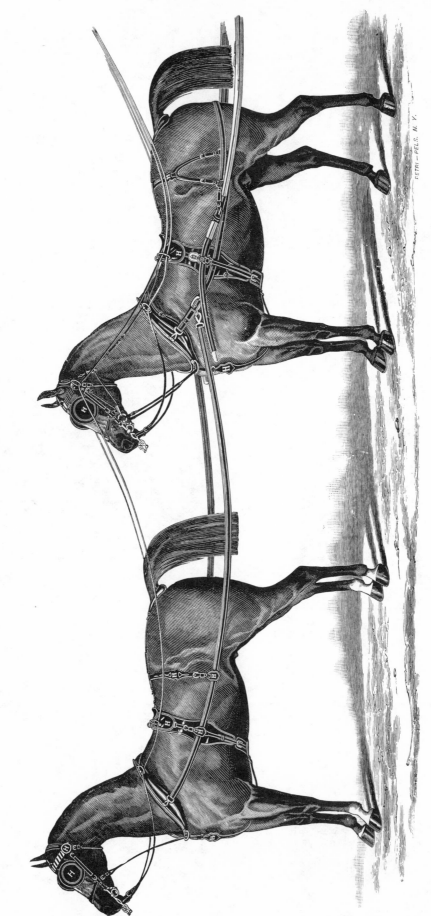

1744—Price furnished upon application. Give the Style of Cart or Carriage for which it is to be used.

TANDEM HARNESS.

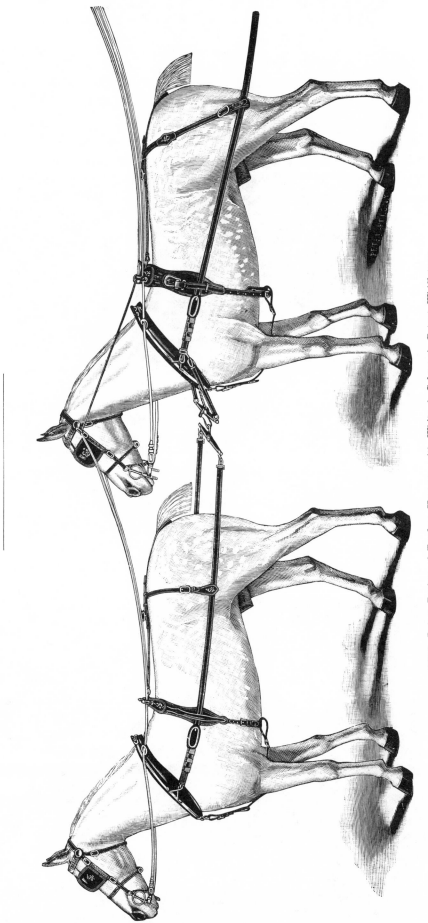

1745—Latest Design of Tandem Harness, with White & Coleman's Patent Whiffletrees.

SINGLE HARNESS.

1746—Sun Bonnet, to protect the Head from the Sun, made on Wire Frame and of Light Striped Muslin with Fringe. Fastened by the Frame Wire running down into the Cheek of the Bridle behind Rosette.

1747—Hansom Cab Harness on hand and made to order in styles to suit buyers.

SINGLE HARNESS.

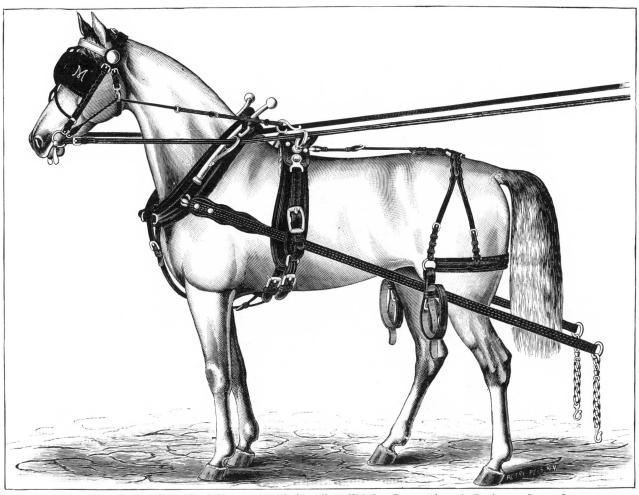

1748—First Quality, Heavy Draft Harness, furnished in Silver, Nickel or Brass.   Always in Stock or made to order.

1749—Medium Weight Delivery Harness, with Silver, Nickel or Brass Furniture.   Always in Stock or made to order.

HEAVY DRAFT HARNESS.

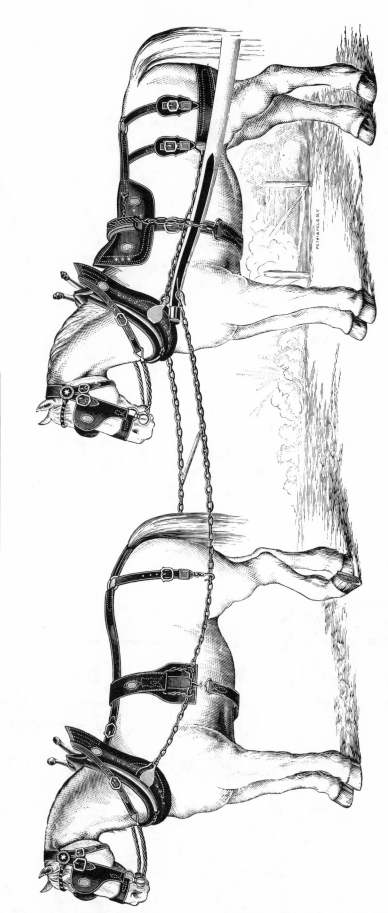

1750—This cut shows a strong, well made Wheel-cart Harness and Lead Harness attached, adapted to heavy Work.

MULE-CART HARNESS.

1751

This cut shows a good, strong, well-made Mule-cart Harness, with Lead Harness attached.

1752

This cut shows a plain, strong Mule-cart Harness, with Lead Harness attached. Contractors and Large Operators furnished with these goods at low prices.

Save ✳ Your ✳ Horses

And Double their Value by Using

✳❦ THE "MOGUL" DRAUGHT SPRINGS. ❦✳

SPRING DISTENDED, SHOWING THE DOUBLE SPRINGS.

INTERIOR LINK DISTENDED.

The Mogul Draught Springs are to be attached to the traces, at the whiffletrees or at the hames.

There have been many inventions and devices made for trace-springs, but **none like the Mogul Springs.**

This is what the Mogul Springs will do, **absolutely and literally,** as proved by over one million in use:

They completely obviate all sudden jerks and strains in passing over holes and impediments on the road.

They do absolutely prevent all injuries from the collar, ruptures, and the bursting of blood vessels from sudden violent strains.

They entirely heal up collar wounds and bruises; old sores will heal after beginning to use the Mogul Springs.

They do balking. Vicious horses become gentle and docile by using them.

They do actually increase the working power of the Horse fully twenty-five per cent.

They will increase the working life and value of the Horse.

Their elasticity will not give out, and they will not break under any strain, exceeding many times the power of any horse.

They work as well with the empty wagon as when it is heavily loaded.

They are made of different elastic strength, to suit any kind of a vehicle.

With ordinary care they will last for years.

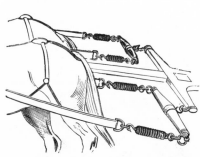

The parts of a MOGUL DRAUGHT SPRING are two spiral springs, one within the other, wound in opposite directions around two long links. The springs are wound in opposite directions, to compensate each other for loss of elasticity, and to overcome any tendency to bend or leave a straight line when contracting; while the links prevent breaking or overstraining the springs.

Mogul Springs attached to the rings in the whiffletrees by open links.

INTERIOR LINK CLOSED.

Mogul Springs attached by open links to the collar, as for cart horses, mine mules, &c.

ADOPTED BY	IN GENERAL USE AMONG
U. S. GOVERNMENT ORDNANCE DEPARTMENT, OVER ONE HUNDRED FIRE DEPARTMENTS.	THE LARGEST MINING COMPANIES AND ALL THOSE WHO DO HEAVY TEAMING.

Weight of each wagon (and whether double or single horse), also maximum load carried, should accompany each inquiry or order.

Prices, Catalogues, Directions for Attachment and full particulars furnished by

C. M. MOSEMAN & BROS.

128 CHAMBERS ST.,   NEW YORK CITY.

CART HARNESS.

1754—This cut shows a strong, well made Cart or Heavy Truck, Van or Dray Harness.

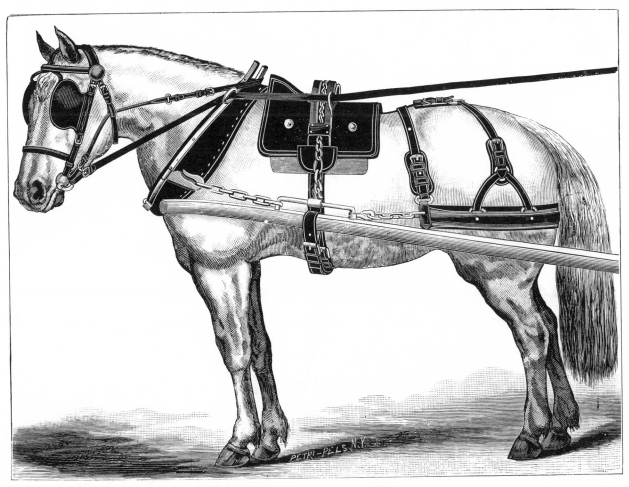

1755—Cart Harness complete, ready for use.

CART SADDLES.

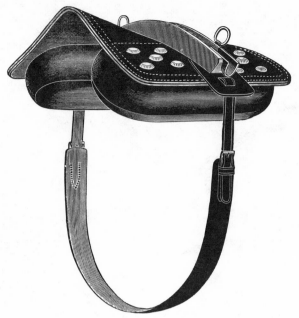

1756—Double Cover Cart Saddle, Tree Fitted for Loose Chain to take Tug with Hook.

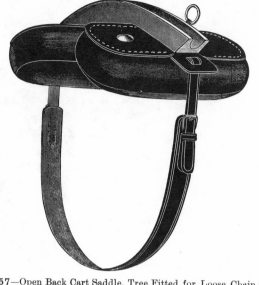

1757—Open Back Cart Saddle, Tree Fitted for Loose Chain to take Tug with Hook.

1758—Double Cover, with Moulded Edge and Bridge, Hook Bar over Tree, Hook and Terrets finished in Brass or Nickel.

1759—Back Band Chain to take Tug with Hook.

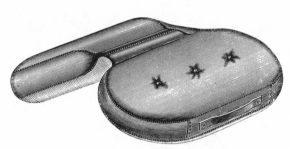

1760—Fancy Leather Cart Saddle Pad.

1763—Brown Duck Cart Saddle Pad.

1761—Iron Shaft Tug, with 5 Link Chain and Swivel for Cart Saddle, with Hook Bar over the Tree.

1762—Iron Shaft Tug, with hook to be used on Saddle that has a loose Chain over Tree.

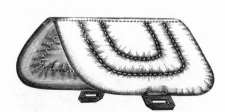

1764—White Duck Cart Saddle Pad.

1765—Feed Bag, with Leather Bottom and sides and Patent Ventilator.

1766—Feed Bag, with Leather Bottom and Patent Ventilator.

1767—Feed Bag, with Plain Wood Bottom.

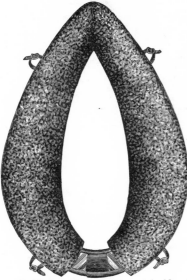

1770—Tufted Wool Pad to put inside of Horse Collar.

1768—Tufted Wool Pad for top of Collar.

1769—The "Comfort" Saddle Pad gives free ventilation.

1771—Tufted Wool Pad for inside of Breast Collar.

1772—Tufted Wool, with Leather Top Pad for Harness Saddle.

1773—Sore Back Saddle, with Iron Frame.

1774—Sore Back Saddle without Frame.

1775—Fine Sheepskin Sweat Collar, Faced with Hair and Linen Lined.

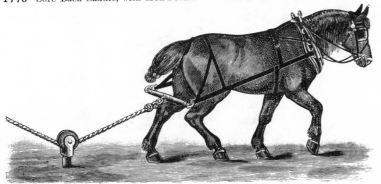

1776—Hoisting Harness—Always Ready.

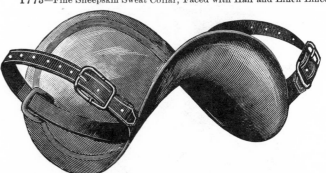

1777—Zinc Collar Pad in different sizes; to prevent the Collar from chafing the top of the neck.

"SUCCESS" SWEAT COLLARS.

No. 1 ALL BROWN DRILL.

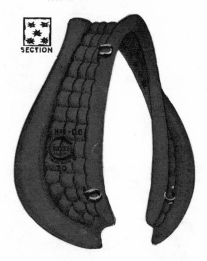

No. 1 ENAMELED-WHITE DRILL.

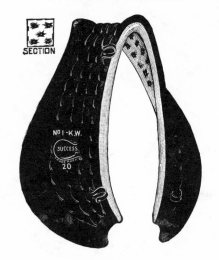

No. 1 BROWN-WHITE DRILL.

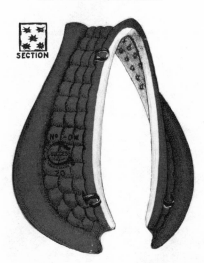

No. 1 ALL WHITE DRILL.

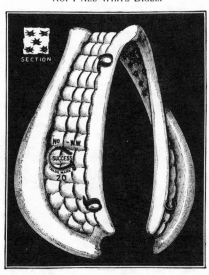

"SUCCESS" SWEAT COLLARS.

NO. 8.

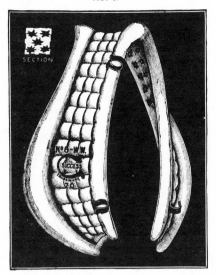

NO. 16.

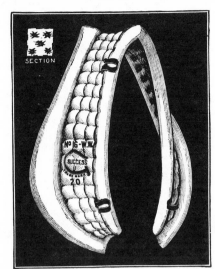

NO. 40.

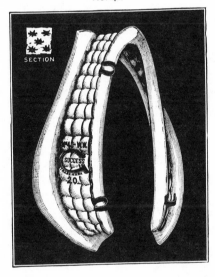

No. 1 measures 12 inches at the draft.
No. 8   " $11\frac{1}{2}$ "   "   "
No. 16   "   11   "   "   "
No. 24   " $10\frac{1}{2}$ "   "   "
No. 32   "   10   "   "   "
No. 40   " $9\frac{1}{2}$ "   "   "

Each number is made in Enameled-White, All Brown, Brown-White and All White Drill. See other side for illustrations of styles named. Other styles made to order.

The materials used throughout are the best known for the purpose. The Drills are heavy; the Hair a Deer-Goat mixture; the Hooks very elastic; the Stitch the only anti-chafing in use; the Workmanship the best. "SUCCESS" is not the cheapest in the beginning, but in the end.

NO. 24.

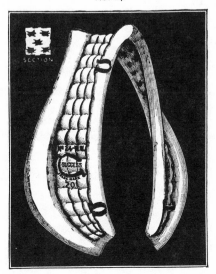

NO. 32.

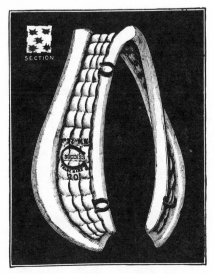

Riding and Driving Bits

SECTION.

All Goods shown in this Section furnished at Lowest Wholesale Prices.

RIDING AND DRIVING BITS.

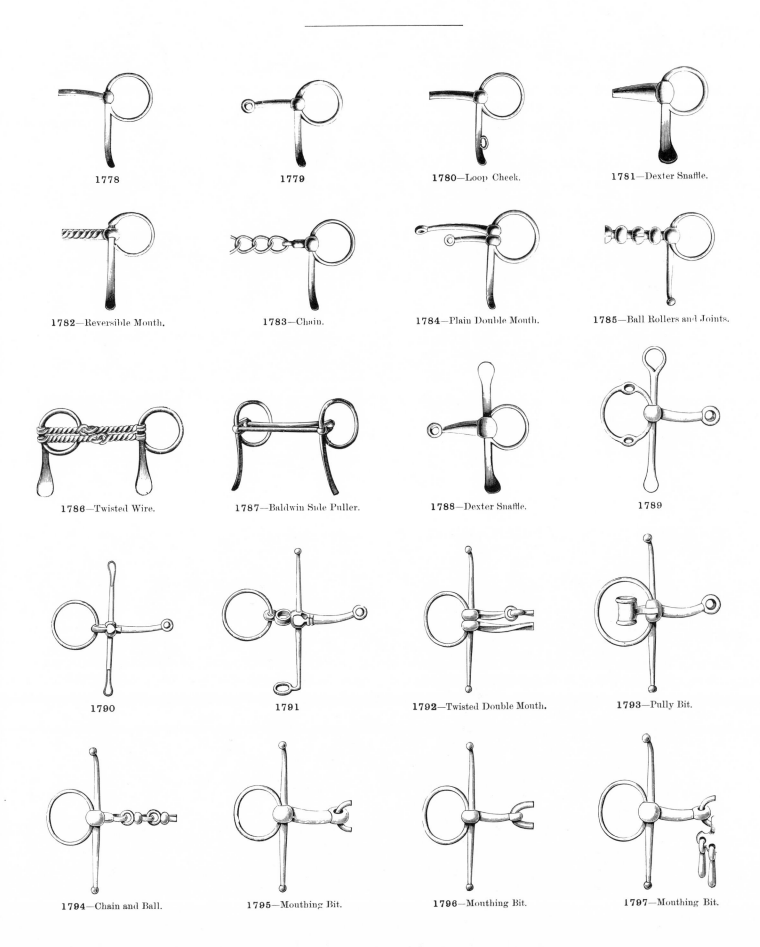

1778

1779

1780—Loop Cheek.

1781—Dexter Snaffle.

1782—Reversible Mouth.

1783—Chain.

1784—Plain Double Mouth.

1785—Ball Rollers and Joints.

1786—Twisted Wire.

1787—Baldwin Side Puller.

1788—Dexter Snaffle.

1789

1790

1791

1792—Twisted Double Mouth.

1793—Pully Bit.

1794—Chain and Ball.

1795—Mouthing Bit.

1796—Mouthing Bit.

1797—Mouthing Bit.

RIDING AND DRIVING BITS.

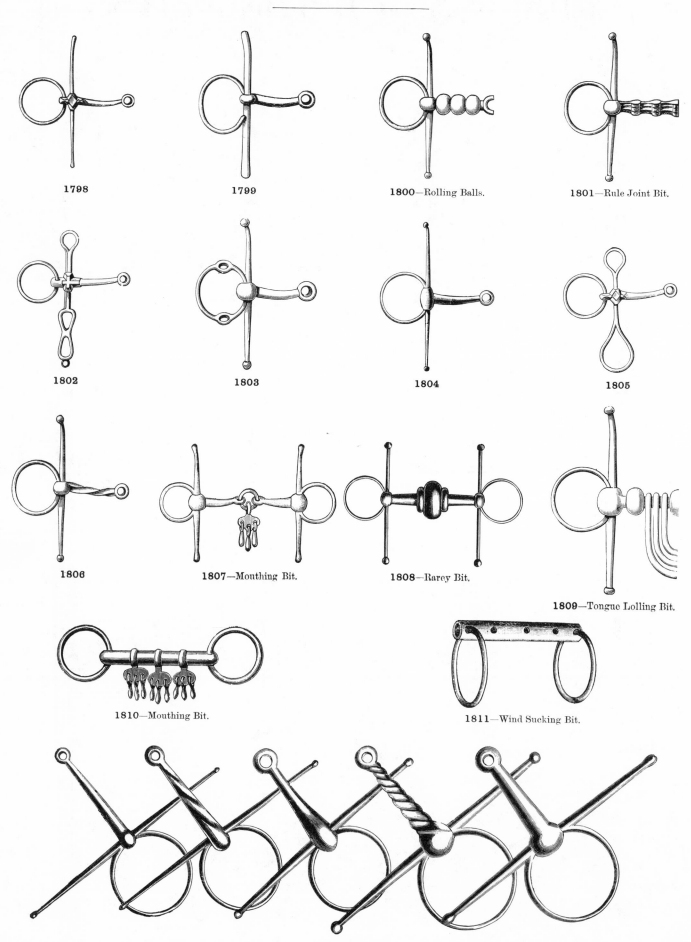

1798

1799

1800—Rolling Balls.

1801—Rule Joint Bit.

1802

1803

1804

1805

1806

1807—Mouthing Bit.

1808—Rarey Bit.

1809—Tongue Lolling Bit.

1810—Mouthing Bit.

1811—Wind Sucking Bit.

1812—Exercising Snaffles.

RIDING AND DRIVING BITS.

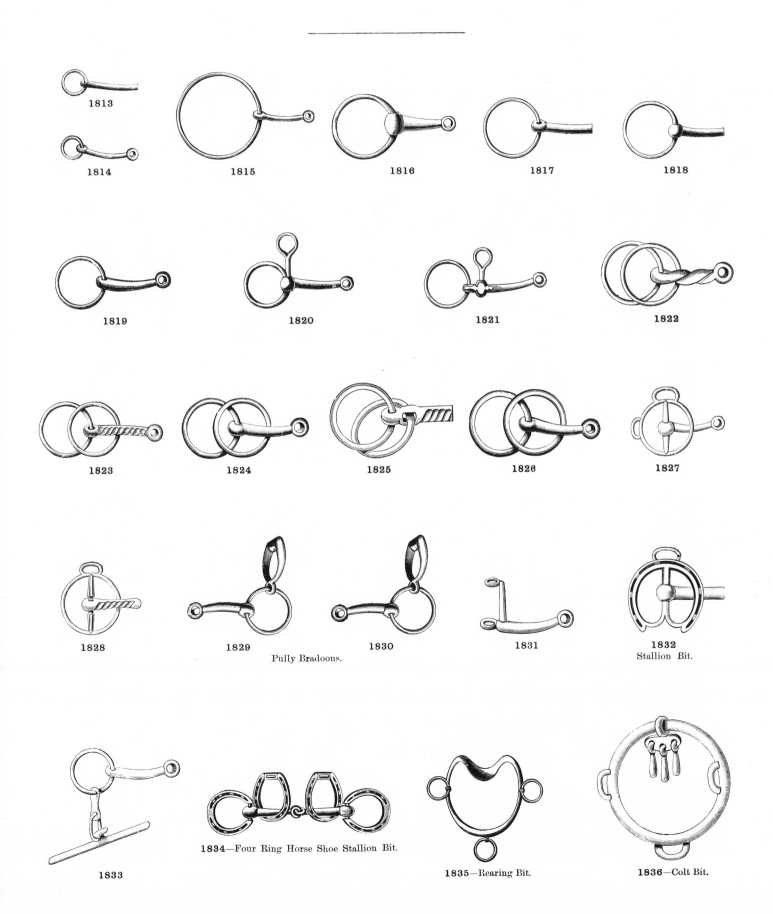

1813

1814

1815

1816

1817

1818

1819

1820

1821

1822

1823

1824

1825

1826

1827

1828

1829

1830
Pully Bradoons.

1831

1832
Stallion Bit.

1833

1834—Four Ring Horse Shoe Stallion Bit.

1835—Rearing Bit.

1836—Colt Bit.

RIDING AND DRIVING BITS.

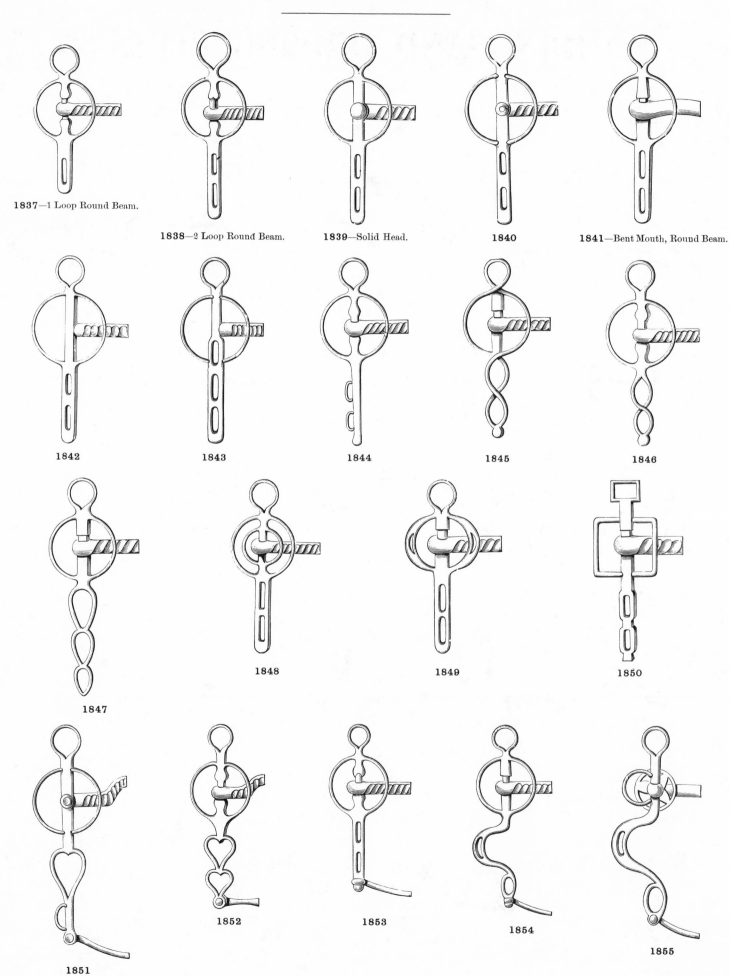

1837—1 Loop Round Beam.

1838—2 Loop Round Beam.   1839—Solid Head.   1840   1841—Bent Mouth, Round Beam.

1842   1843   1844   1845   1846

1847   1848   1849   1850

1851   1852   1853   1854   1855

RIDING AND DRIVING BITS.

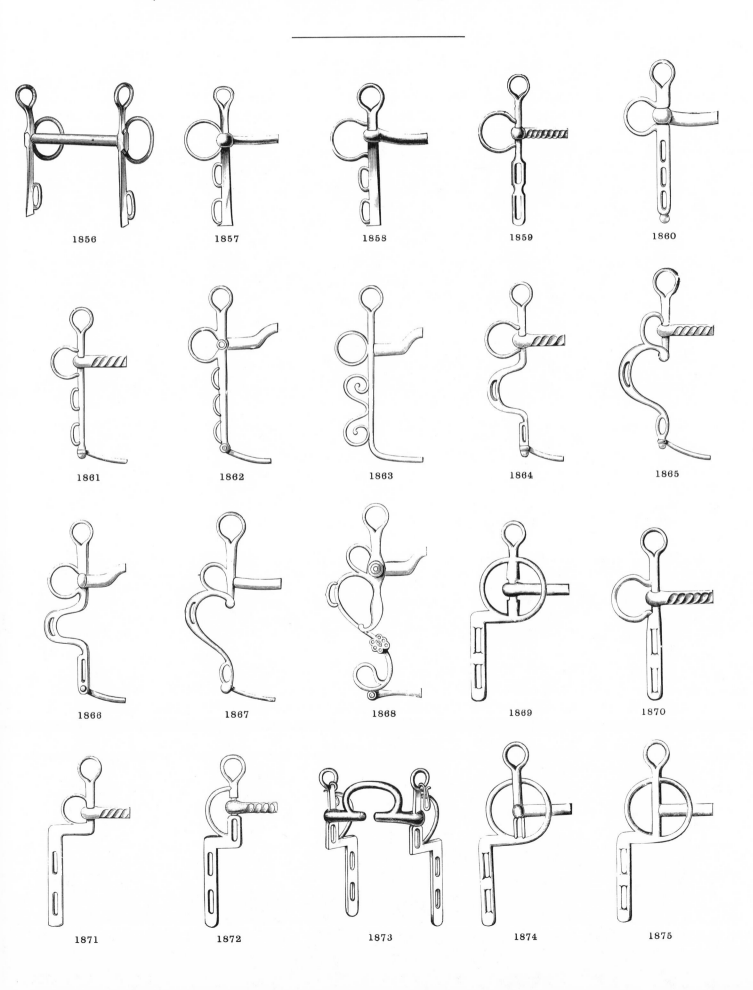

1856   1857   1858   1859   1860

1861   1862   1863   1864   1865

1866   1867   1868   1869   1870

1871   1872   1873   1874   1875

RIDING AND DRIVING BITS.

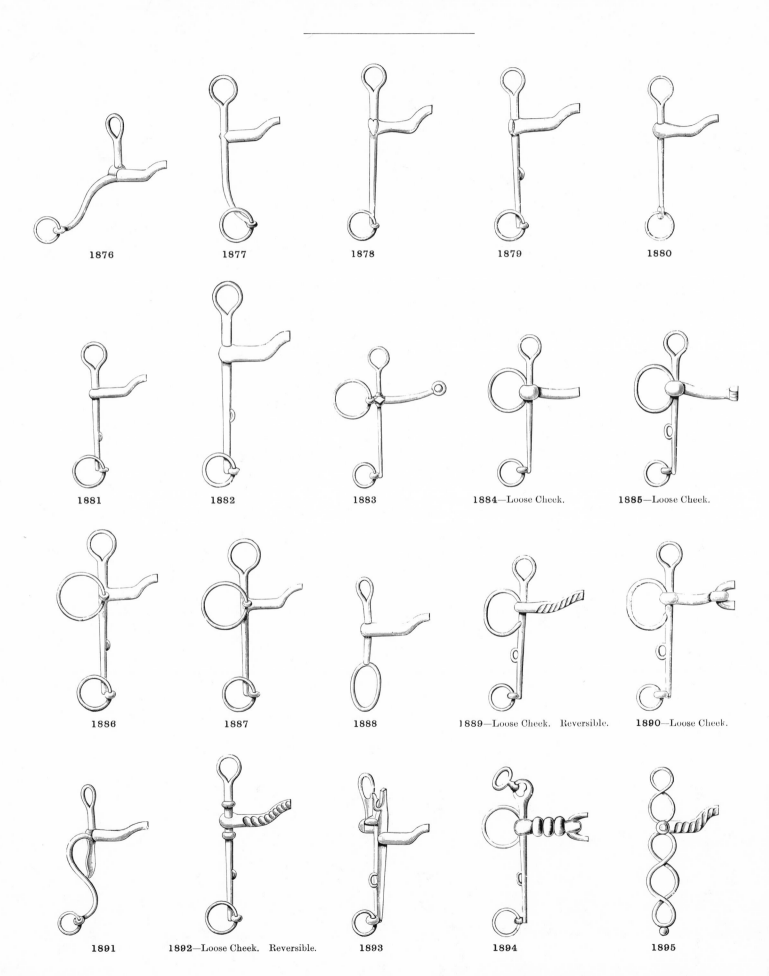

1876   1877   1878   1879   1880

1881   1882   1883   1884—Loose Cheek.   1885—Loose Cheek.

1886   1887   1888   1889—Loose Cheek. Reversible.   1890—Loose Cheek.

1891   1892—Loose Cheek. Reversible.   1893   1894   1895

RIDING AND DRIVING BITS.

1896—Humane Bit, Hard Rubber Covered Mouth.

1897— Humane Bit, Leather Covered Mouth.

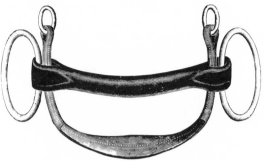

1898—Humane Bit, Round Leather Mouth.

1899—Humane Bit, Flat Leather Mouth.

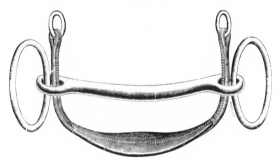

1900—Humane Bit, Plain Metal Mouth.

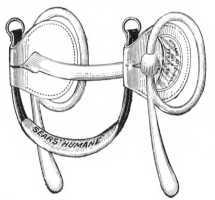

1901—Humane Bit with Leather Safes.

1902—Bostwick's Patent Steel Spring Bit, Leather and Rubber Covered.

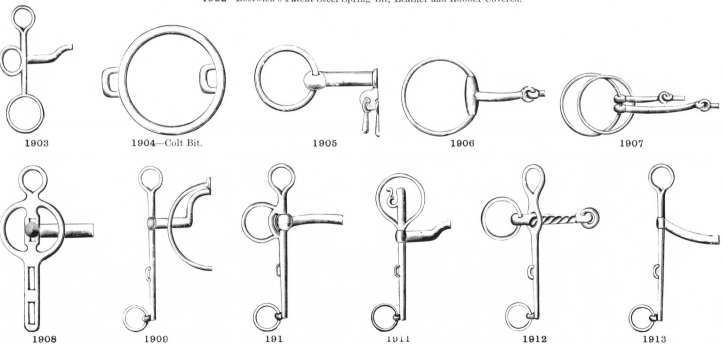

1903   1904—Colt Bit.   1905   1906   1907

1908   1909   191   1911   1912   1913

RIDING AND DRIVING BITS.

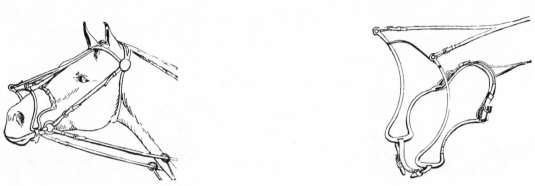

1914—The Raymond Leverage Chin Check.

This device is a perfect Head Controller; its merits can be seen at a glance. It is Simple. It is Humane. It is Effective. It is Easily Adjusted. There is no opposing force in the mouth. It works independent of the driving bit and keeps the mouth closed, thus dispensing with a nose band. It has a powerful impact leverage that resists the most stubborn effort to put the head down and choke.

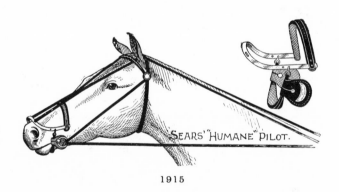

SEARS' "HUMANE" PILOT.

1915

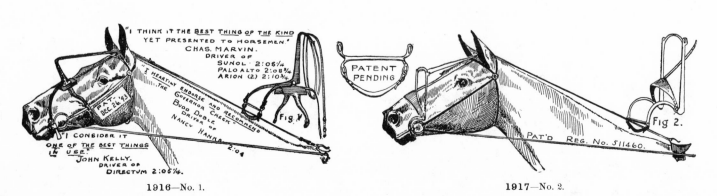

1916—No. 1.

1917—No. 2.

The Governor Check, No. 1 and No. 2.

RIDING AND DRIVING BITS.

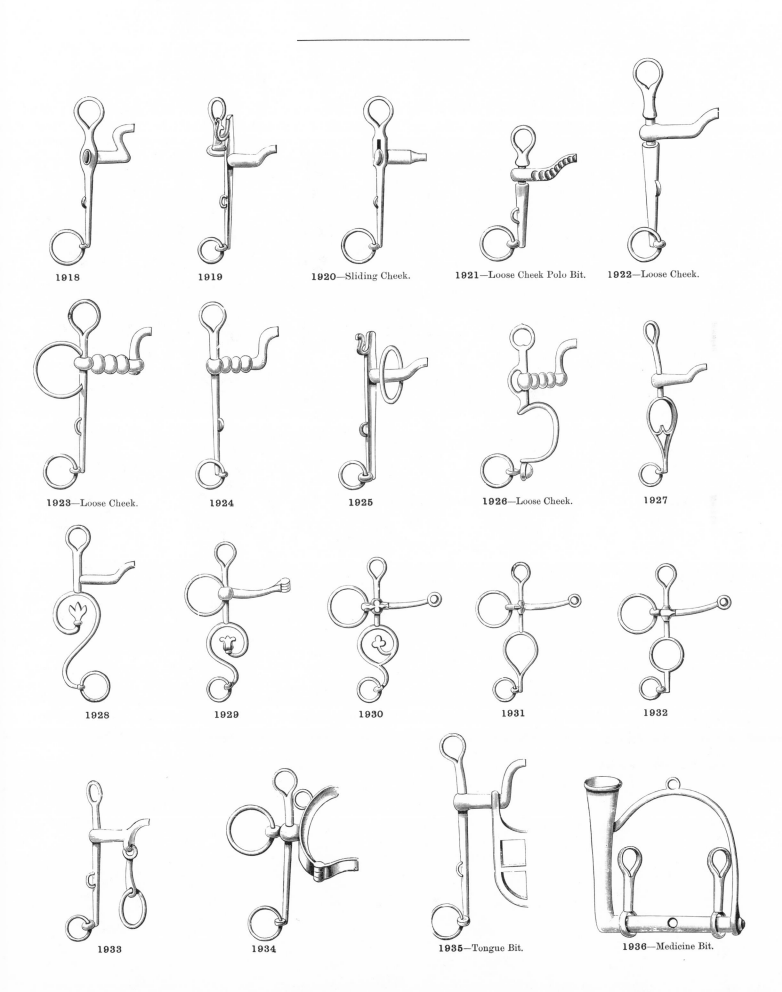

1918

1919

1920—Sliding Cheek.

1921—Loose Cheek Polo Bit.

1922—Loose Cheek.

1923—Loose Cheek.

1924

1925

1926—Loose Cheek.

1927

1928

1929

1930

1931

1932

1933

1934

1935—Tongue Bit.

1936—Medicine Bit.

RIDING AND DRIVING BITS.

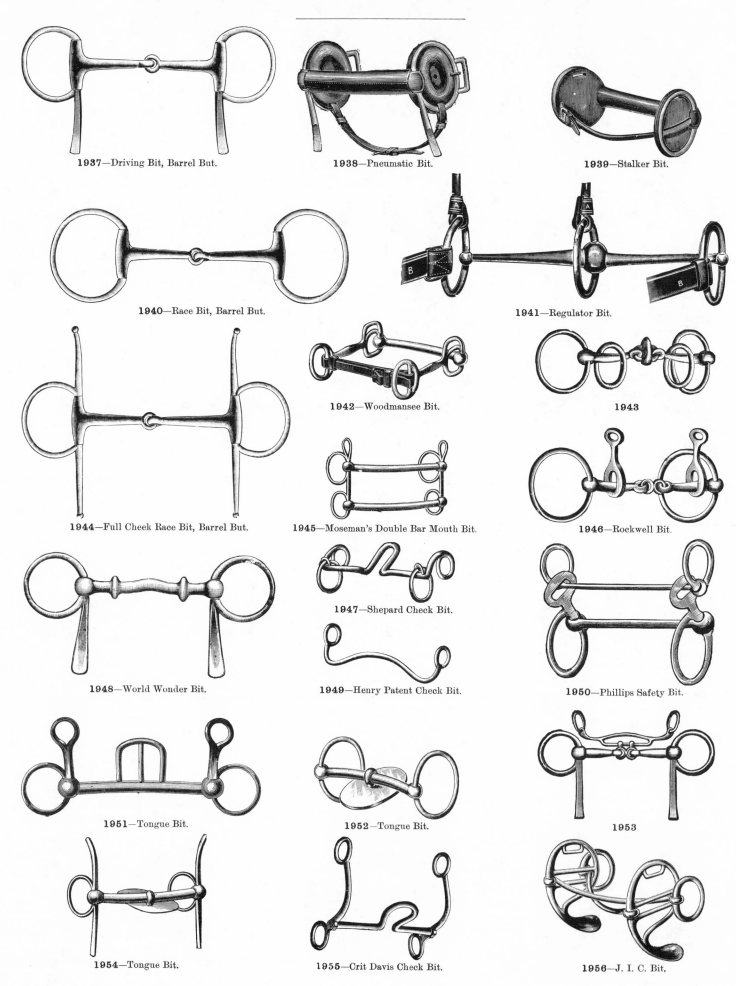

1937—Driving Bit, Barrel But.

1938—Pneumatic Bit.

1939—Stalker Bit.

1940—Race Bit, Barrel But.

1941—Regulator Bit.

1942—Woodmansee Bit.

1943

1944—Full Cheek Race Bit, Barrel But.

1945—Moseman's Double Bar Mouth Bit.

1946—Rockwell Bit.

1947—Shepard Check Bit.

1948—World Wonder Bit.

1949—Henry Patent Check Bit.

1950—Phillips Safety Bit.

1951—Tongue Bit.

1952—Tongue Bit.

1953

1954—Tongue Bit.

1955—Crit Davis Check Bit.

1956—J. I. C. Bit.

RUBBER MOUTH DRIVING BITS.

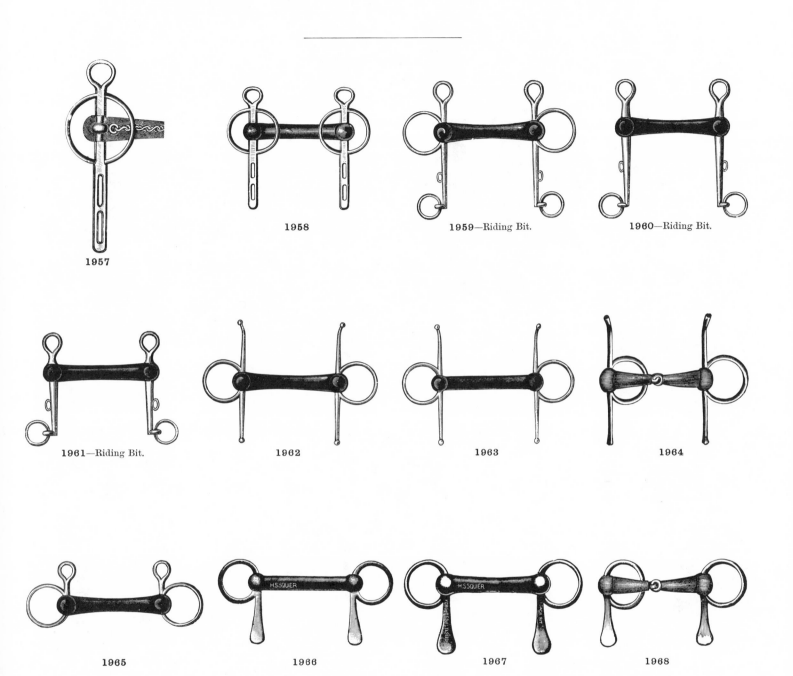

1957

1958

1959—Riding Bit.

1960—Riding Bit.

1961—Riding Bit.

1962

1963

1964

1965

1966

1967

1968

1969

1970

1971—Bit Burr.

1972—Tongue Bit.

RIDING AND DRIVING BITS.

1973

1974

1975

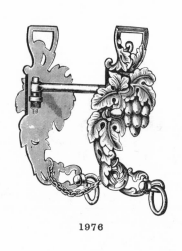

1976

1977

1978

1979

Whip Sockets and Whips

SECTION.

All Goods shown in this Section furnished at Lowest Wholesale Prices.

"DO NOT CUT THIS BOOK."

Every consumer or dealer in Harness and Saddlery, no matter in what part of the world he does business, will promote his own interests by sending us **ONE DOLLAR** and receiving in return a copy of this complete Illustrated Guide Book. It is the key to success in the prosecution of business. He cannot afford to be without the knowledge it contains of every department of the trade. It will surely serve as a lamp to light him through the many perplexities which are incidental to the Harness Industry.

With this Book in your possession you are at liberty to write to us, or to any manufacturer or dealer in Harness or Saddlery Goods with whom you do business, asking questions or sending orders, and either will know just what you want if you will mention "Moseman's Book" and give the "Number" under the article you wish to know about, or mention the picture of the article you may have under consideration at the time.

In any event, **DO NOT CUT THIS BOOK!** but simply give "Number" of the article you wish to obtain.

We are, yours for business,

C. M. MOSEMAN & BROTHER,

126 & 128 Chambers Street,

New York, U. S. A.

WHIP SOCKETS.

1980   1981   1982   1983   1984

1985   1986   1987—Rubber Lining.   1988

1989   1990   1991   1992   1993

WHIPS.

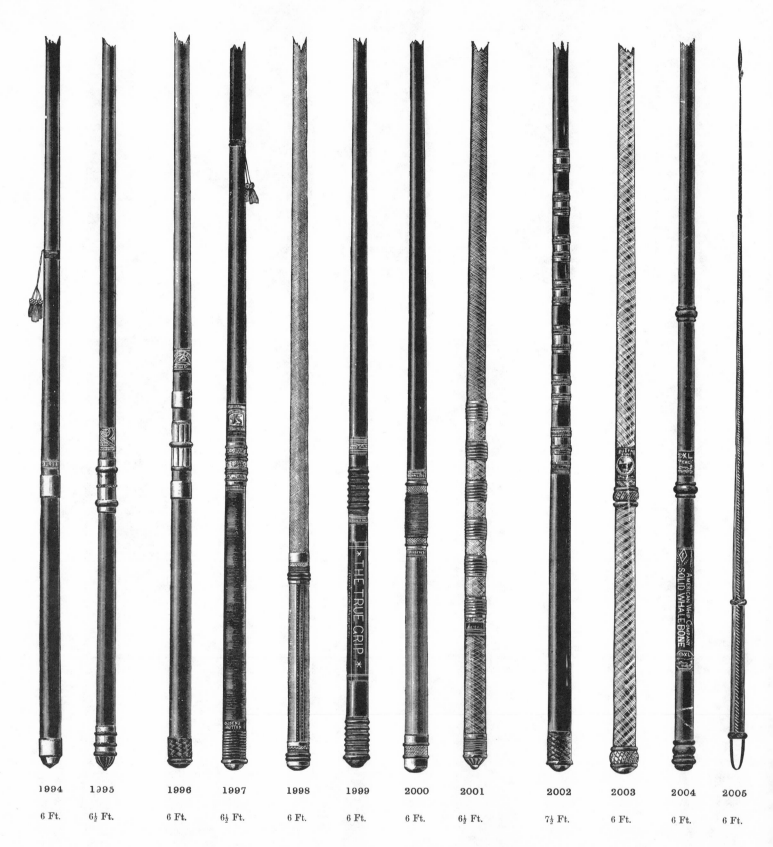

1994	1995	1996	1997	1998	1999	2000	2001	2002	2003	2004	2005
6 Ft.	6½ Ft.	6 Ft.	6½ Ft.	6 Ft.	6 Ft.	6 Ft.	6½ Ft.	7½ Ft.	6 Ft.	6 Ft.	6 Ft.

Ordinary and Medium Class of American Raw Hide and Java Filled Whips.

WHIPS.

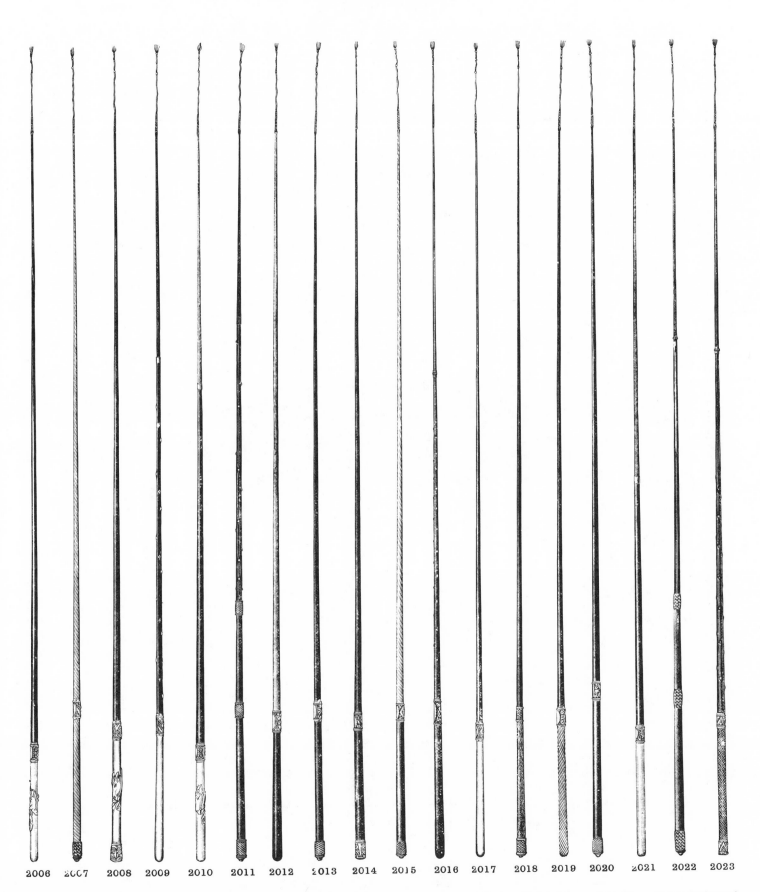

2006 2007 2008 2009 2010 2011 2012 2013 2014 2015 2016 2017 2018 2019 2020 2021 2022 2023

Woodbury, Truit, Coburn, and other makes of fine American Bone Road Driving Whips Mounted with Various Styles of Ivory, Gold, Silver, Ebony, Snakewood and other Plain and Ornamental Handles, finished with Cotton, Linen, Silk and Gut Coverings.

WHIPS.

We are handling ASHFORD'S make; the firm was established in 1790 and they were appointed by Royal Warrant makers to Her Majesty, the Queen, in 1844. Their Whips are somewhere about the best that are made, any way we have not seen any better or, of course, we should not have taken them up. We have made special arrangements as to shipments, prices and terms so that we are able to sell their highest class Whips, either at wholesale or retail, at quite exceptionally moderate prices. We are carrying a considerable stock and have most of the following lines, which are illustrated, in our store in New York, but, as we are having regular shipments, we can get any line we do not happen to have in stock, from the manufactory in England in a short time.

On this page and the next will be found their latest novelties; on the following pages will be found their regular standard lines.

C. M. MOSEMAN & BROTHER.

ASHFORD'S PRESENTATION CASE OF WHIPS.

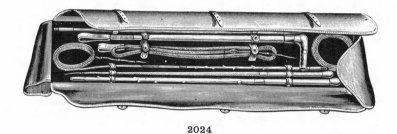

2024

Containing the following Whips, all of the highest quality and finish: HOLLY CARRIAGE WHIP, with Russia Leather Handle and Interchangeable Carriage, 4-in-hand and Gut and Whalebone Buggy Tops. (Making three distinct Whips). MALACCA CANE HUNTING CROP, with Thong (Stag Horn Hook), and a GUT AND WHALEBONE CUTTING WHIP, with Russia Leather Handle.

The case is of best grained cowhide and is lined with Doe Skin and Velvet. The straps are made long enough to enable umbrellas, walking sticks or fishing rods to be strapped to the case when traveling.

BUILT CANE DRIVING WHIP.

PATENTED.

2025

With Russia Leather Handle.   Electro Mounts.   Sterling Silver Mounts.

These Whips are built from the choicest East India Mottled Bamboo Cane, in six sections, split and shaped by hand and cemented together with waterproof cement, exactly like the best salmon and trout fishing rods. They handle exceedingly well, are very durable and always keep straight. They are made suitable for either Gig, Coupe or Pair Horse, as may be required.

WHIPS.

COACHING WHIP WITH HORN.

2026

Pig Skin Handle, best Holly Stick, with 12 inch Horn, 18 inch Horn, and 24 inch Horn.

FOUR-IN-HAND WHIP, ON FRAME.

2027

Electro and Sterling Silver Mounts.

INTERCHANGEABLE FOUR-IN-HAND AND PAIR HORSE WHIP, ON FRAME.

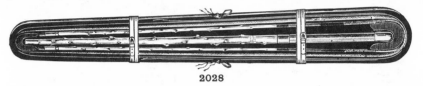

2028

Electro and Sterling Silver Mounts.

LADIES PARASOL WHIP.

2029

Russia Leather Handle, Electro and Silver Mounts.   Ivory Handle, Electro and Silver Mounts.   Silk and Silk Lining, any color.

SPRING TOP (patent) CARRIAGE WHIPS, Latest Patterns.
THE "SHAFTO."

2030

Selected Holly.   Handle covered **all over** with Pig Skin.   Very neat and stylish.

YE "OLD TIMES."

2031

This is the old coaching style, with lapped doe-skin handle.

THE "DOWN-THE-ROAD."

2032

Neat and modern.   Looks well and wears well.   The handle and mounts are covered with narrow strips of Pig Skin.

The Hollies used for the above Whips are all English grown and are the first selection, and have all had about five years careful seasoning.
Colors range from Lemon to Nut Brown.   They are all "Ashford's exclusive patterns.

WHIPS.

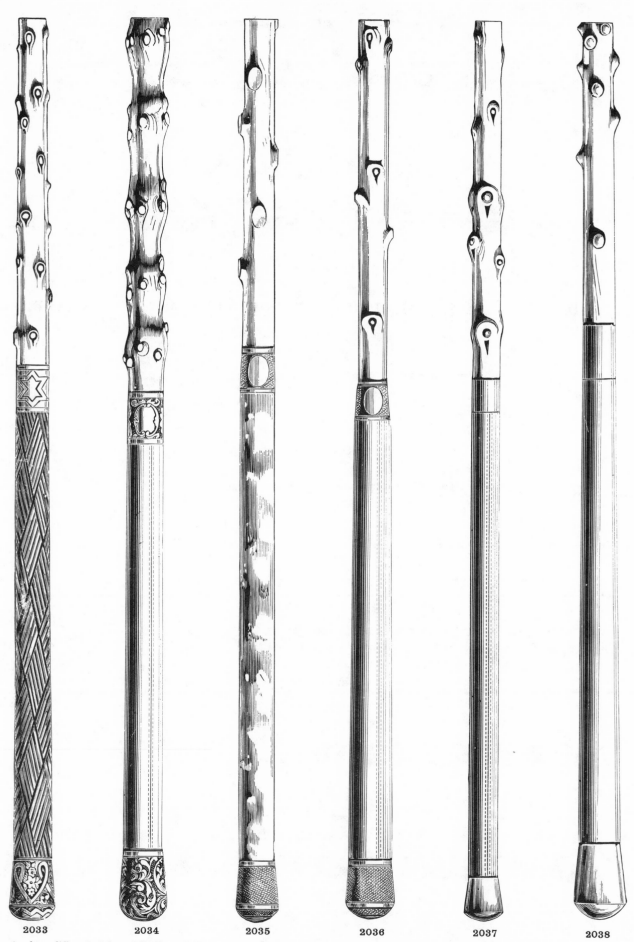

2033   2034   2035   2036   2037   2038

These cuts show different styles of Holly and Yew Sticks, with Ivory, Leather and other Handles, with Plain and Chased Mounts, for English-made
Quill-top Coach, Dog-cart and other Whips, for Gents' Ladies' and Children's use.

WHIPS.

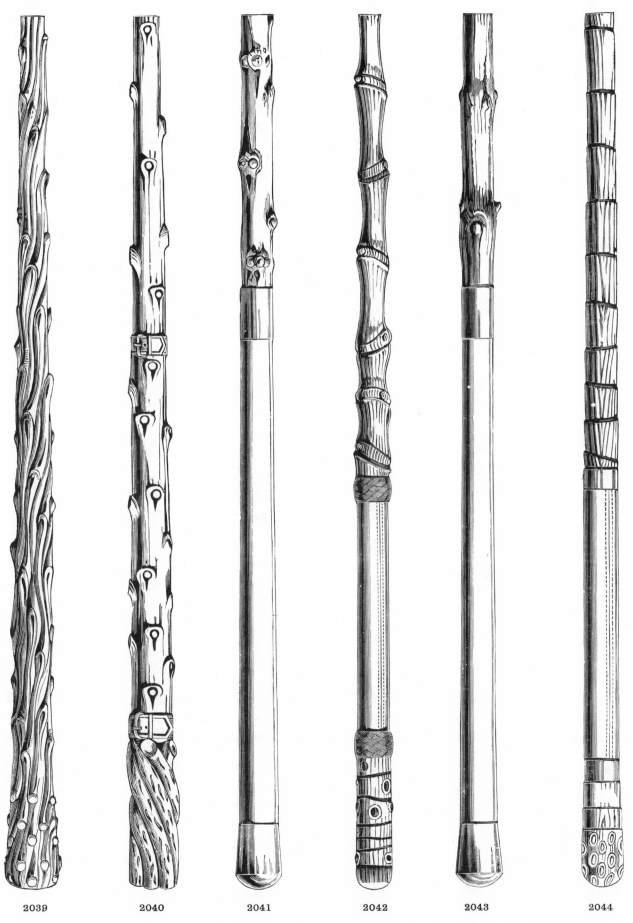

2039   2040   2041   2042   2043   2044

These cuts show different styles of English Holly, Thorn, Wangee, Bamboo and Lance-wood Sticks for Quill Top Coach, and other English-made Whips
for Gents', Ladies and Children's use.

DRIVING WHIPS.

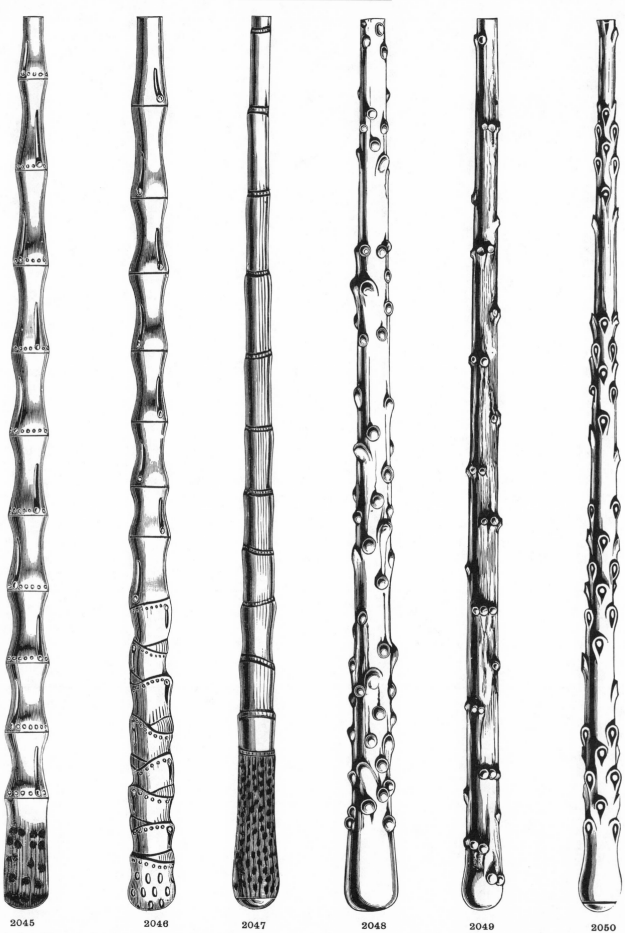

| 2045 | 2046 | 2047 | 2048 | 2049 | 2050 |

These cuts show different styles of Wangee, Bamboo, Root, Holly and Yew Sticks for English-made Quill-top, Dog-cart, Village-cart, Pony-cart, Phæton and other use.   Light, Heavy, Long or Short, as desired.   These Whips are made for us by the best makers of England and America.

WHIPS.

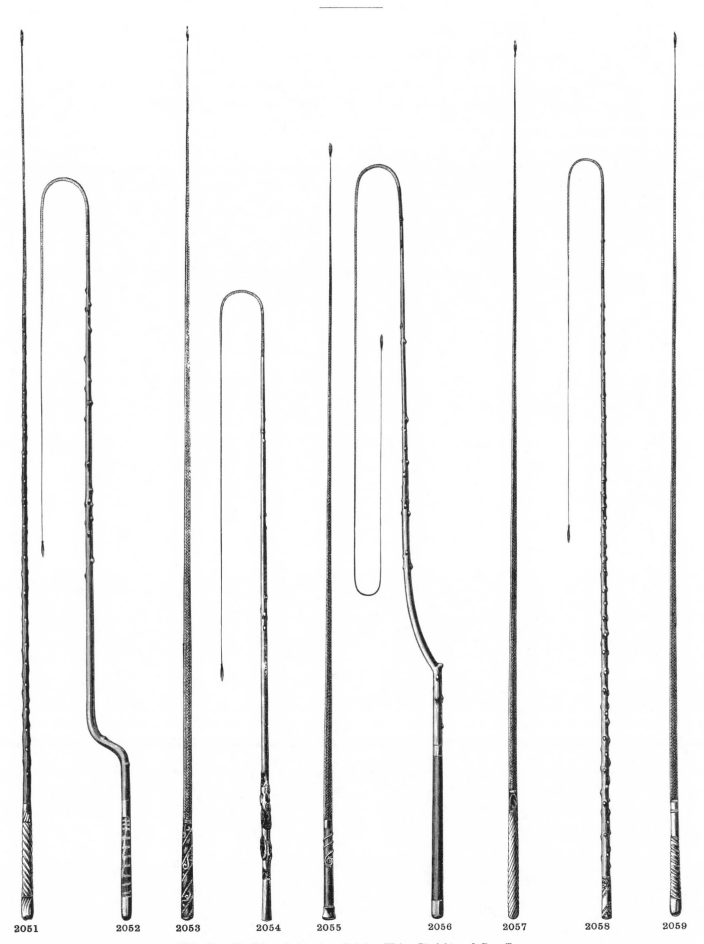

| 2051 | 2052 | 2053 | 2054 | 2055 | 2056 | 2057 | 2058 | 2059 |

High Class English and American Driving Whips, Straight and Bow Top.

WHIPS.

Ashford's Standard Patterns of English Holly Driving Whips.

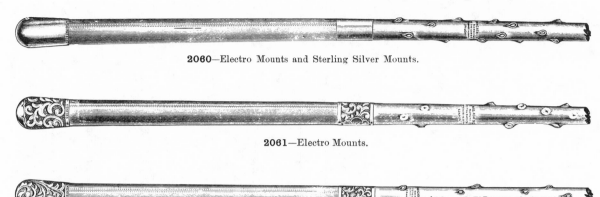

2060—Electro Mounts and Sterling Silver Mounts.

2061—Electro Mounts.

2062—Electro Mounts and Sterling Silver Mounts.

This Whip is made in every way as well as it is possible to make a Whip.   It can be had any weight for Gig, Coupe or heavy Pair of Horse use.

ASHFORD'S JOCKEY WHIPS.

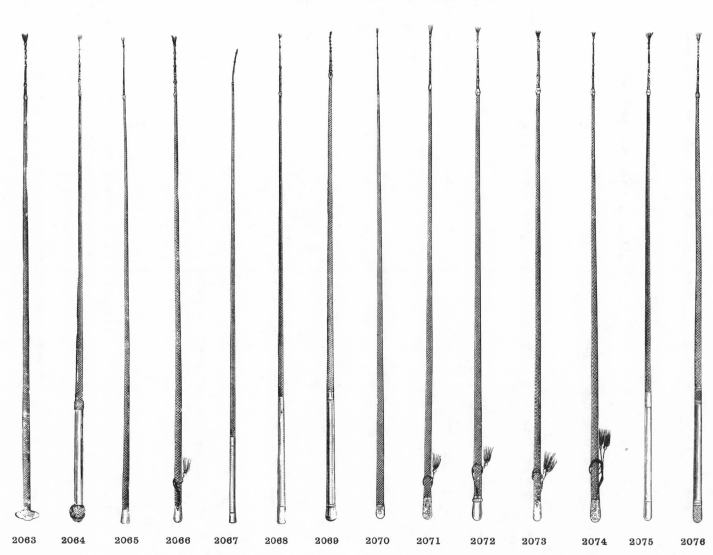

2063   2064   2065   2066   2067   2068   2069   2070   2071   2072   2073   2074   2075   2076

RIDING WHIPS.

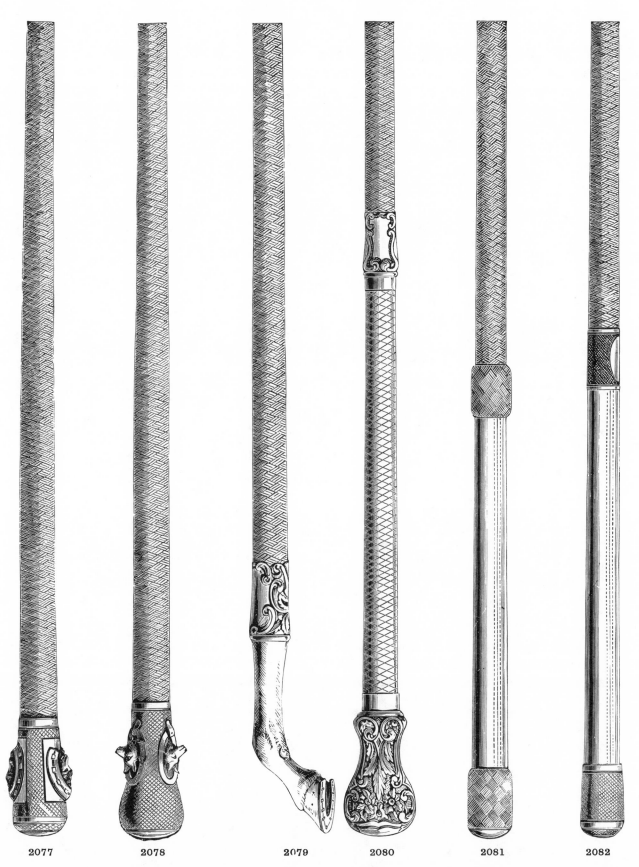

2077   2078   2079   2080   2081   2082

These cuts show different styles of Riding Whips, with Gut and Thread Finish, Plain or Highly Mounted. Made directly for us by the best makers of England, such as **Swain & Adeney, Joseph Carver, Zair-Schomberg,** and others.

WHIPS.

ASHFORD'S LADIES' TWIG WHIPS.

Plain Mounts.   **Fancy Mounts.**

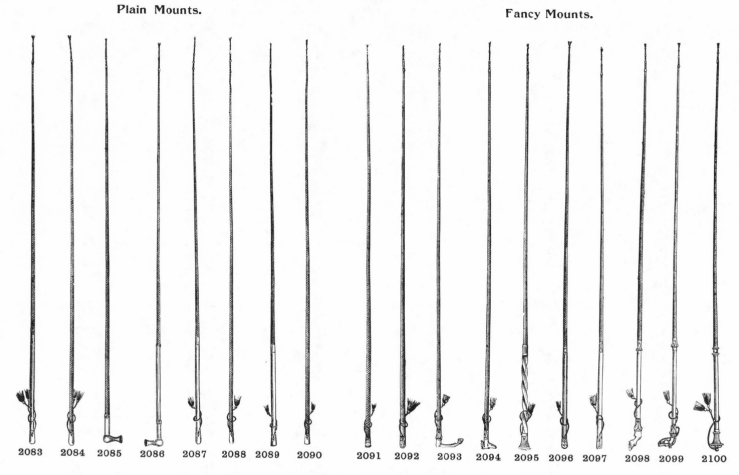

2083 2084 2085 2086 2087 2088 2089 2090   2091 2092 2093 2094 2095 2096 2097 2098 2099 2100

All Whalebone Stock and Finest Selected Gut.

2083—Electro Mounts,	Sterling Silver Mounts.	2091—German Silver Mounts.
2084—Electro Mounts,	Sterling Silver Mounts.	2092—Electro Mounts.
2085—Electro Mounts,	Gilt Mounts.	2093—Electro Mounts.
2086—Electro Mounts,	Gilt Mounts.	2094—Electro Mounts.
2087—Electro Mounts,	Sterling Silver Mounts.	2095—Electro Mounts.
2088—Electro Mounts,	Sterling Silver Mounts.	2096—German Silver Mounts.
2089—German Silver Mounts,	Electro Mounts.	2097—Electro Mounts.
2090—German Silver Mounts,	Electro Mounts.	2098—Electro Mounts.
		2099—Electro Mounts.
		2100—Electro Mounts.

ASHFORD'S DOG WHIPS.

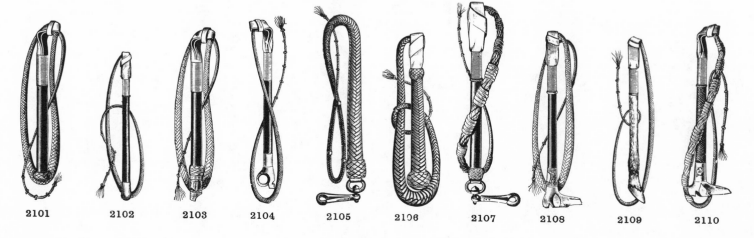

2101   2102   2103   2104   2105   2106   2107   2108   2109   2110

WHIPS.

ASHFORD'S HUNTING CROPS.

DRAGON CANES. (Light Weight.)

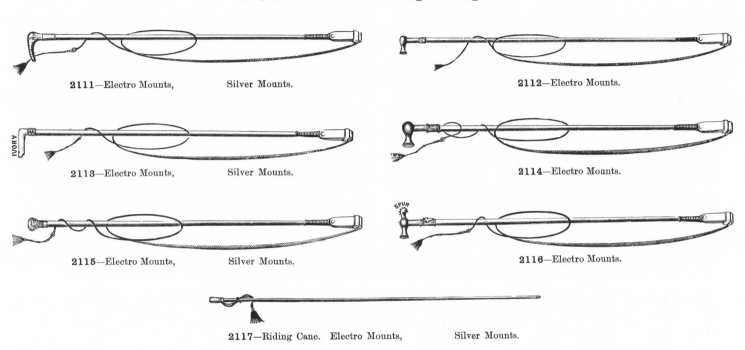

2111—Electro Mounts,   Silver Mounts.

2112—Electro Mounts.

2113—Electro Mounts,   Silver Mounts.

2114—Electro Mounts.

2115—Electro Mounts,   Silver Mounts.

2116—Electro Mounts.

2117—Riding Cane. Electro Mounts,   Silver Mounts.

MALACCA CANES. (Full Weight.)

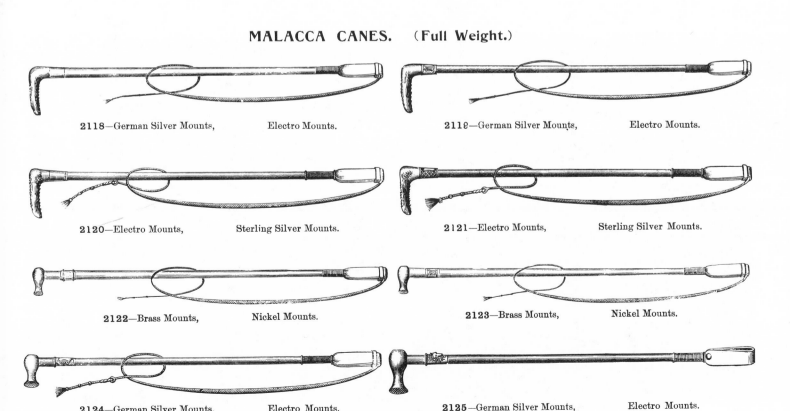

2118—German Silver Mounts,   Electro Mounts.

2119—German Silver Mounts,   Electro Mounts.

2120—Electro Mounts,   Sterling Silver Mounts.

2121—Electro Mounts,   Sterling Silver Mounts.

2122—Brass Mounts,   Nickel Mounts.

2123—Brass Mounts,   Nickel Mounts.

2124—German Silver Mounts,   Electro Mounts.

2125—German Silver Mounts,   Electro Mounts.

RIDING WHIPS.

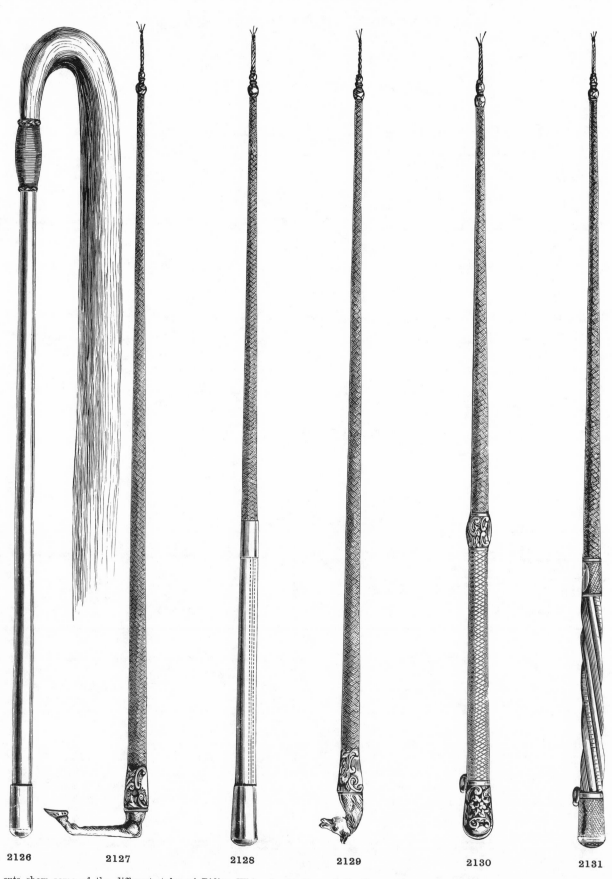

2126   2127   2128   2129   2130   2131

These cuts show some of the different styles of Riding Whips for Ladies and Gentlemen, mounted in Ivory, Silver, Gold, etc. Made for us
by the best makers of the world, such as **Swain & Adeney, Joseph Carver, Zair-Schomberg,** and others.

FANCY RIDING WHIPS.

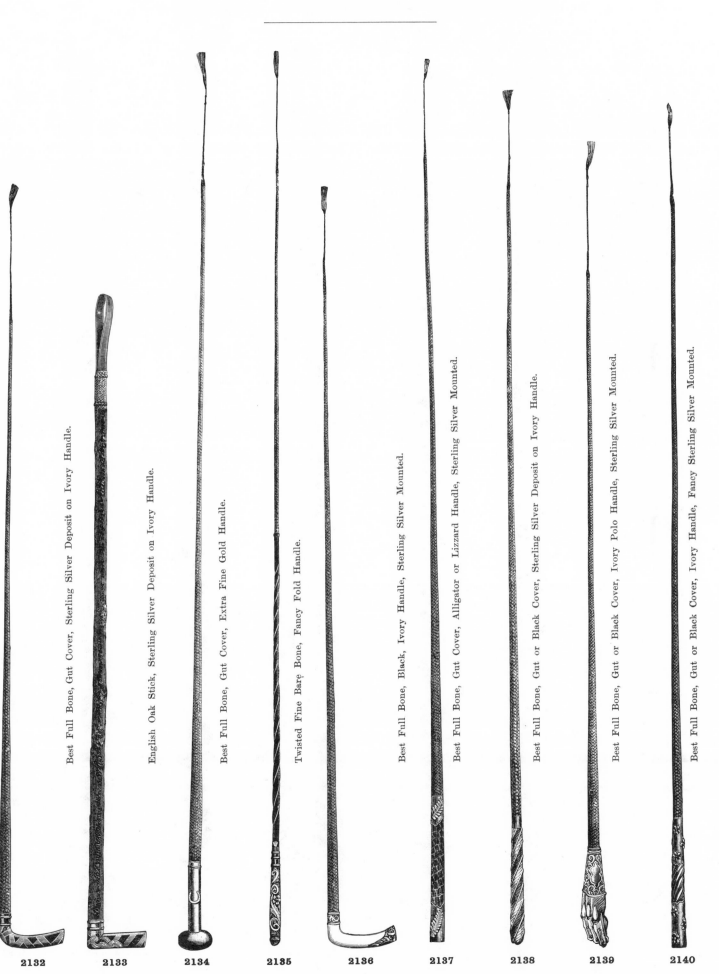

Best Full Bone, Gut Cover, Sterling Silver Deposit on Ivory Handle.

English Oak Stick, Sterling Silver Deposit on Ivory Handle.

Best Full Bone, Gut Cover, Extra Fine Gold Handle.

Twisted Fine Bare Bone, Fancy Fold Handle.

Best Full Bone, Black, Ivory Handle, Sterling Silver Mounted.

Best Full Bone, Gut Cover, Alligator or Lizzard Handle, Sterling Silver Mounted.

Best Full Bone, Gut or Black Cover, Sterling Silver Deposit on Ivory Handle.

Best Full Bone, Gut or Black Cover, Ivory Polo Handle, Sterling Silver Mounted.

Best Full Bone, Gut or Black Cover, Ivory Handle, Fancy Sterling Silver Mounted.

2132   2133   2134   2135   2136   2137   2138   2139   2140

PLAIN GUT RIDING WHIPS.

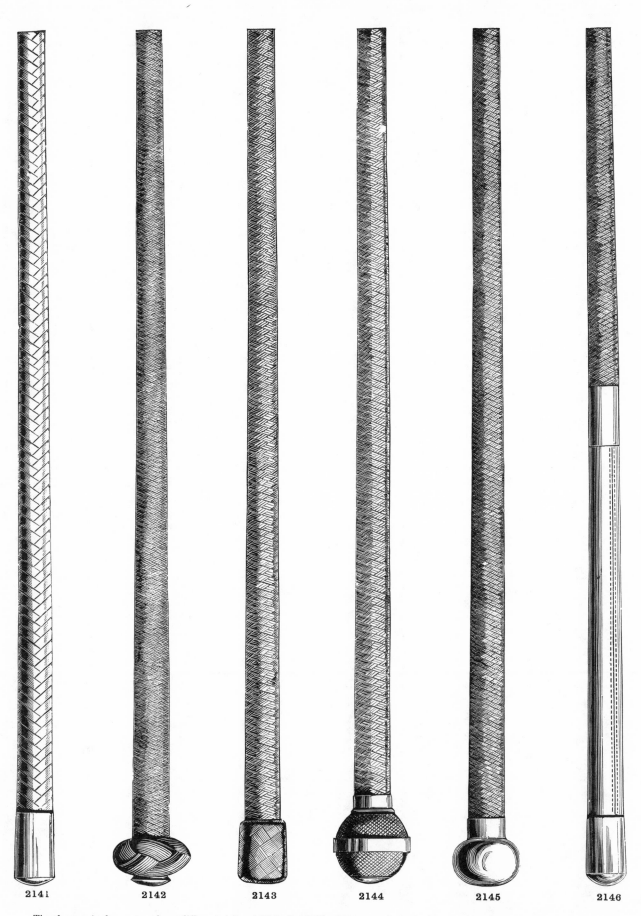

2141   2142   2143   2144   2145   2146

The above cuts show some of our different styles of Plain Gut Riding Whips, made for Ladies' and Gentlemen, or for race purposes.

Made for us by the best makers of England and America.

RACE WHIPS.

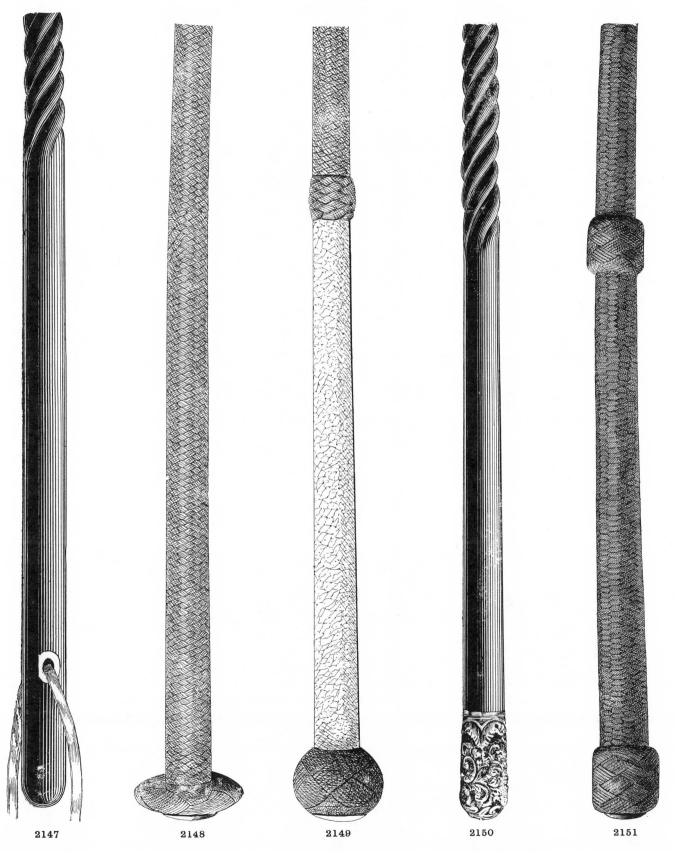

2147
French Twisted Willow.

2148
Gut and Bone Race Whip.

2149
Gut and Bone, with Leather Covered Handle, Race Whip.

2150
French Twisted Willow, Silver Mounts.

2151
Gut and Bone Race Whip.

HUNTING CROPS.

2152   2154   2156

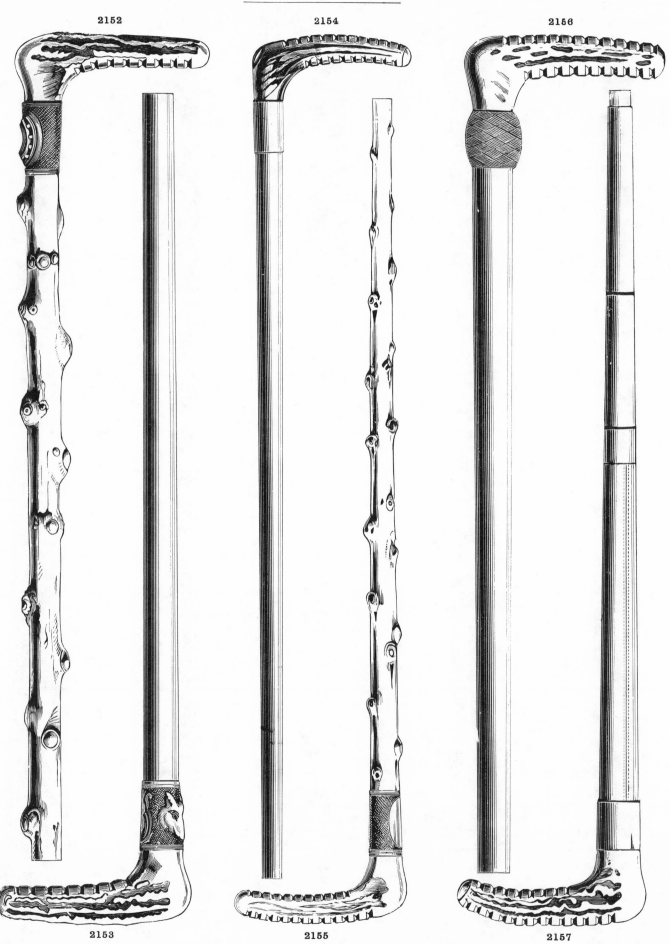

2153   2155   2157

These cuts show different styles of Hunting Crops adapted to the wants of Ladies and Gentlemen. All Crops made for us by the best makers of England and America.

HUNTING CROPS.

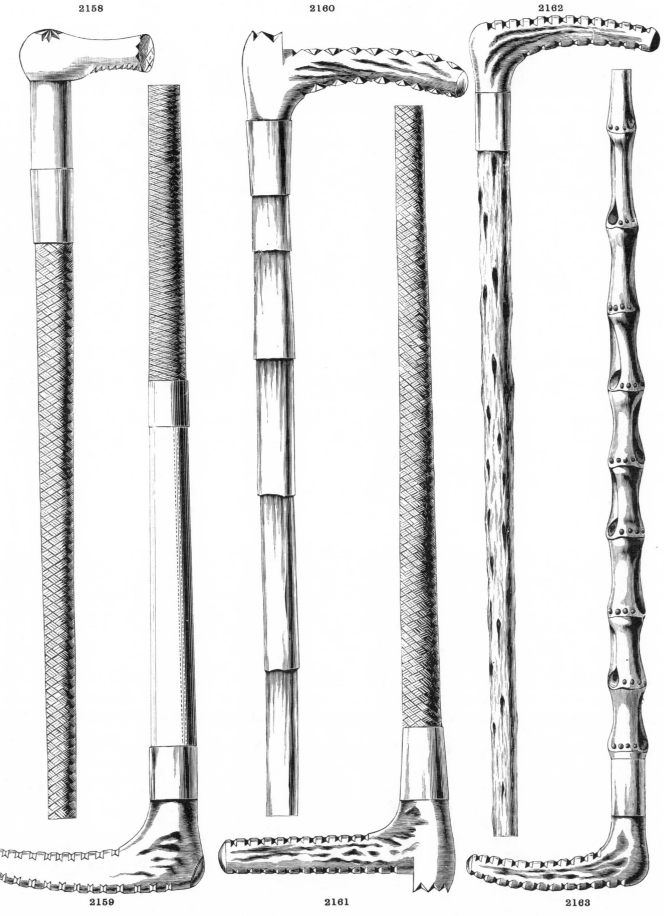

2158   2160   2162

2159   2161   2163

These cuts show different styles of Hunting Crops, with Gut, Malacca, Bamboo, Wangee and Holly Sticks, with Buckhorn or Silver Handles.

HUNTING CROPS.

2164   2166   2168

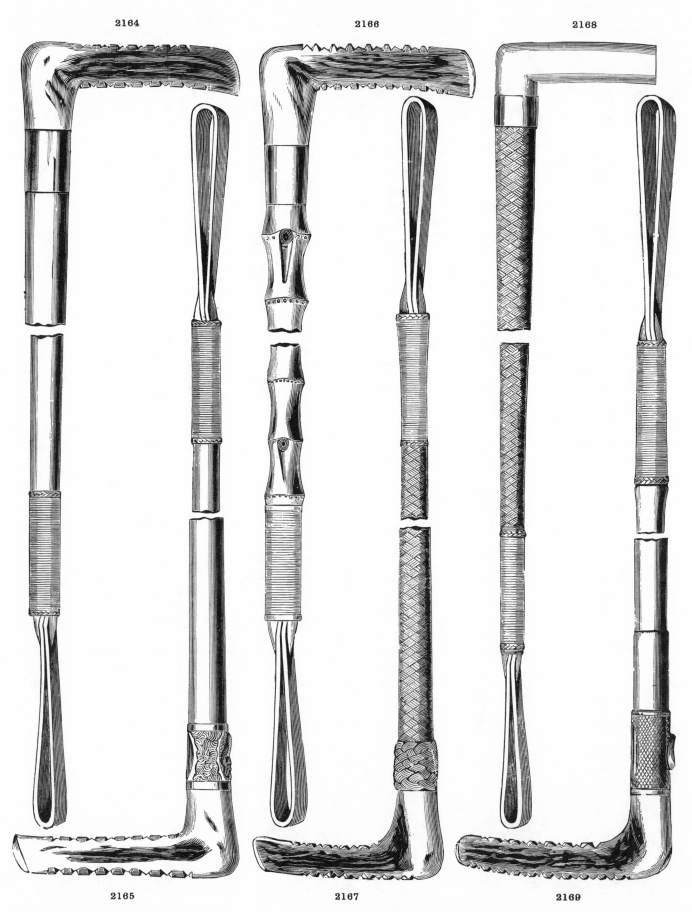

2165   2167   2169

These cuts show different styles of Hunting Crops, with Buckhorn and Ivory Handles.   Made for us by the best makers of England and America.

WHIPS AND WHIP HOLDERS.

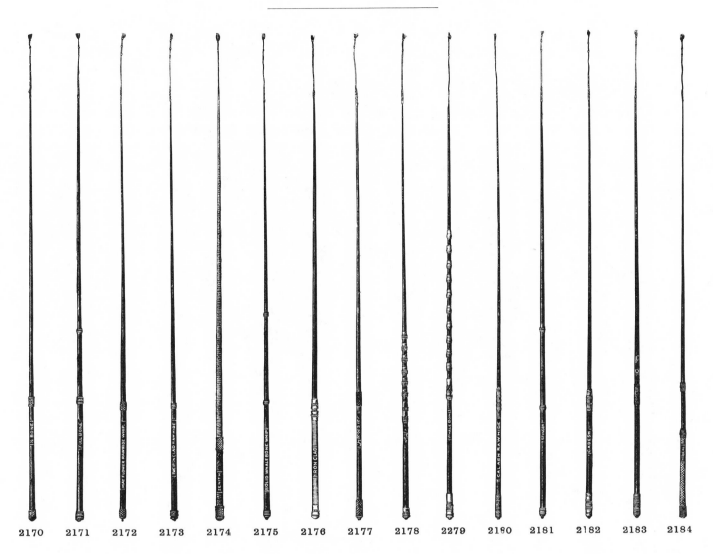

| 2170 | 2171 | 2172 | 2173 | 2174 | 2175 | 2176 | 2177 | 2178 | 2279 | 2180 | 2181 | 2182 | 2183 | 2184 |

2185—Steel Whip Holder for 12 Whips.

Rosewood, Mahogany and Oak Whip Holders.

2186—To hold 4 Holly and 12 Bone Whips.

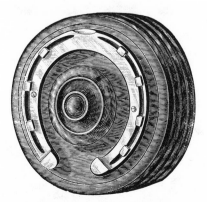

2187—To hold 4 Holly Whips.

PAT. JUNE 2D 1896.

2188—Temple's Patent Whip Stand for showing Whips. Will hold 36 Whips.

Jackets

Caps and Breeches

RIDING JACKETS, CAPS, BREECHES AND BOOTS, TO SUIT THE REQUIREMENTS OF ALL TASTES OR STABLES.

Jackets

Caps and Breeches

SPECIAL SETS OF COLORS MADE TO ORDER AT SHORT NOTICE. WATERPROOF RACING OUTFITS READY FOR IMMEDIATE DELIVERY

Four-in-Hand and Double

Harness Ornaments, Etc.

SECTION.

All Goods shown in this Section furnished at Lowest Wholesale Prices.

2189—BUYING PRIZE WINNERS AT TATTERSALLS.

USEFUL ORNAMENTS.

2190—Clock for Stable Office, Club Rooms, etc.

2191—Clocks for Stable Office, Club Rooms, etc.

2192
Clock for Stable Office, Club Rooms, etc.

2193—Watch and Mirror Case,
for inside of close carriages.

2194   **2195**   **2196**

Watch and Case with Rein Holder for the Dashboard of Carriages.

2197—Watch and Bracelet Case for Ladies' or Gent's Wrist.

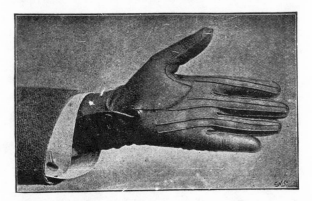

2198—Fowne's Patent Grip Driving Gloves.

DRIVING SUNDRIES.

2199—Eye Shields or Spectacles, with Wire Screen.

2200   2201   2202

Lamb's Patent Mica Eye Shields for Ladies and Gentlemen.   For use in Windy and Dusty Weather.

2203—Lehman's Patent Foot Warmers and Fuel.   Can be used in the carriage or house.   One block of fuel will burn slowly 8 hours. No blaze—no smell.

2204—French Patent Leather Hats, Light Strong and Good for Coachmen's use.

2205—Patent Leather Toe Guards to put over the side of she carriage box to prevent toe marks when getting in.

2206   2207   2208
Shoulder Knots for Private Coachmen.

2209
Shopping Basket for inside of Carriages.

HARNESS ORNAMENTS.

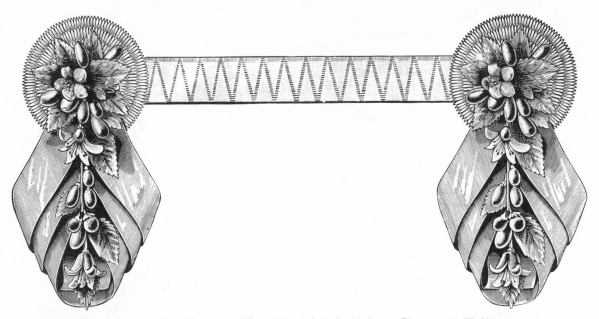

2210—White Silk Bridle Front, Rosettes and Bouttonires, trimmed with Orange Blossoms, for Wedding Turnouts.
Saddle Housings to match.

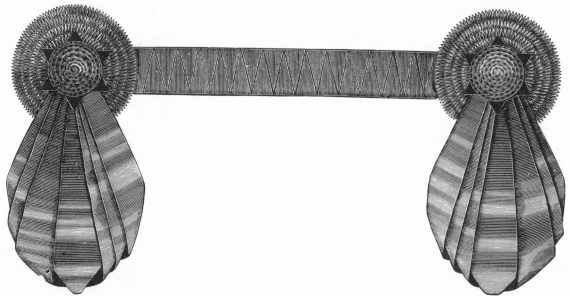

2211—Black Silk Bridle Front and Rosettes for Livery Mourning.   Saddle Housings to match.

2212   2213   2215   2216   2217

2214

Fine French Flowers for Horses Heads, Livery and Private use.

HARNESS ORNAMENTS.

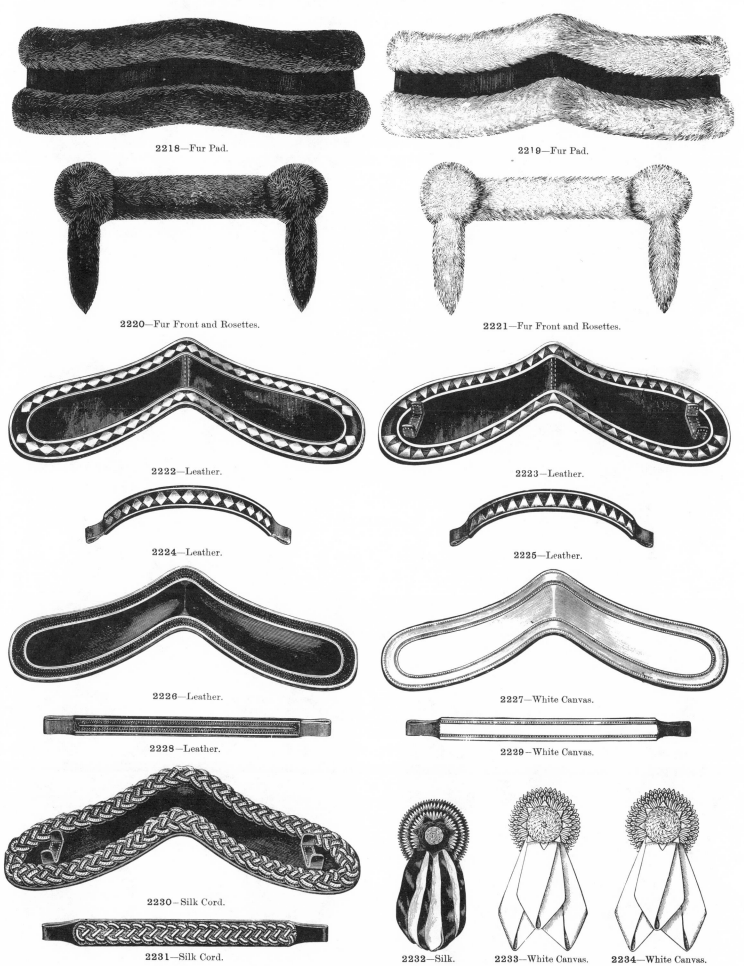

2218—Fur Pad.

2219—Fur Pad.

2220—Fur Front and Rosettes.

2221—Fur Front and Rosettes.

2222—Leather.

2223—Leather.

2224—Leather.

2225—Leather.

2226—Leather.

2227—White Canvas.

2228—Leather.

2229—White Canvas.

2230—Silk Cord.

2231—Silk Cord.

2232—Silk.   2233—White Canvas.   2234—White Canvas.

Harness Saddle Pads in various Patterns and Colors of Leather, Silk or Wool, with Fronts and Rosettes to match.

ROSETTES AND MONOGRAMS.

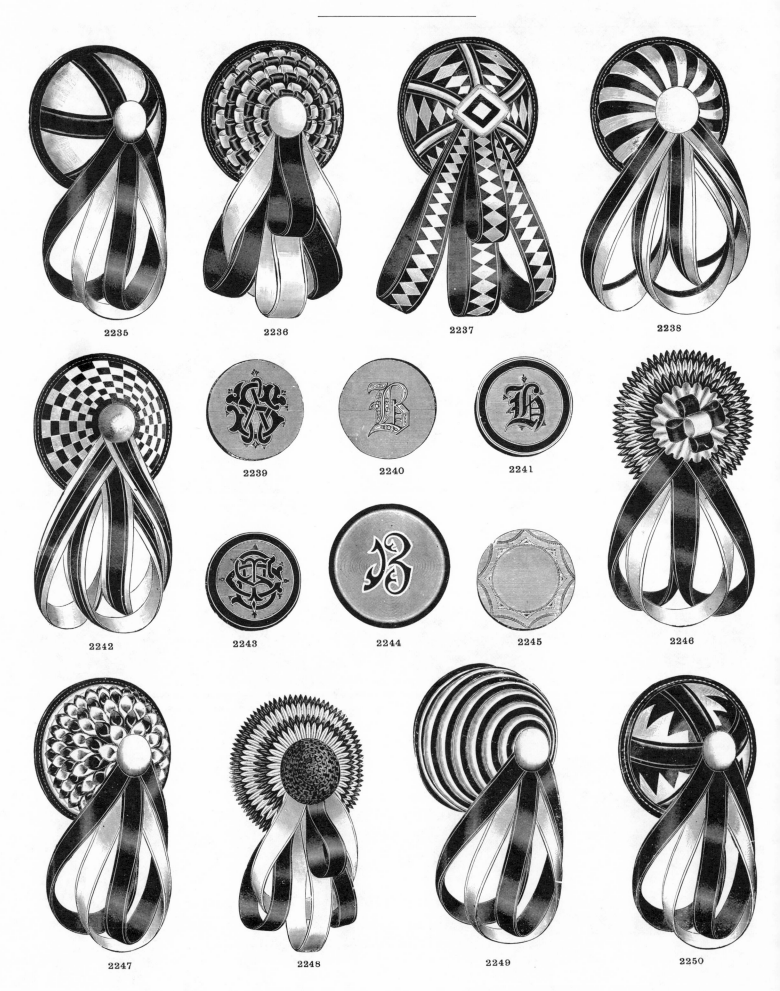

2235   2236   2237   2238

2242   2239   2240   2241

2243   2244   2245   2246

2247   2248   2249   2250

BRIDLE FRONTS.

2251

2252

2253

2254

2255

2256

2257

2258

2259

2260

2261

BRIDLE FRONTS.

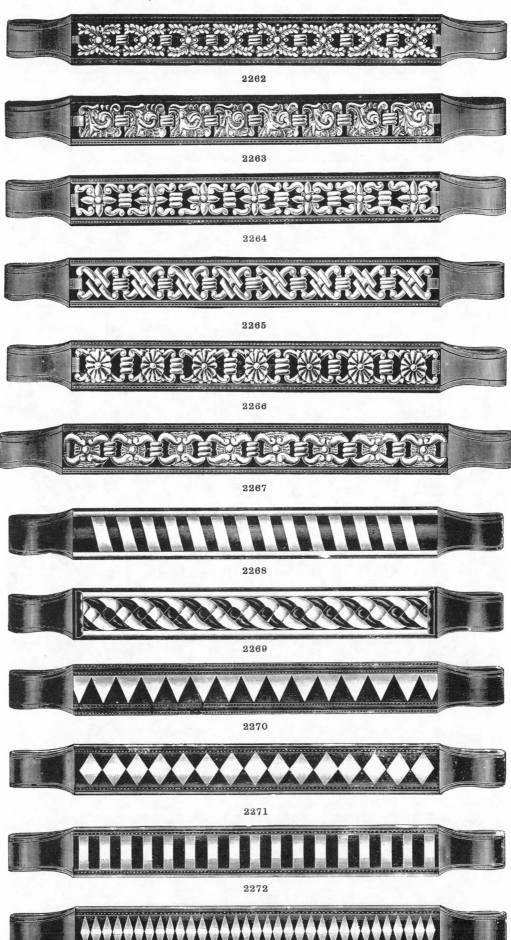

2262

2263

2264

2265

2266

2267

2268

2269

2270

2271

2272

2273

BRIDLE FRONTS, CURB CHAINS AND HOOKS.

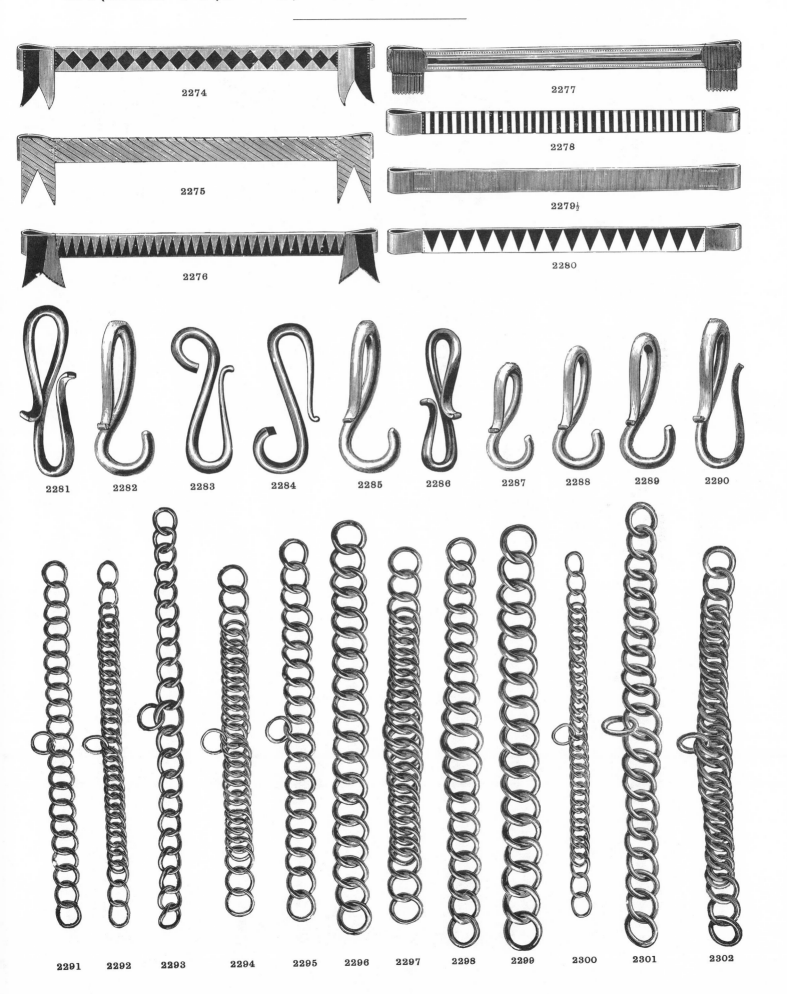

2274

2275

2276

2277

2278

2279½

2280

2281 2282 2283 2284 2285 2286 2287 2288 2289 2290

2291 2292 2293 2294 2295 2296 2297 2298 2299 2300 2301 2302

MONOGRAMS AND CRESTS.

2303   2304   2305   2306

2307   2308   2309   2310

2311   2312   2313   2314   2315

2316   2317   2318   2319

2320   2321   2322   2323

MISCELLANEOUS.

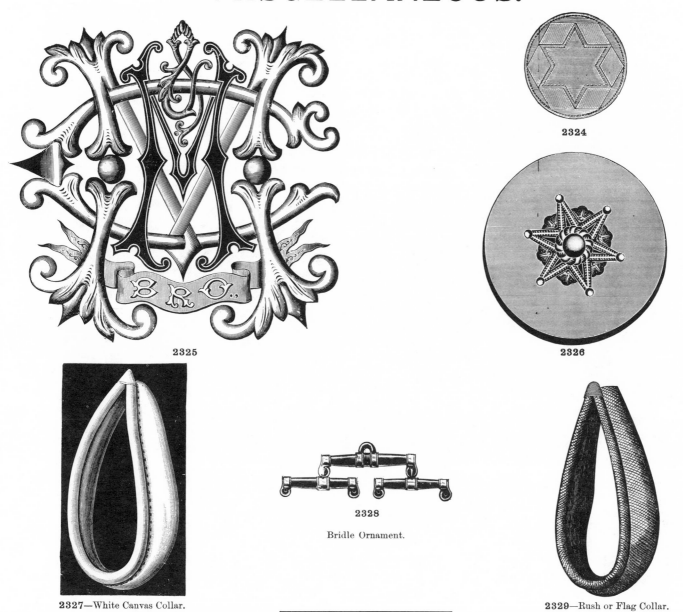

2325

2324

2326

2327—White Canvas Collar.

2328

Bridle Ornament.

2329—Rush or Flag Collar.

Directions for Measuring a Horse for a Collar.

2330

2331

To measure the neck, place your hand on top and get the number of inches in a straight line to bottom of neck, as shown on drawing. If you have a collar that fits your horse, measure as shown on drawing of collar. Inside measure only is wanted.

ADJUSTABLE SUPPORTER.

For Wagon Pole or Shafts.

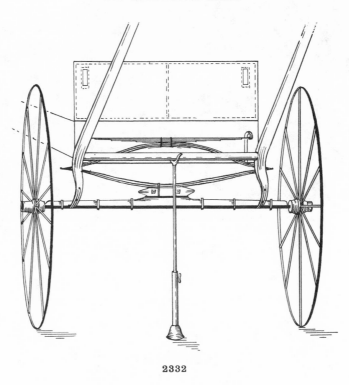

2332

FOWNES' DRIVING GLOVES.

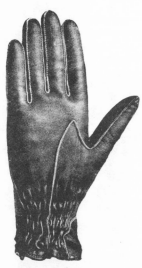

**Fownes'
Patent Sleighing.**

2333

**Fownes'
Lisle Thread Tilburyed.**

2334

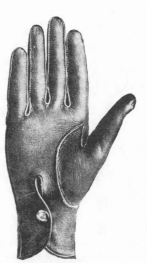

**Fownes'
Celebrated Driving**

2335

2336—Fownes' Patent Grip Driving

DOUBLE HARNESS

SECTION.

All Goods shown in this Section furnished at Lowest Wholesale Prices.

"DO NOT CUT THIS BOOK."

Every consumer or dealer in Harness and Saddlery, no matter in what part of the world he does business, will promote his own interests by sending us **ONE DOLLAR** and receiving in return a copy of this complete Illustrated Guide Book. It is the key to success in the prosecution of business. He cannot afford to be without the knowledge it contains of every department of the trade. It will surely serve as a lamp to light him through the many perplexities which are incidental to the Harness Industry.

With this Book in your possession you are at liberty to write to us, or to any manufacturer or dealer in Harness or Saddlery Goods with whom you do business, asking questions or sending orders, and either will know just what you want if you will mention "MOSEMAN'S BOOK" and give the "NUMBER" under the article you wish to know about, or mention the picture of the article you may have under consideration at the time.

In any event, **DO NOT CUT THIS BOOK!** but simply give "Number" of the article you wish to obtain.

We are, yours for business,

C. M. MOSEMAN & BROTHER,

126 & 128 CHAMBERS STREET,

NEW YORK, U. S. A.

2337—On the road behind a pair of Trotters.

DOUBLE HARNESS.

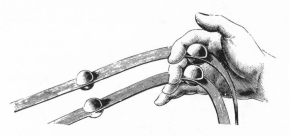

2338—Adjustable Wooden Buttons to put on Driving Reins.

2339—Adjustable Loop or Holder to put on Driving Reins.

2340—Breast Collar to use on light Double Harness, instead of Hame Collar.

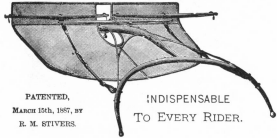

UNIQUE POLE SCREEN.

PATENTED,
MARCH 15th, 1887, BY
R. M. STIVERS.

INDISPENSABLE
TO EVERY RIDER.

PROTECTS DRIVER AND VEHICLE. GOGGLES FOR EYES NOT NEEDED.
ONE SCREEN CAN BE USED FOR DIFFERENT WAGONS
EXCELLENT FOR SLEIGHING   STOPS BALLS.

2341

2342—Pair Horse Trotting and Road Harness, finished in Leather and Rubber Trimmings; also Silver, Gilt and Brass.

Furnished in various grades and styles.

POSTILION HARNESS.

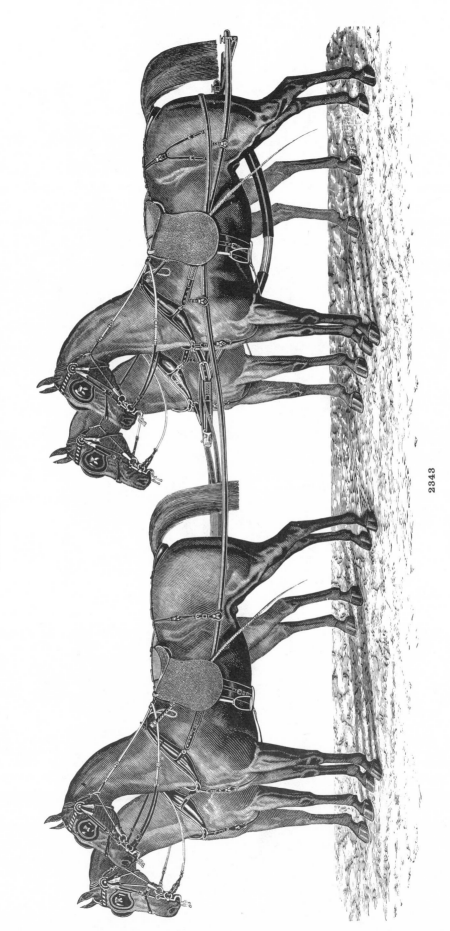

2343

Furnished to order in various grades.

FOUR-IN-HAND HARNESS.

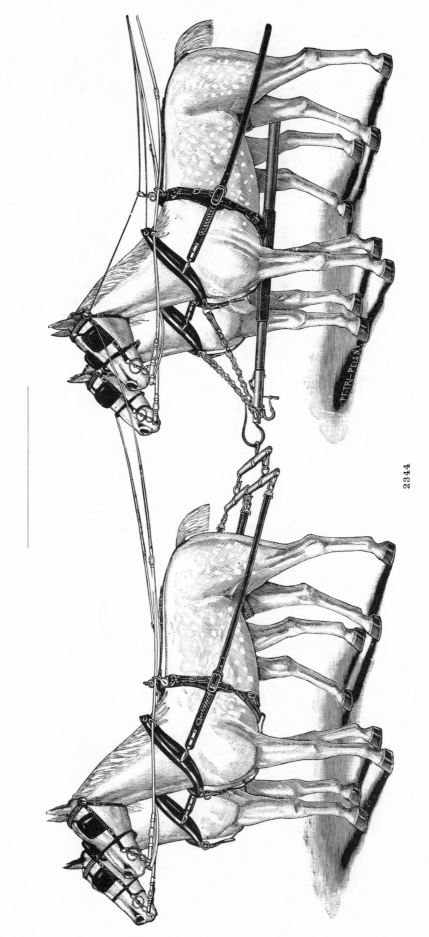

2344

All the latest Designs in Four-in-Hand Harness furnished at short notice.

FOUR-IN-HAND COACH HARNESS.

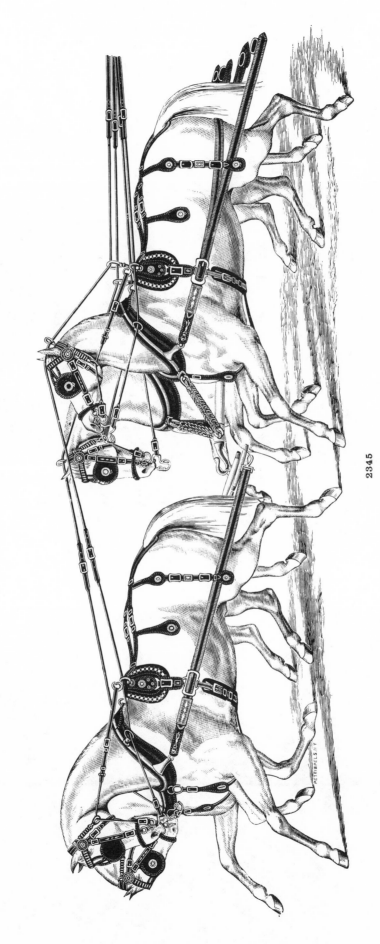

2345

Orders for the above Harness will be executed in modern fashion, equipped with the latest patterns in Trimmings, Pad Housings, Monograms, Crests, Fronts, Bits, etc.

Special designs and requirements carried out when full particulars are given.

DOUBLE HARNESS.

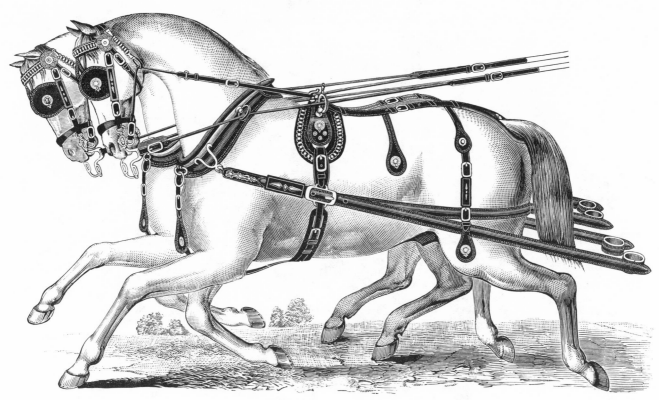

2346 Fine Coach Harness.

2347—Process of Breaking a Four-in-Hand on the Diamond Ranch of G. D. Rainsford of Wyoming.

DOUBLE HARNESS.

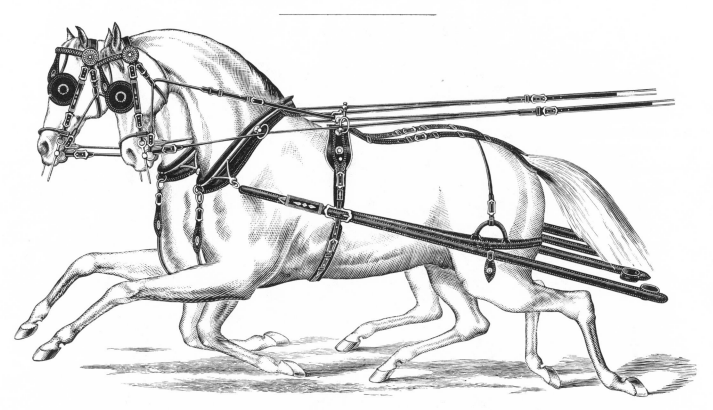

2348—Medium Coach, Wagonette or Rockaway Harness.

2349—Medium Heavy Coach or Carry-all Harness. Good for Country or City Livery use.

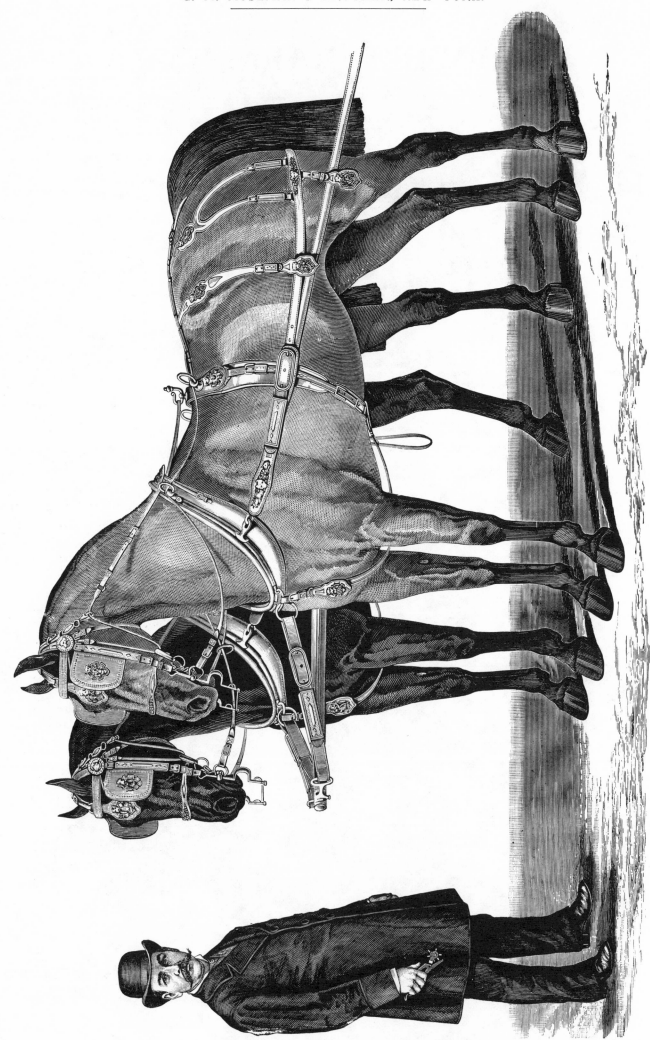

2350—WILLIAM, our trusty equine tailor, will come and measure your Horses and fit any description of Harness if specially desired.

2351—High Class and Comfortable Winter Requisites, such as Blankets, Robes, Capes and Gloves, furnished entire in every grade at short notice.

DOUBLE HARNESS.

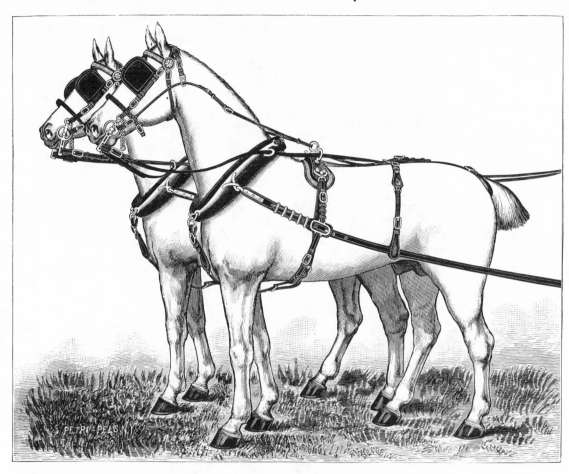

2352—Pair Horse Long Tug Coach Harness, with Metal Loops on Hame Tugs, finished in Silver, Brass or Solid Nickel Silver.

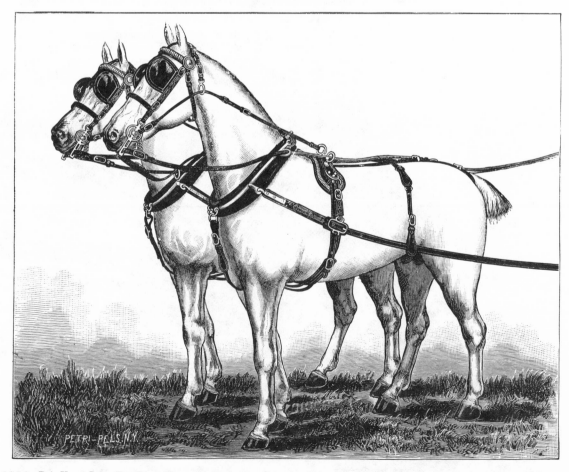

2353—Pair Horse Long Tug Coach Harness, with Leather Loops on Hame Tugs, finished in Silver, Brass or Solid Nickel Silver.

DOUBLE HARNESS.

2354—Pair Horse Short Tug Coach Harness, in Silver, Nickel or Brass.

2355—Pair Horse Short Tug Coach Harness, in Silver, Nickel or Brass.

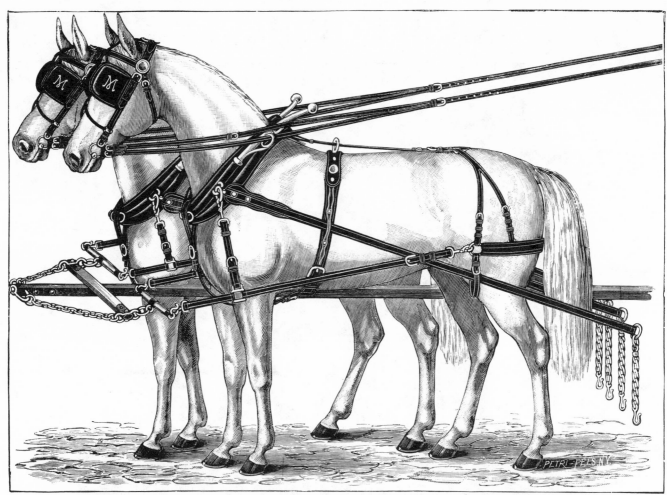

2356—Pair Horse Draught Harness, with High Ball Top Hames and Whiffletree Backers, finished in Silver, Nickel, Brass or Japan, in various grades.

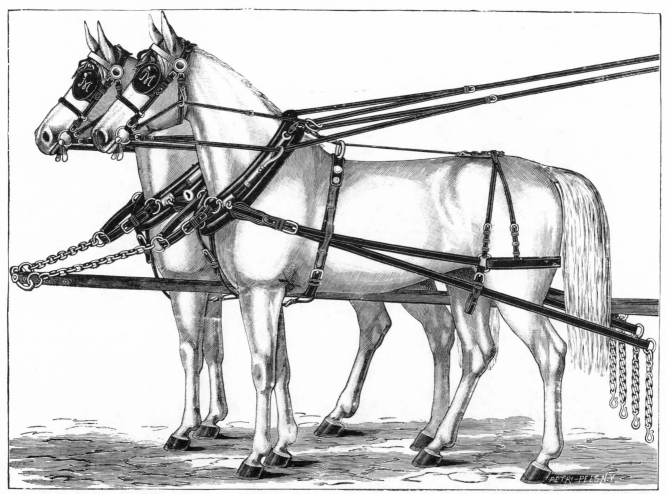

2357—Pair Horse Draught Harness, with Low Top Hames and Side Breeching Straps, finished in Silver, Nickel, Brass or Japan, in various grades.

DOUBLE HARNESS.

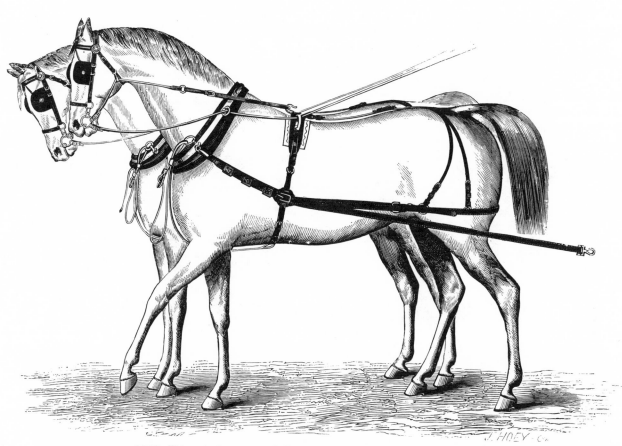

2358—This cut shows a good Harness for farm and for marketing produce.

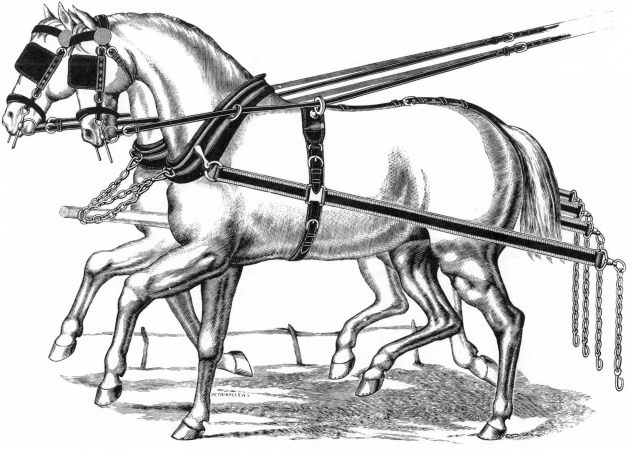

2359—This cut shows a strong well-made double Truck or Business Harness, adapted for heavy hauling.

CHAINS AND SNAPS.

2360—54 inch Fine Tinned Halter Chains, Snap on both ends, or with T on one end and Snap on the other.

2361—36 inch Fine Tinned Rack Chains, Snap on both ends.

2362—Swivel Back Band Chain for Dump Cart Harness.

2363—Stall Chains in lengths of 12 and 18 inches for Strap at one end.

2364—Stall Chain for Strap at each end.

2365—French Steel Carriage Pole Chains.
Double Curb Link.

2366—French Steel Carriage Pole Chains.
Single Curb Link.

2367—French Steel Carriage Pole Chains.
Cable Link.

SNAPS.

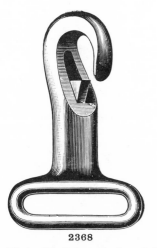   

2368   **2369**   **2370**   **2371**—Swivel.

Blackwell's Patent Single and Double Snaps, in Brass, Silver, Nickel or Tinned Finish. All Sizes of Eyes from $\frac{3}{4}$ to $1\frac{3}{4}$ inch, also Round and Open Eyes for Rope and other purposes.

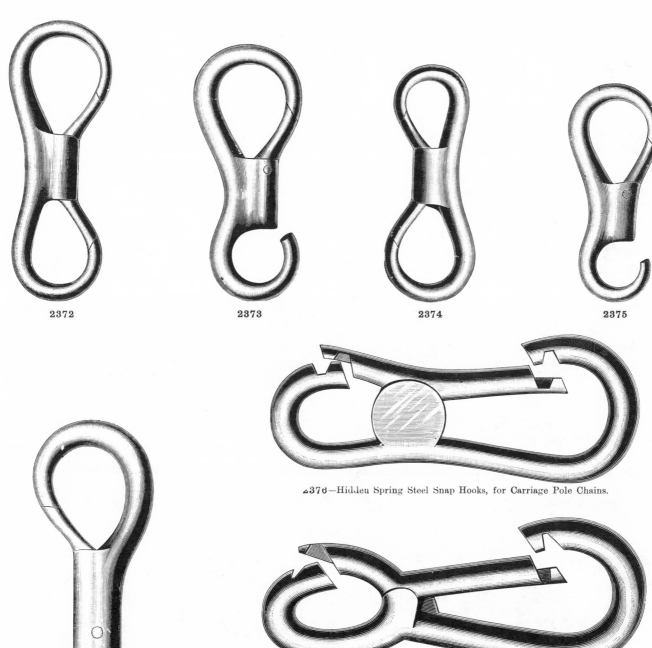

2372   **2373**   **2374**   **2375**

2376—Hidden Spring Steel Snap Hooks, for Carriage Pole Chains.

2377—Spring Hook Heads, for Riding and Dog Whips, Canes, Pillar Reins, etc.

2378—Steel Spring Snap Hooks, for Carriage Pole Chains.

2379

2381

2382

2383

2380

2384

2385

2387

2388

2389

2390

2386

2391

2392

2394

2396

2397

2398

2399

2393

2395

2400

2401

2402

2403

2404

2405

2406

2407

Covert's Patent Snaps for Harness and Rope Tie use.   All sizes from $\frac{5}{8}$ to $2\frac{1}{2}$ inch Eye.

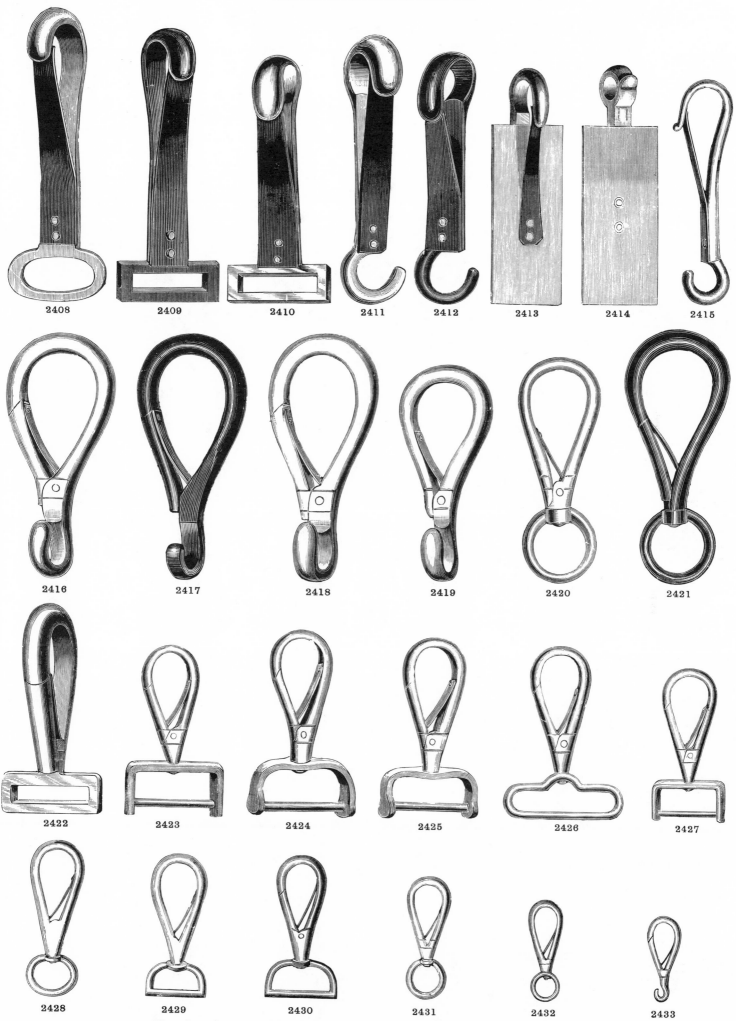

2408   2409   2410   2411   2412   2413   2414   2415

2416   2417   2418   2419   2420   2421

2422   2423   2424   2425   2426   2427

2428   2429   2430   2431   2432   2433

Silver, Brass, Tinned or Japanned Snaps of various kinds, of English and American Make.

CARRIAGE ROBES

FOR SPRING, SUMMER, AUTUMN AND WINTER USE.

Carriage Robes in Box, Beaver, Momie and other Cloths; also, in Bedford Cords, Corduroys, Linens, Plushes, Furs and other goods of imported and domestic make. Made up in the best and latest fashion for Coaching, Tandem and ordinary driving purposes, in Black, Blue, Green, Drab, Maroon, Wine and other colors.

Always in stock, ready for inspection or immediate shipment.

HIGH GRADE SILK AND MOHAIR PLUSHES A SPECIALTY.

Horse Clothing and Fly Nets

SECTION.

All Goods shown in this Section furnished at Lowest Wholesale Prices.

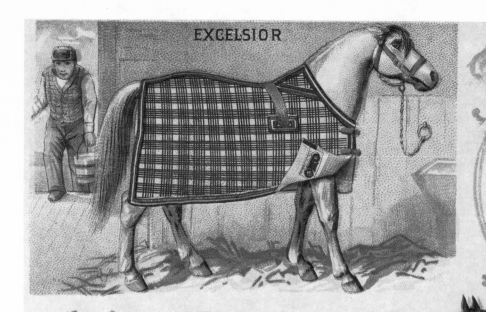

EXCELSIOR

This cut shows the CHASE EXCELSIOR. It has no equal for strength.

Government test shows this Blanket one-third Stronger than all similar Blankets.

The CHASE ADJUSTABLE BLANKETS are guaranteed to fit any Horse weighing 900 to 1400 lbs. Only one size needed. They are well made, well stayed, and have two strong surcingles with patent flat snaps.

Made in 50 different styles including the EXCELSIOR.

The CHASE SUPERFINE WOOL SQUARES are the Best Wool Blankets made, and their

WATERPROOF FAWNS are recognized as the standard of the kind.

Made in all regular sizes and weights.

The CHASE PLUSH ROBES are the only Robes that do not shed their plush.

Look for the name CHASE sewed on the corner of each Robe.

400 ARTISTIC PATTERNS.

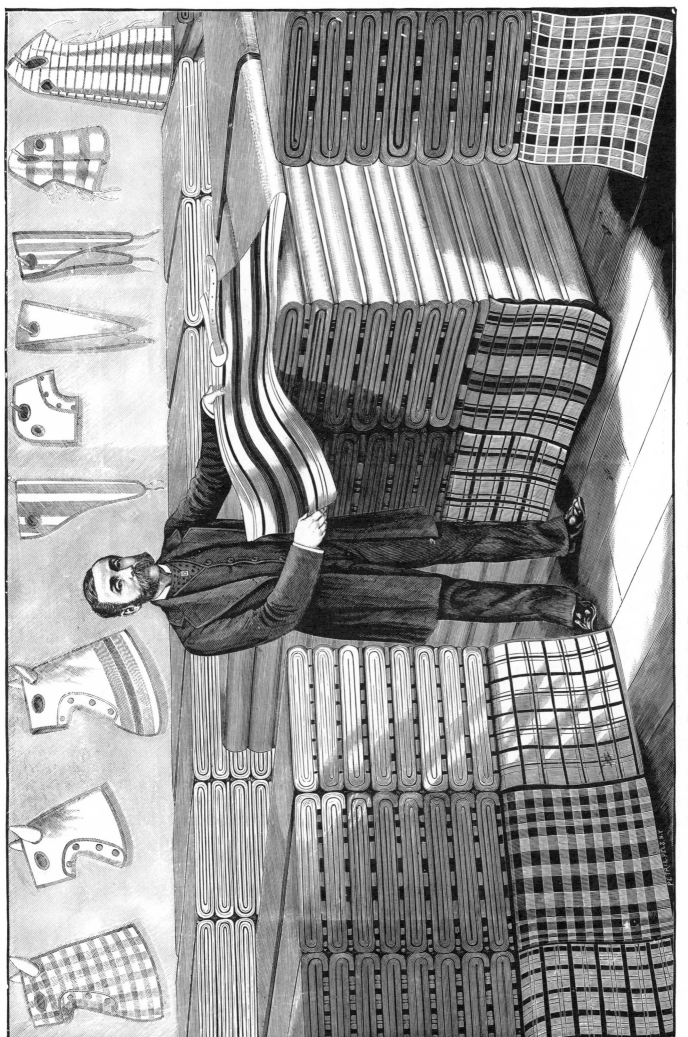

2424 —Section of our Horse Clothing Show Room.   New Styles and Patterns of these Goods brought out every year.

HORSE CLOTHING.

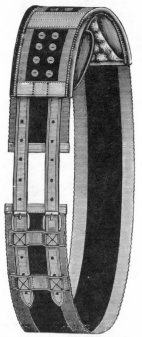
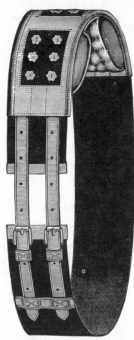
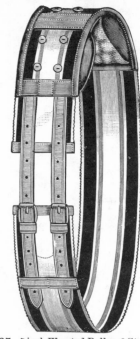
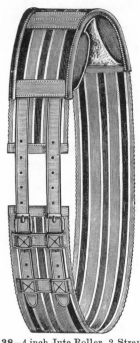

2435—5 inch Worsted Roller, 2 Straps. **2436**—5 inch Worsted Roller, 2 Straps. **2437**—5 inch Worsted Roller, 2 Straps. **2438**—4 inch Jute Roller, 2 Straps.

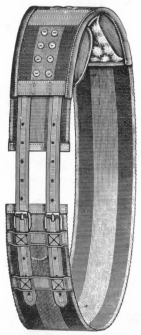
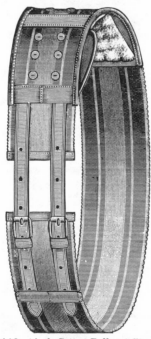
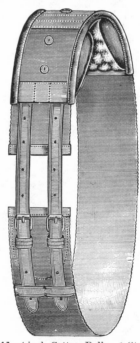
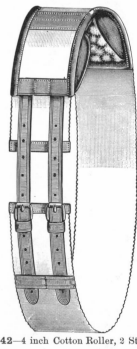

2439—4 inch Cotton Roller, 2 Straps. **2440**—4 inch Cotton Roller, 2 Straps. **2441**—4 inch Cotton Roller, 2 Straps. **2442**—4 inch Cotton Roller, 2 Straps.

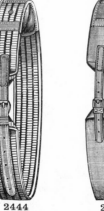

2443 **2444** **2445** **2446** **2447** **2448** **2449**

Cotton Surcingles, with Pads.   Cotton Surcingles, without Pads.

HORSE CLOTHING.

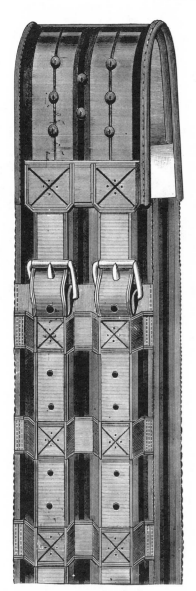

2450—2 Strap Roller.

2451—1 Strap Roller.

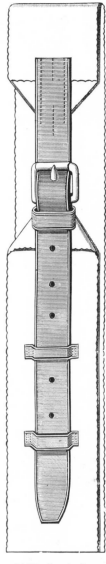

2452—Surcingle.

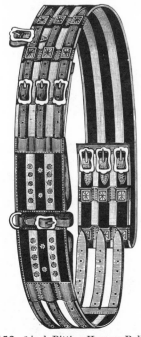

2453—6 inch Bitting Harness Roller.

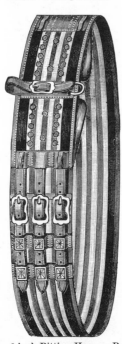

2454—6 inch Bitting Harness Roller.

Made of Worsted or Cotton.

2455—6 inch Bitting Harness Roller.

HORSE CLOTHING.

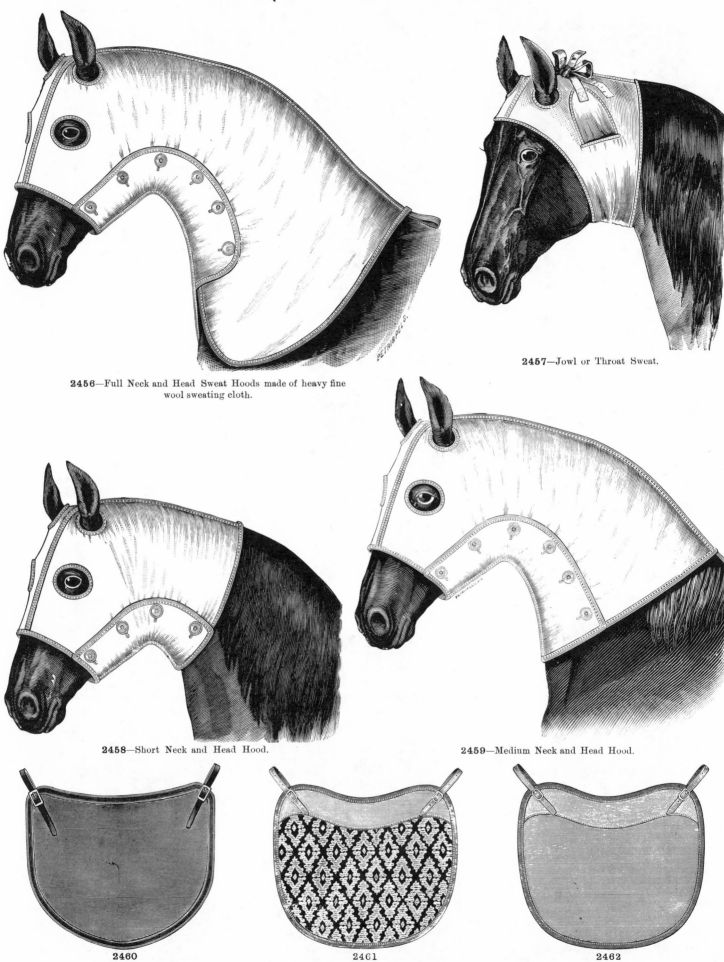

2456—Full Neck and Head Sweat Hoods made of heavy fine wool sweating cloth.

2457—Jowl or Throat Sweat.

2458—Short Neck and Head Hood.

2459—Medium Neck and Head Hood.

2460

2461

2462

Breast Blankets in Fawn, Blue and other colors. Made of Carpet, Kersey and other Cloths.

HORSE CLOTHING.

2463—Road Blanket, 90 × 96 inches, Medium and Heavy Weights, of High Class Wool, Beautiful Patterns and Colors.

2464—Road Blanket, 90 × 96 inches, Medium and Heavy Weights, of High Class Wool, Beautiful Patterns and Colors.

HORSE CLOTHING.

2465—Road Blanket, 90 × 96 inches, Medium and Heavy Weights, of High Class Wool, in Beautiful Patterns and Colors.

2466—Road Blanket, 90 × 96 inches, Medium and Heavy Weights, of High Class Wool, in Beautiful Patterns and Colors.

HORSE CLOTHING.

2467—Road Blanket, 90 × 96 inches, Medium and Heavy Weights, of High Class Wool, in Beautiful Patterns and Colors.

2468—Road Blanket, 90 × 96 inches, Medium and Heavy Weights, of High Class Wool, in Beautiful Patterns and Colors.

HORSE CLOTHING.

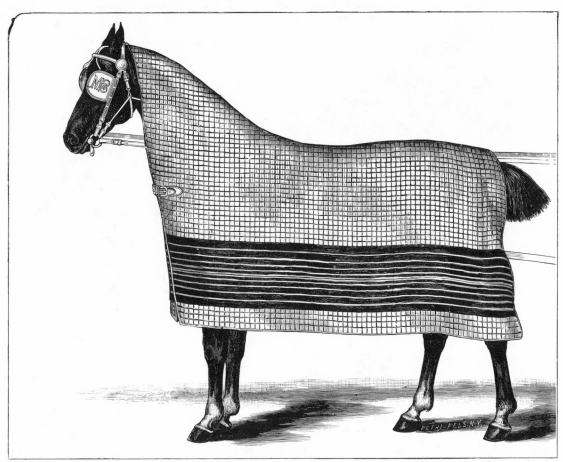

2469—Road Blanket and Summer Cooler, 90 × 96 inches, light and Medium Weights, in Beautiful Patterns and Colors.

2470—Road Blanket, 90 × 96 inches, Medium and Heavy Weights, of High Class Wool, in Beautiful Patterns and Colors.

2471—Road Blanket, 90 × 96 inches, Medium and Heavy Weights, of High Class Wool, in Beautiful Patterns and Colors.

2472—Road Blanket, 90 × 96 inches, Medium and Heavy Weights, of High Class Wool, in Beautiful Patterns and Colors.

HORSE CLOTHING.

2473—Road Blanket, 90 × 96 inches, Medium and Heavy Weight, of High Class Wool, in Beautiful Patterns and Colors.

2474—Wool Sweating-out Blanket, 90 × 96 inches, 7½ to 8½ pounds each, White, Ground, Blue and Yellow, or Red Stripes.

HORSE CLOTHING.

2475—Sweating-out Blanket, 90 × 96 inches.   New Styles and Patterns every year.

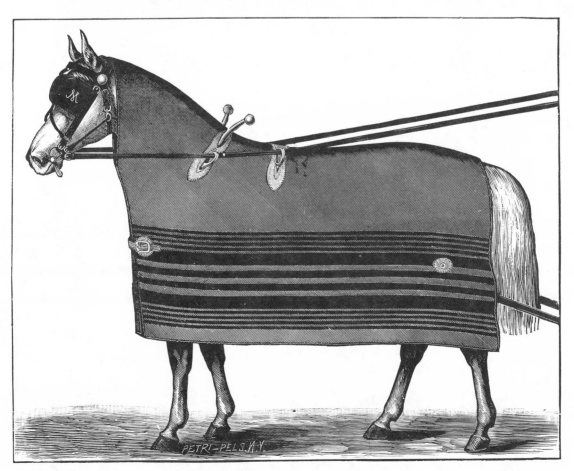

2476—Fawn Colored Blanket, 90 × 96 inches, with Red Stripes, fitted to use over Harness.   These come in different sizes and weights.

2477

2478   2479

Above cuts show some of the different Plaids or Checks in Fine Kersey that may be used in making up Suits of Clothing, all of which and many others we have on
hand or can furnish at short notice.   A large variety of completed Suits ready for immediate delivery, both home made and imported.

HORSE CLOTHING.

2480—This cut shows a complete Walking Suit of English Style Horse Clothing.

2481

Suits of Clothing on Hand and made up to suit all tastes.

HORSE CLOTHING.

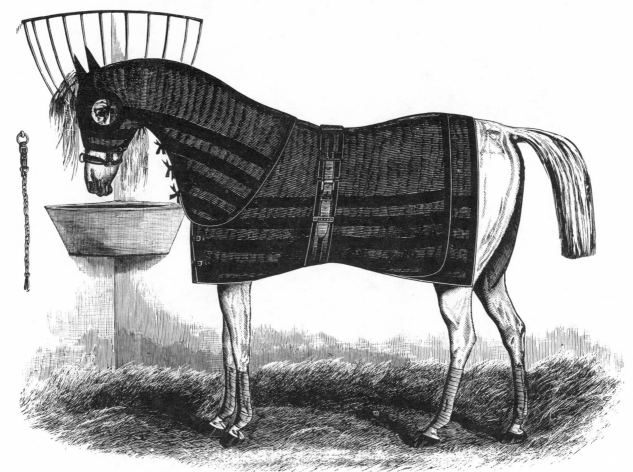

2482—All Wool, Fawn Colored Stable and Exercising Clothing

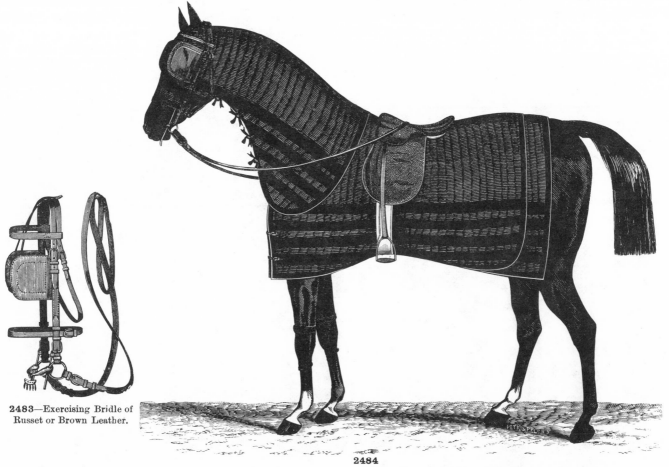

2483—Exercising Bridle of
Russet or Brown Leather.

2484

Saddle, Bridle, Clothes and Knee Caps all ready for the Morning Exercise.

HORSE CLOTHING.

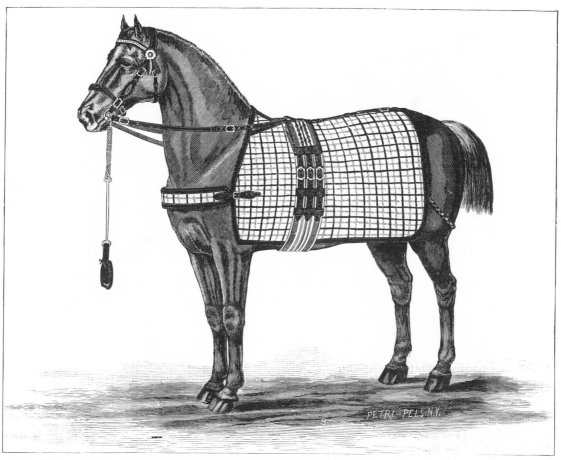

2485—Stallion Blanket in Wool or Linen, with Roller, Breast Plate and Bridle, with Lead Bar, Chain and Strap complete.

2486—Fine Wool Kersey Blanket, in either solid Fawn, Blue, Green or Plaids, trimmed in any color desired. Rollers to match.

2487—Artistic French Pattern Box Stall Dress Blanket, Roller, Roller Cloth and Pad.

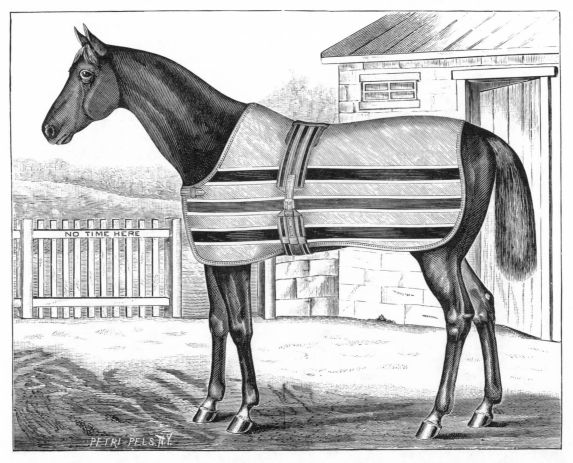

2488—English Jute Wool Lined Stable Blanket, with Roller to match. Very durable, thoroughly made, and well adapted as a shipping Blanket. Three Grades of these Blankets always in stock ready for immediate delivery.

2489—Fine Princess Check or Worsted Summer Blanket or Sheet, made up Light, Neat and as Strong as Goods will allow, well Braced and Stayed in the Neck and Back, furnished in different beautiful Patterns and Colors, with or without Roller and Roller Cloth.

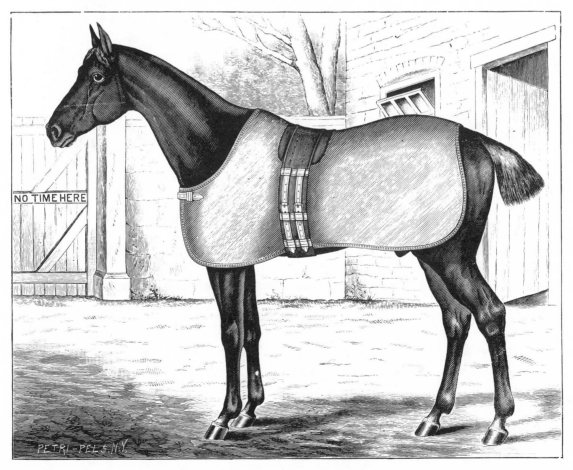

2490—Plain Fawn Colored Duck Stable Sheet, Strong, Durable and Good Looking, Neatly and Properly made for practical use, with or without Roller and Roller Cloth.

HORSE CLOTHING.

2492—Small Blue or Red Check White Ground Linen Sheet for Summer use, Properly and Carefully Made, Neat, Well Sewed Straps and Buckles, Neck Braced and Stayed.

2493—Fancy Plaid Cotton Sheet for Summer use, Neatly Made and Carefully Stayed in Neck.

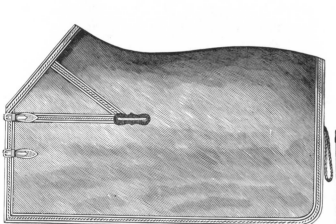

2494—Plain, Strong Brown Linen Sheet, Well Braced, Well Made.

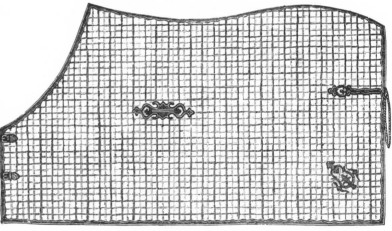

2495—Wool, Summer Kersey Sheet, White Ground, Blue and Lemon Check.

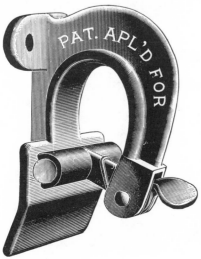

2496—Little Giant Holder.

2497—Little Giant Holder in use.

HORSE CLOTHING.

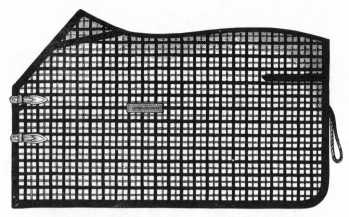

2498—White Ground Wool Summer Kersey, Double Check, 2 Colors.

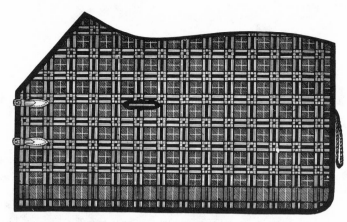

2499—Fawn Ground Summer Kersey, in Single or Double Plaids or Checks.

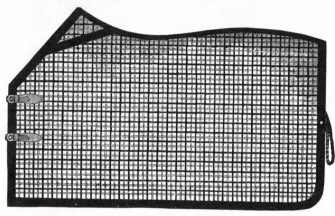

2500—Linen, White Ground, Medium Size Check, in 2 Colors.

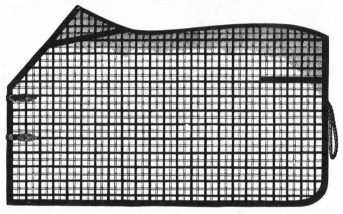

2501—Linen, White Ground, Large Size Check, in 2 Colors.

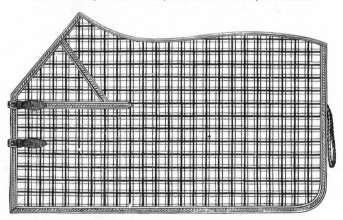

2502—Linen, White Ground, Second Quality.

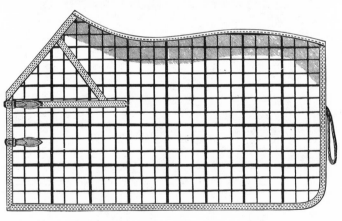

2503—Linen, White Ground, Second Quality.

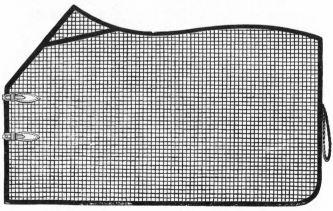

2504—Linen, White Ground, Small Single Color Check.

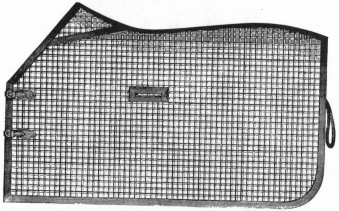

2505—Linen, White Ground, Small, 2 Color Check.

HORSE CLOTHING.

2506—Fine Summer Mosquito Net Sheets in one piece.   2507—Fine Summer Mosquito Net Sheets, in two pieces.

2508   2509

Linsey Woolsey Suits, in all colors as used by Racing Stables while Horses are being exercised on the road.

WATERPROOF COVERINGS.

2510—Waterproof Hunting Coat and Leggings.

2511—Waterproof Coat and Apron Combined.

2512—Oil Cloth Wagon Aprons.

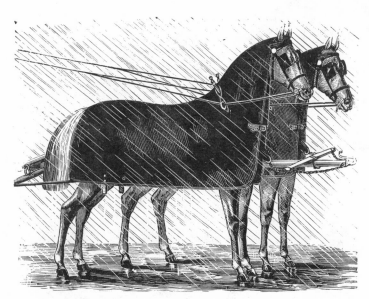

2513—Oil Cloth Horse Covers for Double Harness.

2514—Oil Cloth Horse Cover.

Oiled Cotton Duck Truck Covers, White Canvas Truck Covers, Rubber Coats and Mackintoshes, all sizes.

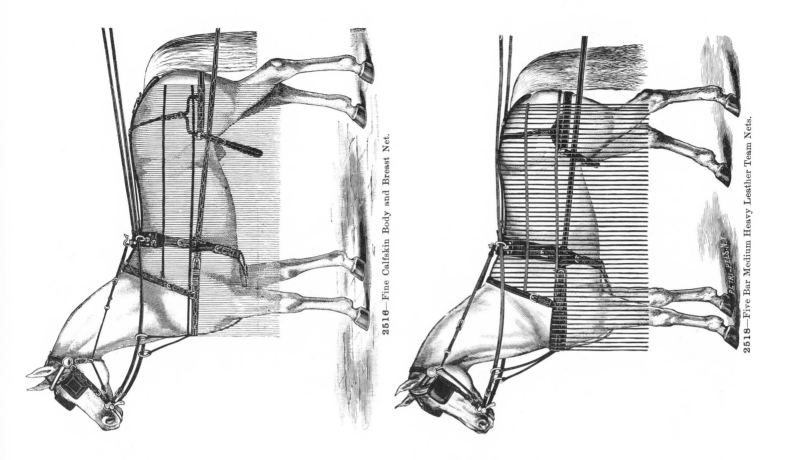

2516—Fine Calfskin Body and Breast Net.

2518—Five Bar Medium Heavy Leather Team Nets.

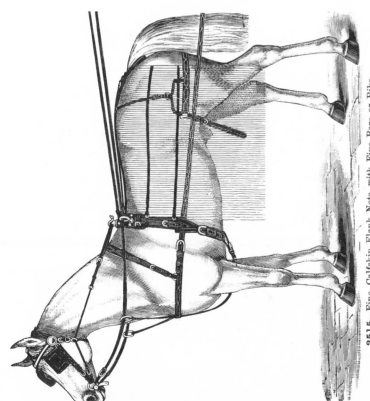

2515—Fine Calfskin Flank Nets, with Five Bars or Ribs.

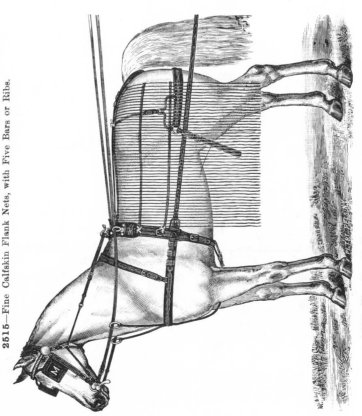

2517—Five Bar Medium Quality Leather Flank Nets.

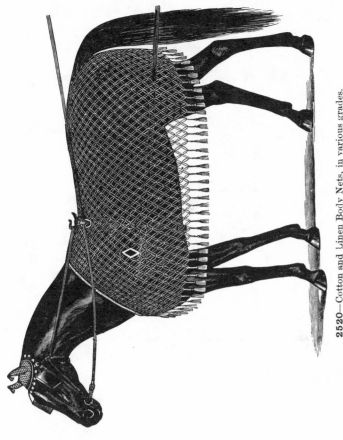

2520—Cotton and Linen Body Nets, in various grades.

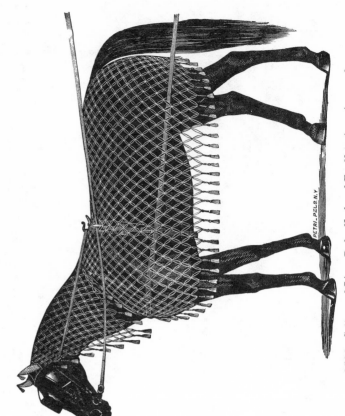

2522—Cotton and Linen Body, Neck and Ear Nets, in various grades.

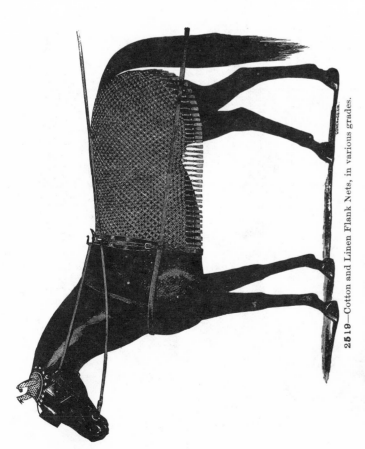

2519—Cotton and Linen Flank Nets, in various grades.

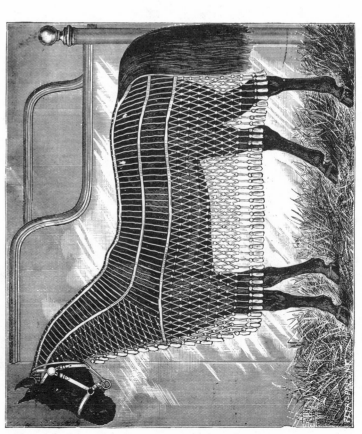

2521—Cotton and Linen Body and Neck Nets, White or Colors, in different grades and patterns.

MISCELLANEOUS.

2523—Black and White Worsted or Cotton Nets for Undertakers' Use.

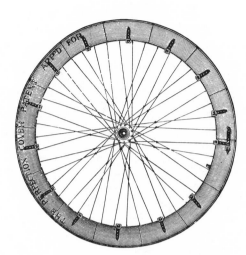

2524—Canvas and Leather Cover for Bicycle Sulky Wheels to prevent injury to Rubber Tires when shipping.

2525—Patent Adjustable Trace Loop for Whiffletree End of Trace.

2526—Heavy Cotton Cord Nets for Working Horses.

2527—Leather or Kersey Cover for Horses Tail to prevent rubbing in the the stall, particularly when shipping on Railroads or Steamships.

2528—Blanket Pin.

A SANITARY BEDDING FOR THE HORSE.

PEAT MOSS IN USE FOR BEDDING

2529

ADVANTAGES:

Prevents Foul Odors.
Even Cheaper than Straw.
Absorbs and Deodorizes the Wet.
The Horse will not Eat it.

Makes a Rich Fertilizer.
Obtains Best Results.
Safe Guard against Vermin.
Sanitary Blessing for all.

The Low Price.
Economy of Labor.
Softness of the Bedding.
Economy in Storage.
Absorbing Power for Gases.
Absorbing Power for Liquids.
Not Soiling the Animals.
Contributing by its own substance to
   increase the Value of the Manure.

Put up in Bales of about 300 pounds each, Six Bales to the Ton.

Clipping Machines, Sleighing Plumes, Chimes and Body Straps of Bells SECTION.

All Goods shown in this Section furnished at Lowest Wholesale Prices.

Horse Chime AND Sleigh Horse-Hair Plumes.

CLARK'S PATENT HORSE CLIPPERS.

Made by W. Clark, Oxford Street, London.

C. M. MOSEMAN & BROTHER, Sole Agents for the United States.

2530—For Horses' Heads. This machine can also be used for cutting human hair when it is desirable to leave it short and even.

2531—For Horses' Legs, Pellies, and parts difficult of access. Being made with strong teeth, they cut tough and wiry hair.

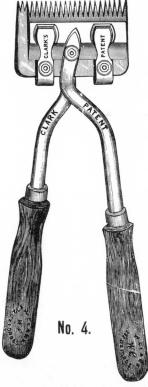

2532—Has been before the public about 25 years, has given the greatest satisfaction, and rules the market in all Europe, America, India, Egypt and the Colonies.

2533—A new patent improved principle, with self-acting spring over the plates, which keeps the machine always on the cut, and gives a softness of action.

Extra Top and Bottom Plates for Clark's Clippers, always in stock.

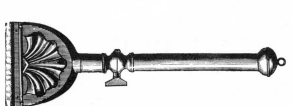

2534—Singeing Lamp for Oil or Alcohol.

2535—Singeing Lamp for Gas.

GILLETTE CLIPPING MACHINES.

2536—Model *B.*

The Gillette Champion Hand Power Clipping Machine.

2537—Model *A.*

The Gillette Bicycle Clipper.

2538—Model *E.*

The Gillette Featherweight Clipper.

2539—Bicycle Clipping Machine in Operation.

GILLETTE CLIPPING MACHINE.

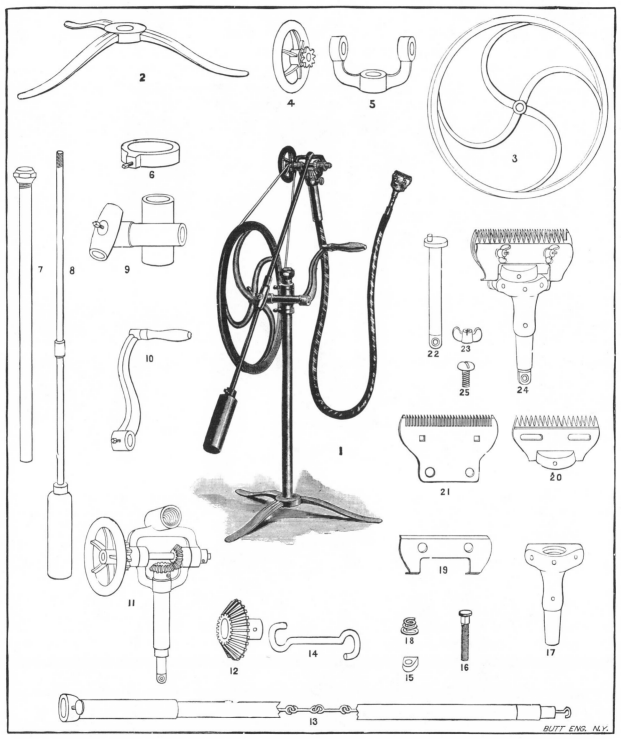

2540

1. Hand Power Clipping Machine, Complete.	9. Swivel, Double.	18. Spring.
2. Base of Machine.	10. Crank Handle.	19. Tension Plate.
3. Large Grooved Wheel.	11. Yoke Complete.	20. Top Vibrating Cutter and Hub.
4. Small Balance Wheel.	12. Gear.	21. Bottom Plate.
5. Part of Yoke.	13. Chain.	22. Crank Shaft for Handle.
6. Collar and Set Screw.	14. Open Link.	23. Fly Nut.
7. Upright Standard.	15. Blank Nut.	24. Handle and Cutter Complete.
8. ¾ Pipe and Weight.	16. Bolt.	25. Round Head Screw.
	17. Handle.	

For Sale by C. M. MOSEMAN & BROTHER, 128 Chambers St., NEW YORK.

PRIEST'S HAIR CLIPPING AND GROOMING MACHINES.

SPECIAL FEATURES:—Ball Bearings, Interchangeable Parts, All Steel Shafts solid or flexible, High Grade Material and Workmanship, Keen Cutters.

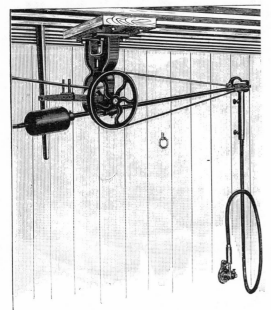

2541—Priest's Single No. 7 Power Clipping Machine.

2542—Priest's No. 10 Vibrating Handle, for all our Flexible Shaft Machines.

2543—Priest's No. 8 Power Grooming Machine.

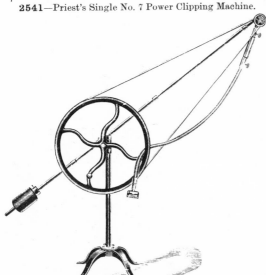

2544—Priest's Flexible Shaft Hand Power Ball Bearing Horse Clipping Machine.

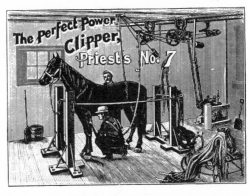

2545—Priest's Rotary Handle, two Patterns for either our Drop Rod or Flexible Shaft Machines.

2546—Priest's Double No. 7 Power Clipping Machine, is also used for Grooming. Capacity with two Operators, one Horse every thirty minutes.

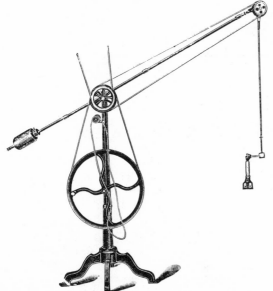

2547—Priest's No. 1 Power Clipping Machine, with Drop Rod and Vibrating Cutter. The Original Power Clipping Machine, with Ball Bearing Balance Wheel.

2548—Priest's No. 2 Power Clipping Machine, with Drop Rod and Rotary Cutter. Ball Bearing Balance Wheel same as No. 1.

2549—Priest's No. 2 Power Clipping Machine, with Flexible Shaft and Vibrating Cutter, Ball Bearings.

PRIEST'S HAIR CLIPPING AND GROOMING MACHINES.

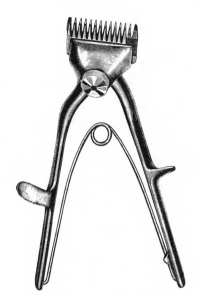

2550—Priest's One Hand Coarse Tooth Clipper,
for Trimming Fetlocks.

2551—Priest's One Hand Fine Tooth Clipper, for
Trimming about the Ears.

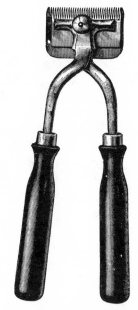

2552—The "Mount Vernon" Extra Quality
Two Hand Horse Clipper.

2553—Priest's No. 3 Power Clipping Machine,
with Drop Rod and Rotary Cutter.

2554—Large Rotary Comb.

2555—Large Rotary Cutter.

2556—Small Rotary Comb.

2557—Small Rotary Cutter.

2558—Priest's No. 10 3-inch Vibrating Cutting
Head, for No. 10 Handle and Nos. 4 and
5 Air Machines.

2559—Priest's Patent 4-inch Vibrating Cutting Head, for all Vibrating
Movements. Drop Rod or Flexible Shaft, except the No. 10.

2560—Priest's No. 10 4-inch Vibrating Cutting Head, for No. 10 and
Nos. 4 and 5 Air Machines.

2561—Priest's Vibrating Handle, Two Patterns,
for either our Flexible Shaft or Drop
Rod Machines.

2562—Priest's Vibrating Cutter, for Shearing
Colt and Dog, and Trimming
Fetlock.

2563—Priest's Patent 3-inch Vibrating Cutting
Head, for all Vibrating Handles. Drop
Rod or Flexible Shaft.

SADDLE CHIMES.

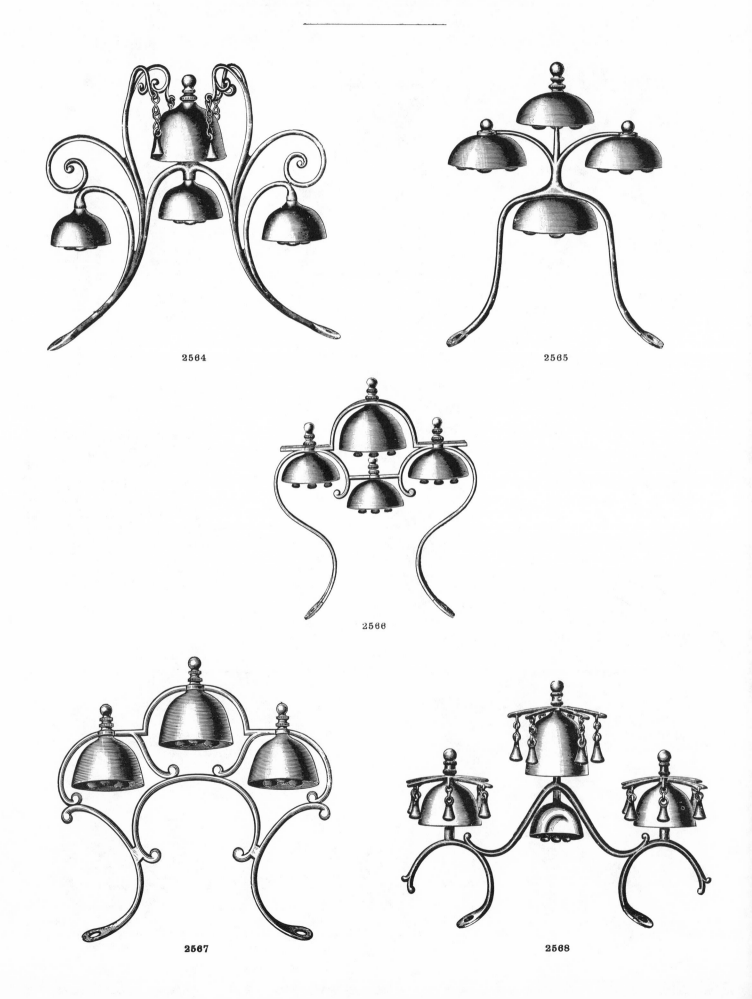

2564

2565

2566

2567

2568

SADDLE CHIMES.

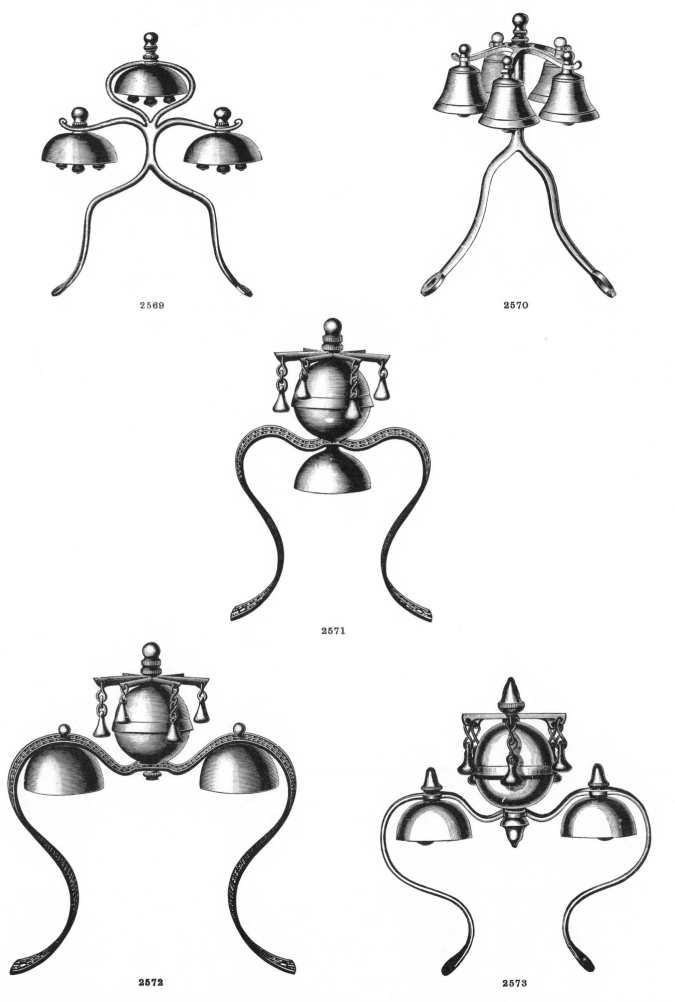

2569

2570

2571

2572

2573

SADDLE CHIMES.

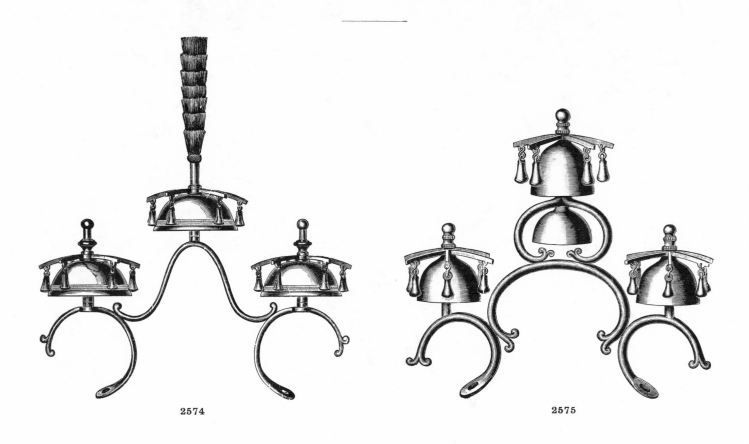

2574   2575

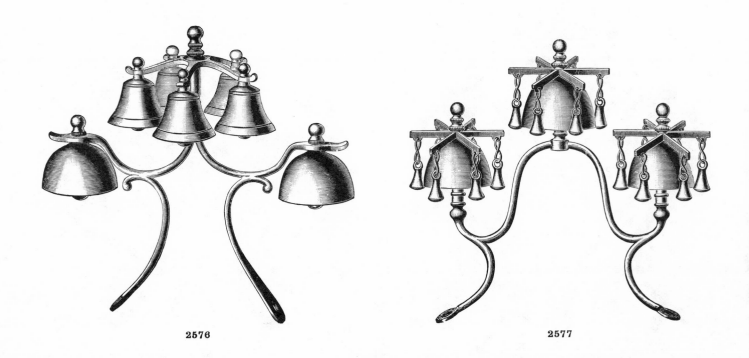

2576   2577

SHAFT AND POLE CHIMES.

2578

2579

2580

2581

2582

2583

2584

2585

2586

2587

2588

2589

2590

2591

2592

2593

2594

2595

BODY STRAPS OF BELLS.

Nickel, Oroide, Brass, Silver and Gold.

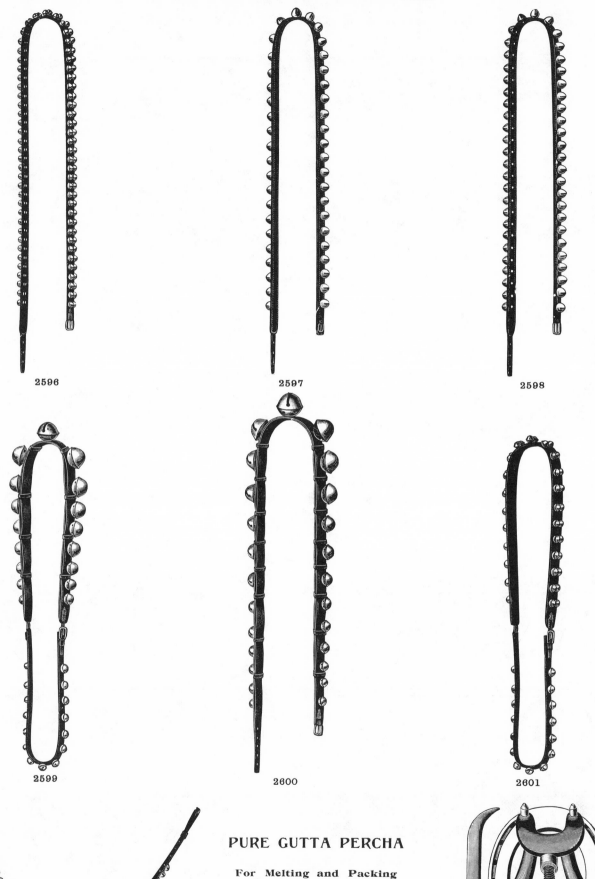

2596　　　　　　　2597　　　　　　　2598

2599　　　　　　　2600　　　　　　　2601

PURE GUTTA PERCHA

For Melting and Packing
in Horses' Feet, to Prevent
Snow Balling.

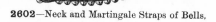

2602—Neck and Martingale Straps of Bells,

2603—Ice Creepers for Horses,

Saddle and Bridle

SECTION.

"DO NOT CUT THIS BOOK."

Every consumer or dealer in Harness and Saddlery, no matter in what part of the world he does business, will promote his own interests by sending us **ONE DOLLAR** and receiving in return a copy of this complete Illustrated Guide Book. It is the key to success in the prosecution of business. He cannot afford to be without the knowledge it contains of every department of the trade. It will surely serve as a lamp to light him through the many perplexities which are incidental to the Harness Industry.

With this Book in your possession you are at liberty to write to us, or to any manufacturer or dealer in Harness or Saddlery Goods with whom you do business, asking questions or sending orders, and either will know just what you want if you will mention "MOSEMAN'S BOOK" and give the "NUMBER" under the article you wish to know about, or mention the picture of the article you may have under consideration at the time.

In any event, **DO NOT CUT THIS BOOK!** but simply give "Number" of the article you wish to obtain.

We are, yours for business,

C. M. MOSEMAN & BROTHER,

126 & 128 CHAMBERS STREET,

NEW YORK, U. S. A.

2604—Sioux on the War Path.

SADDLES.

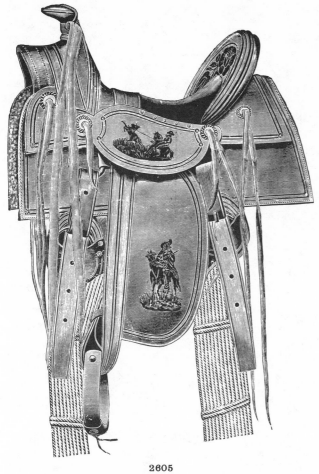

2605

2606

2607

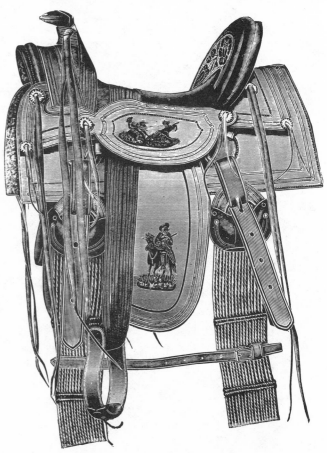

2608

SADDLES.

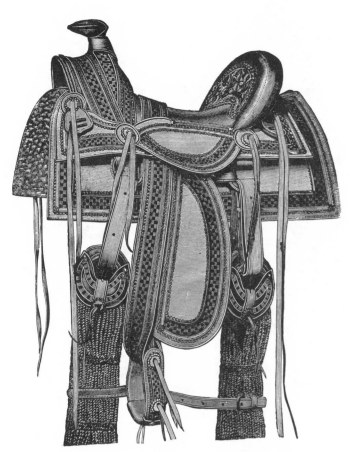

2609

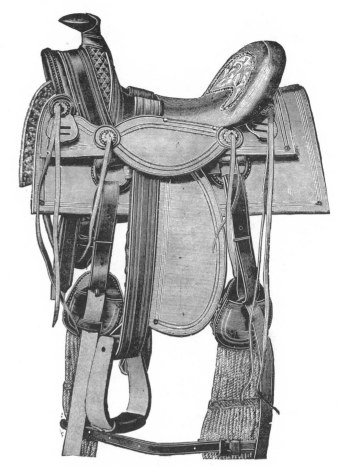

2610

2611

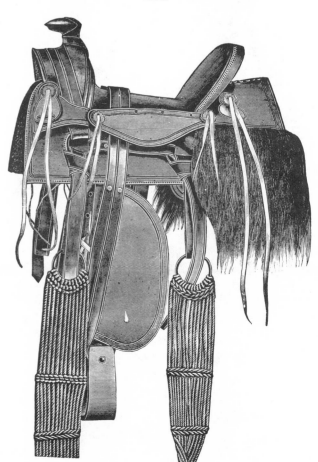

2612

SADDLES.

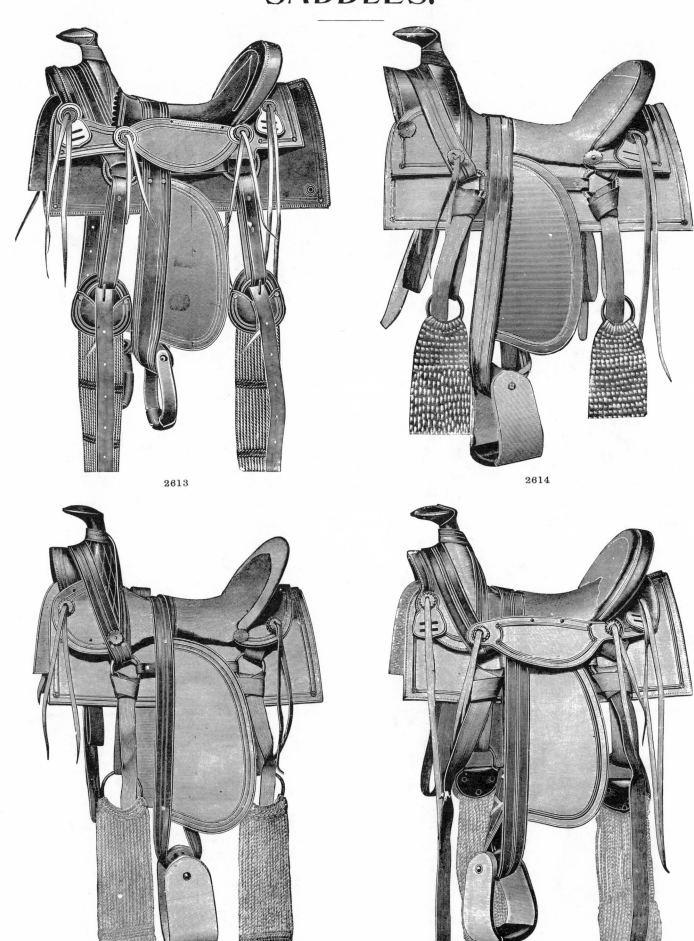

2613　　　　　　　　　　　2614

2615　　　　　　　　　　　2616

SADDLES.

2617

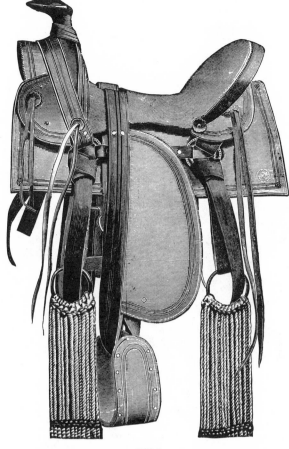

2618

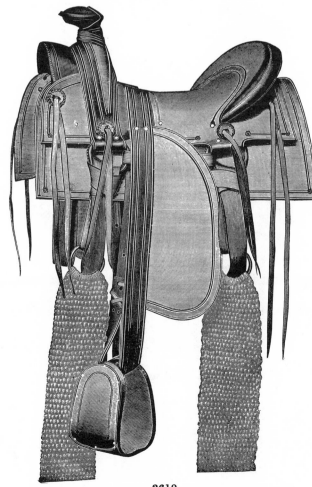

2619

2620

SADDLES.

2621

2622

2623

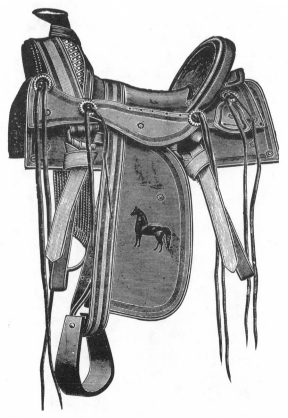

2624

SADDLES.

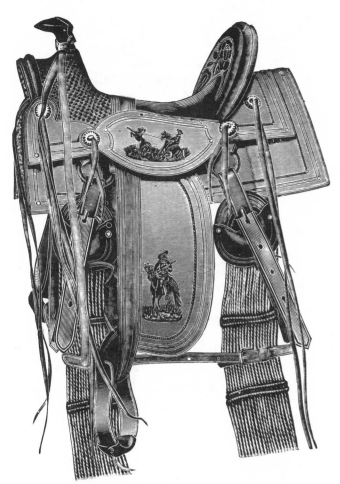

2625

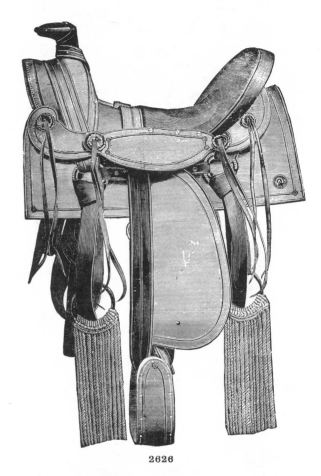

2626

2627

2628

SADDLES.

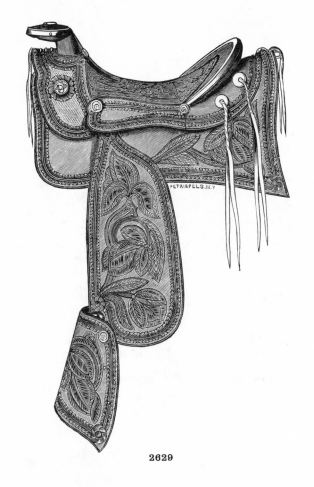

2629

2630

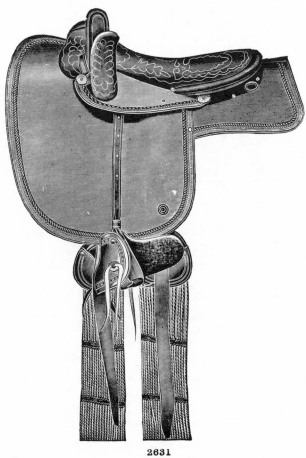

2631

2632

SADDLES.

2633

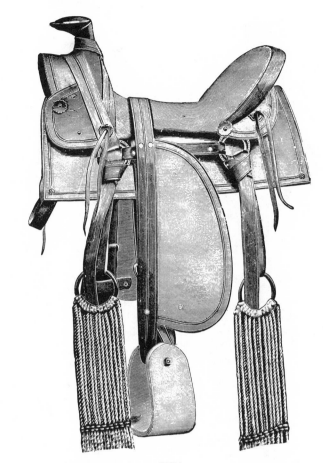

2634

2635

2636

SADDLES.

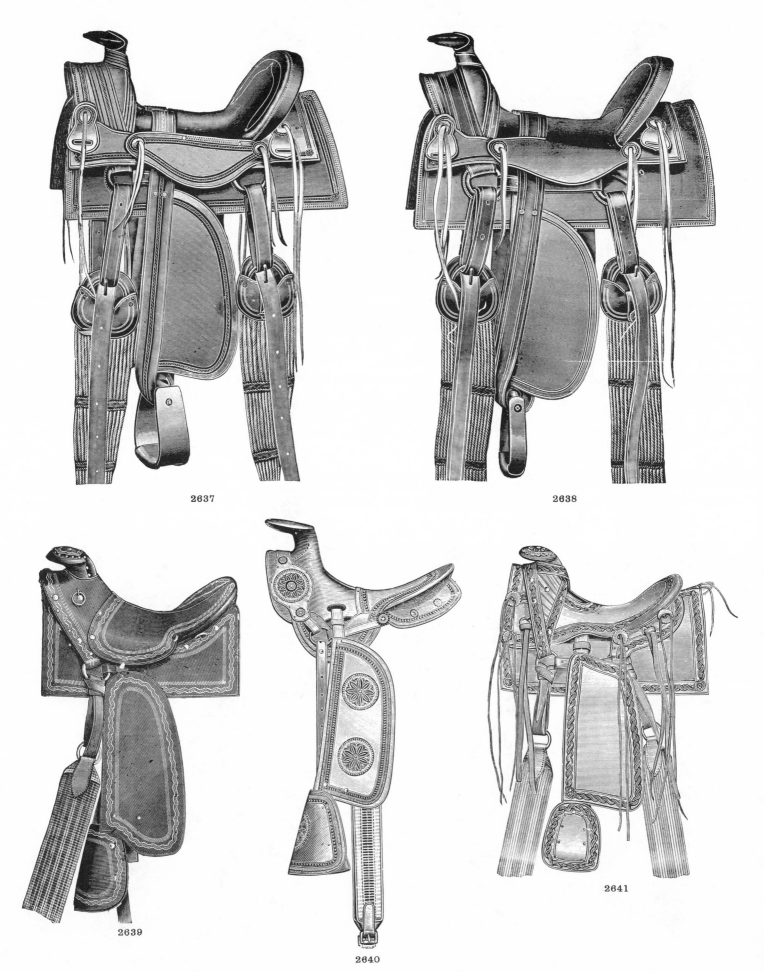

2637

2638

2639

2640

2641

SADDLES.

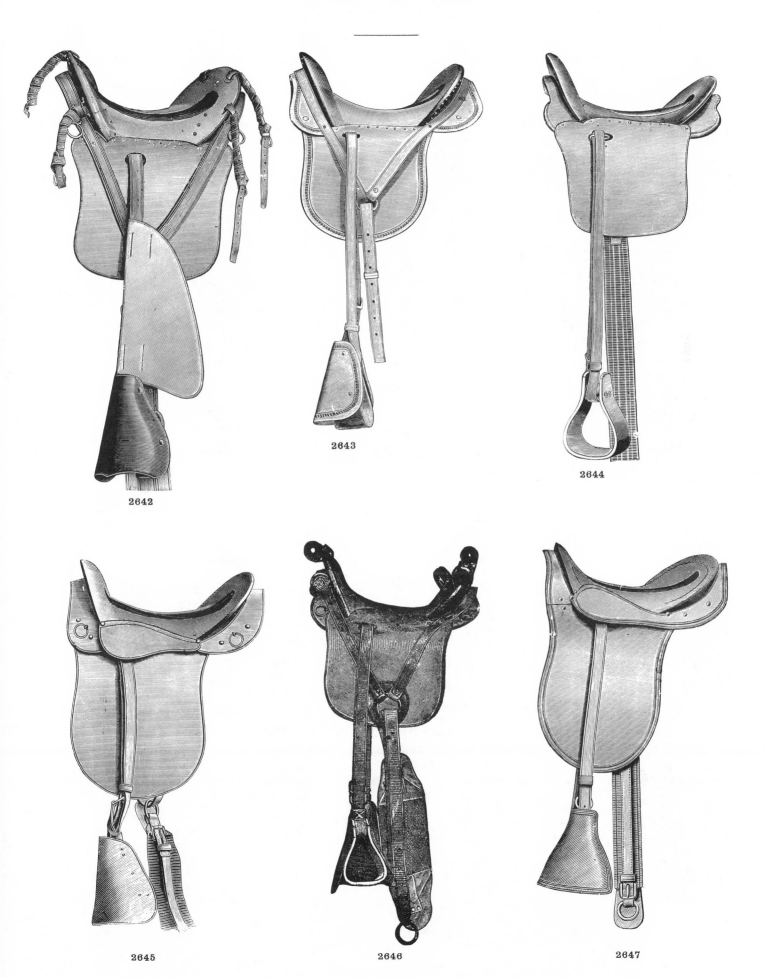

2642

2643

2644

2645

2646

2647

SADDLES.

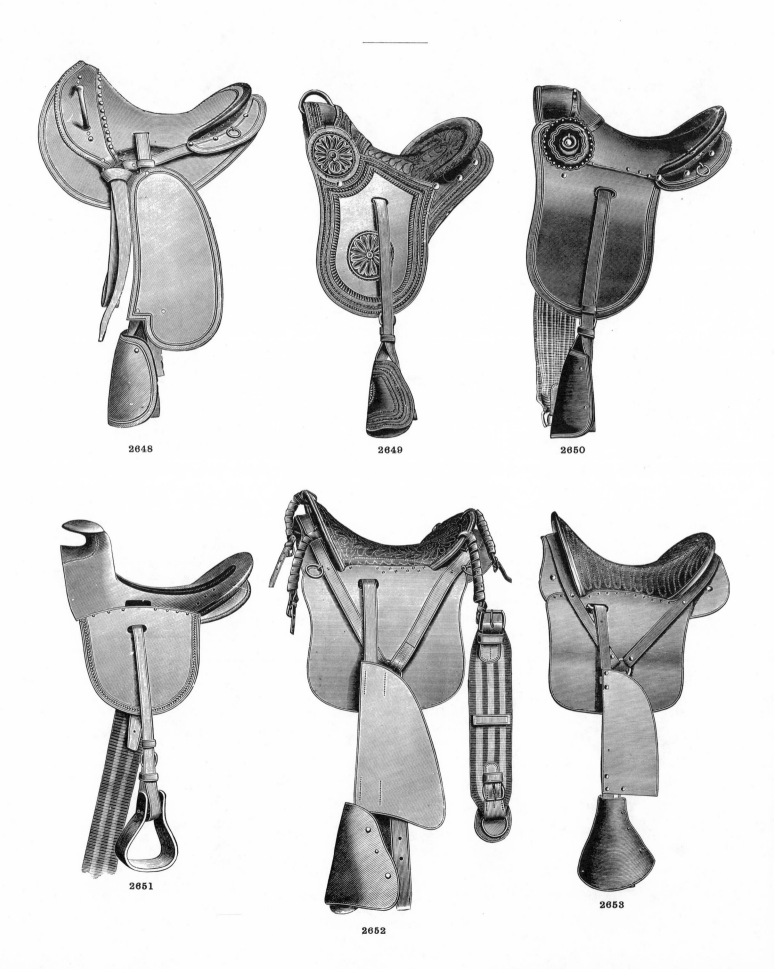

2648   2649   2650

2651   2653

2652

SADDLES.

2654—Waiting.

2655—Ready for the Hunt.

SADDLES.

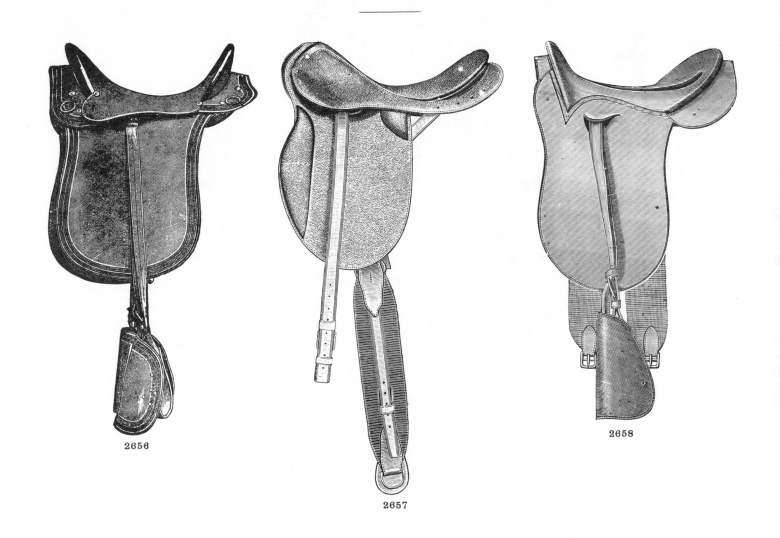

2656

2657

2658

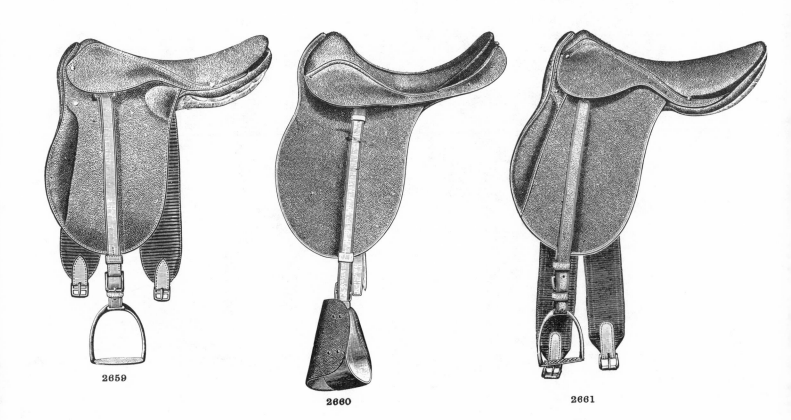

2659

2660

2661

SADDLES.

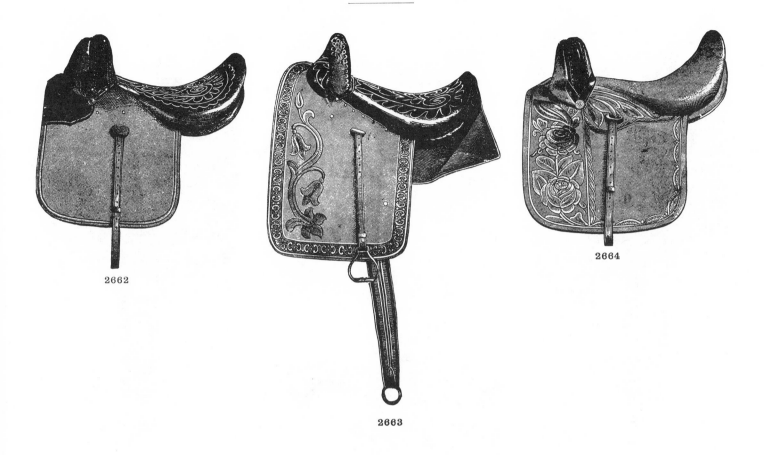

2662

2663

2664

2665

2666

2667

SADDLES.

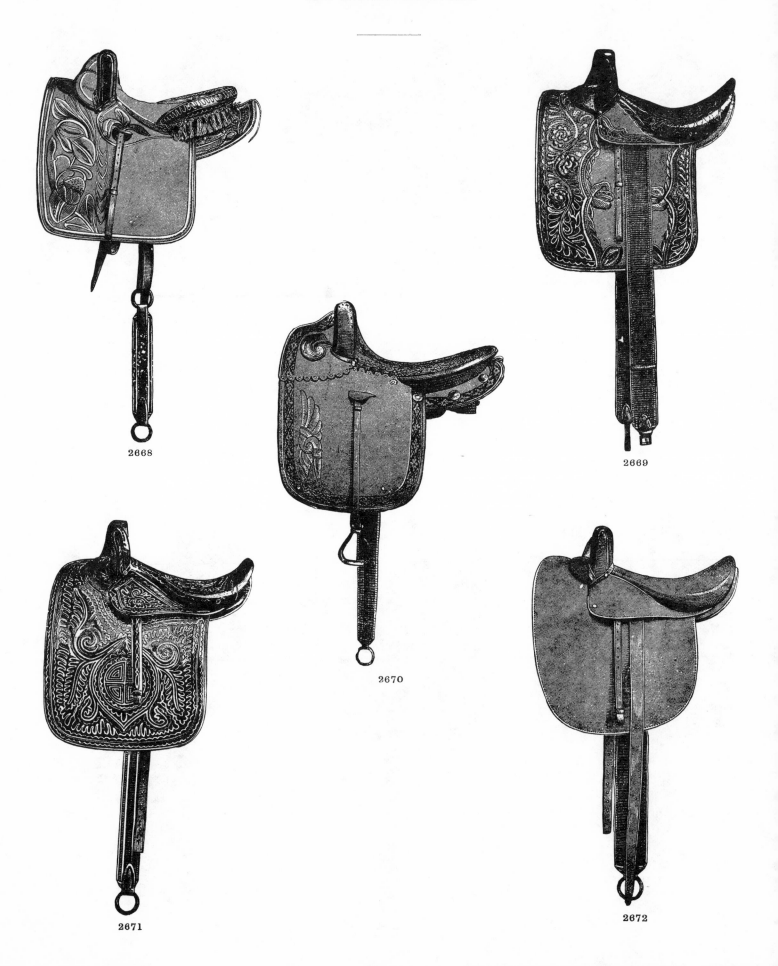

2668

2669

2670

2671

2672

SADDLES.

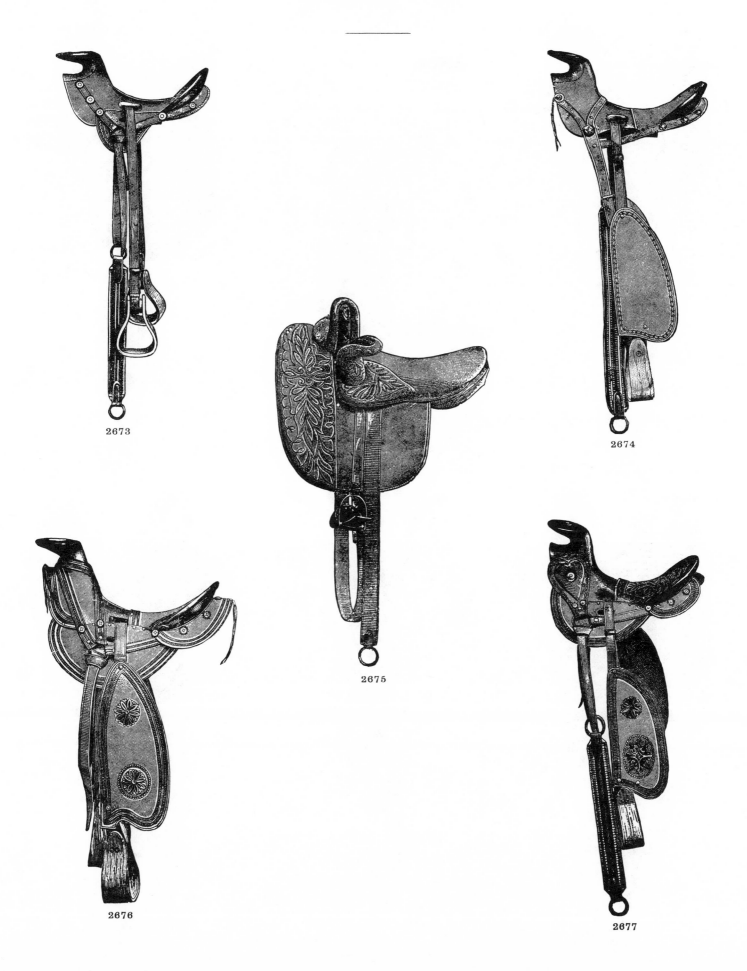

2673

2675

2674

2676

2677

SADDLES.

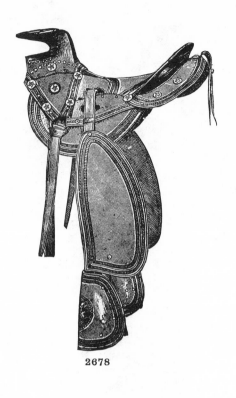

2678

2679

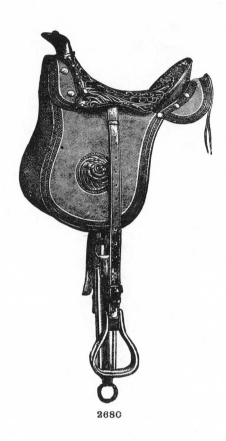

2680

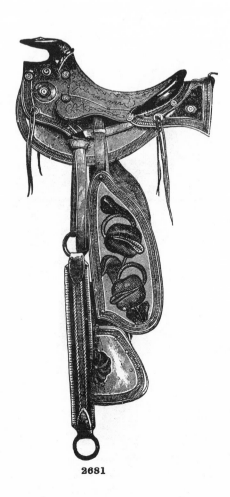

2681

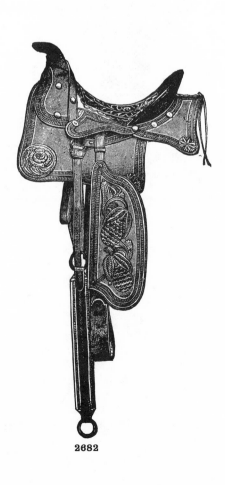

2682

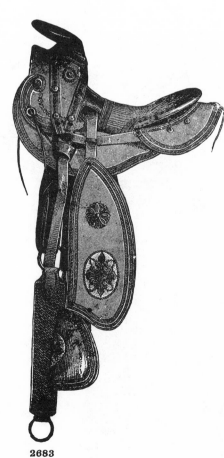

2683

SADDLES.

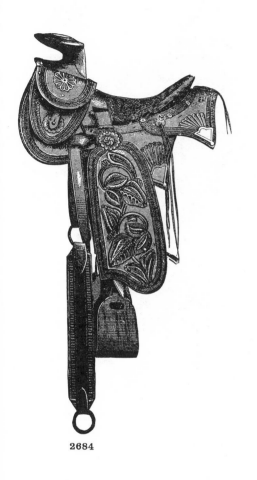

2684

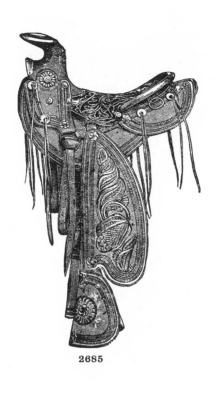

2685

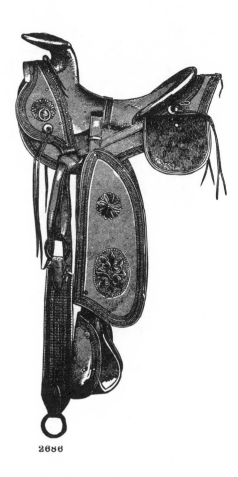

2686

2687

2688

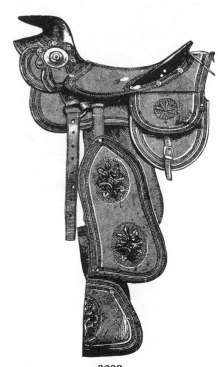

2689

SADDLES.

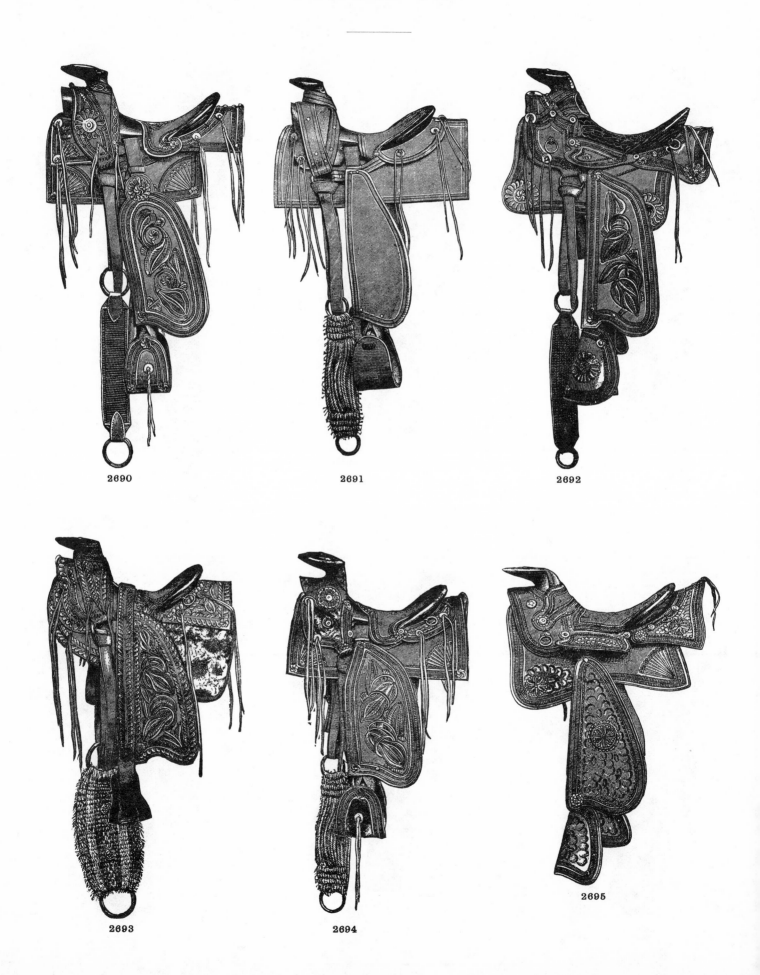

2690   2691   2692

2693   2694   2695

SADDLES.

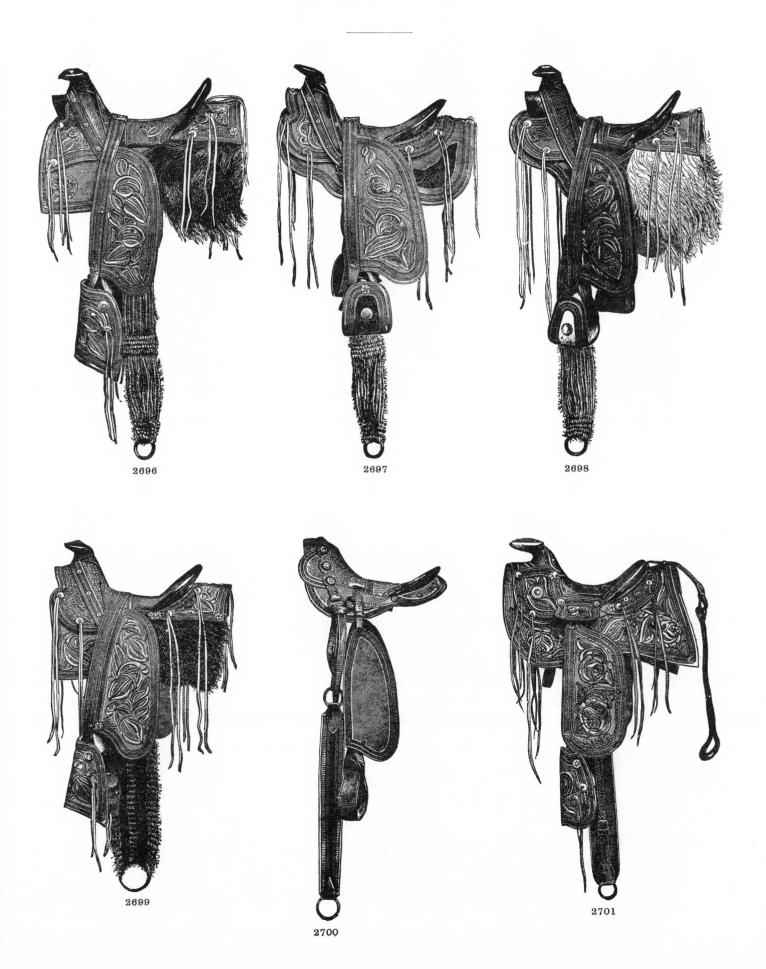

2696

2697

2698

2699

2700

2701

SADDLES.

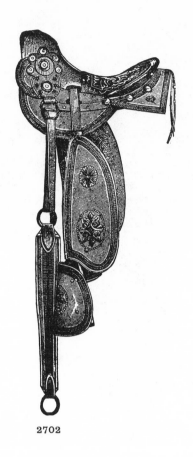

2702

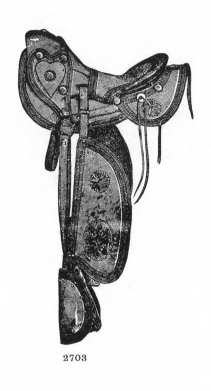

2703

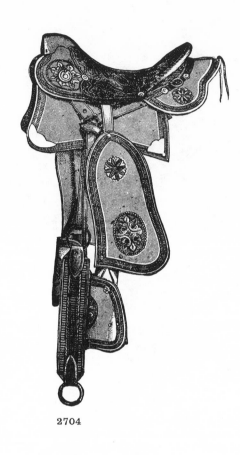

2704

2705

2706

2708

SADDLES.

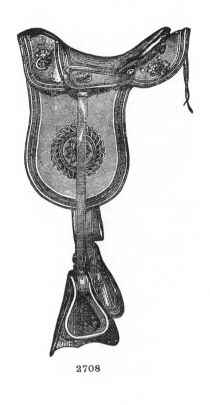

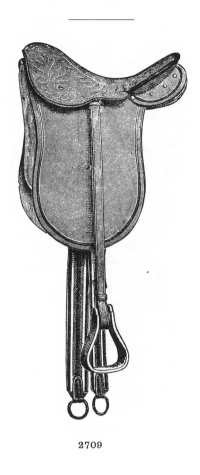

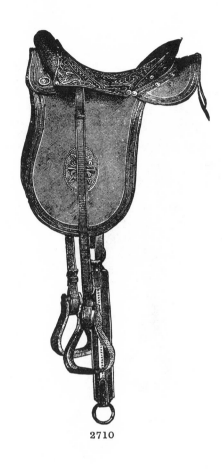

2708

2709

2710

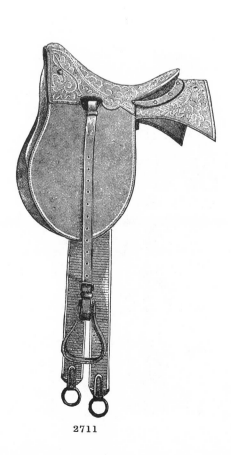

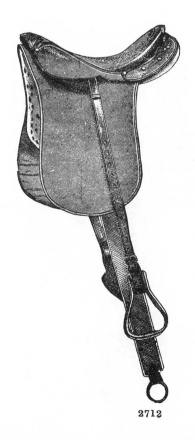

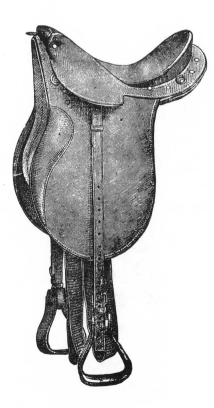

2711

2712

2713

SADDLES.

2714

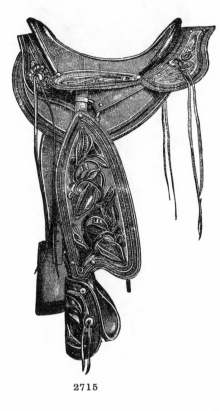

2715

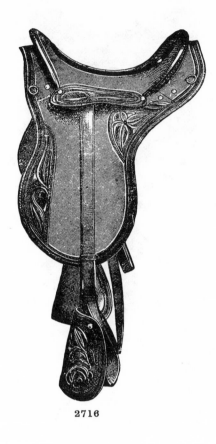

2716

2717

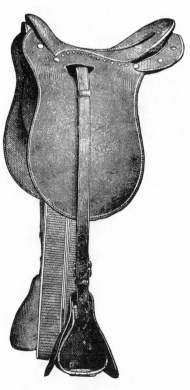

2718

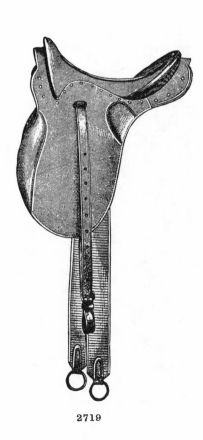

2719

SADDLES.

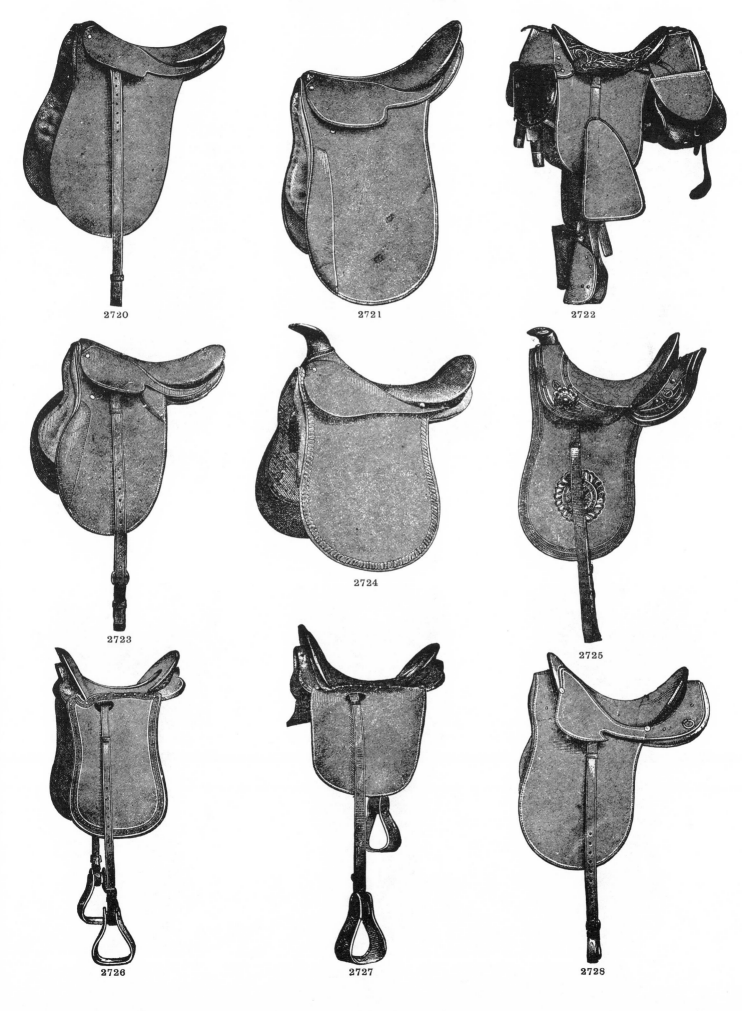

2720

2721

2722

2723

2724

2725

2726

2727

2728

SADDLES.

2730—Saddle Bag.

2729—Police Saddle.   2731—Saddle Bag.   2732—Saddle Bag.   2733—Police Saddle.

2734   2735   2736

SADDLES.

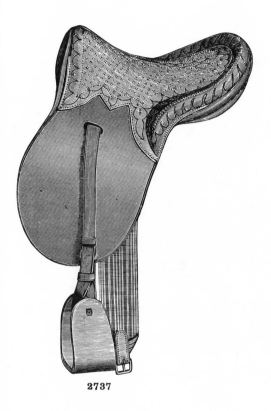

2737

2738

2739– Pony Saddles.

2740

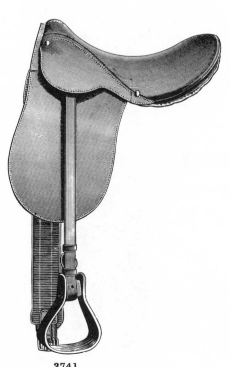

2741

SADDLES.

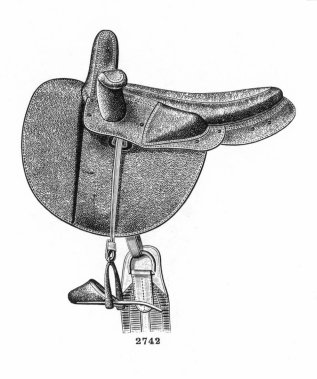

2742

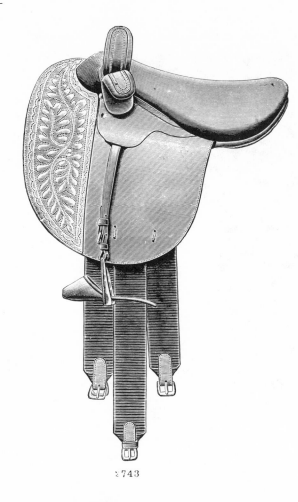

2743

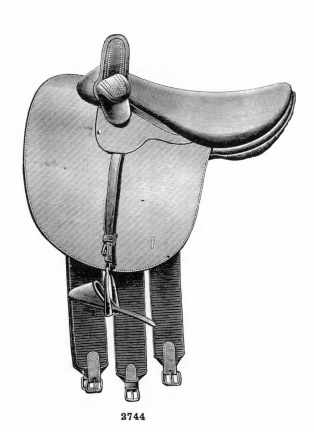

2744

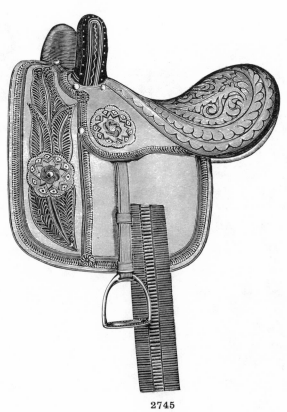

2745

SADDLES.

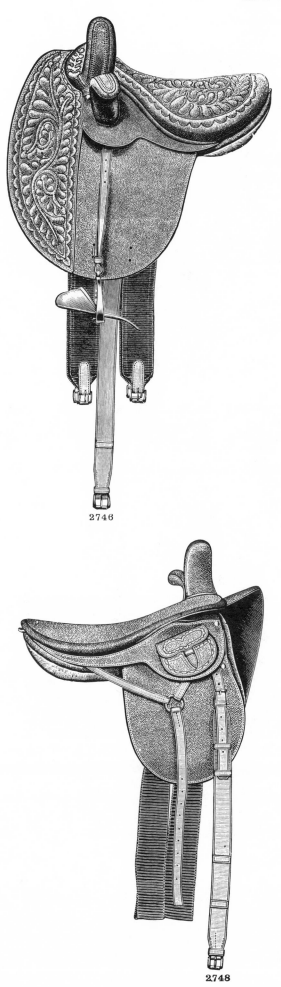

2746

2748

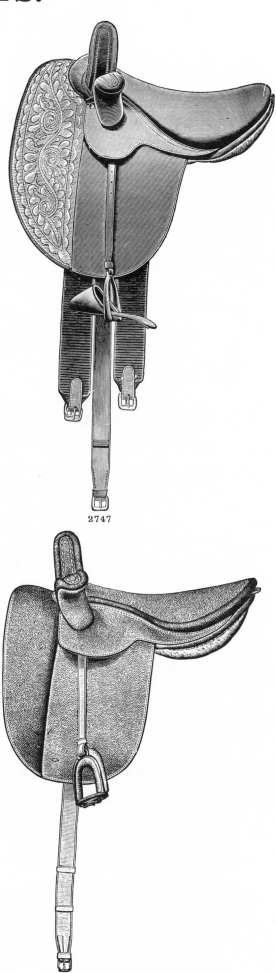

2747

2749

2750

Full Equipments Furnished for Riding Parties.

GENTLEMEN'S SADDLE CLOTHS.

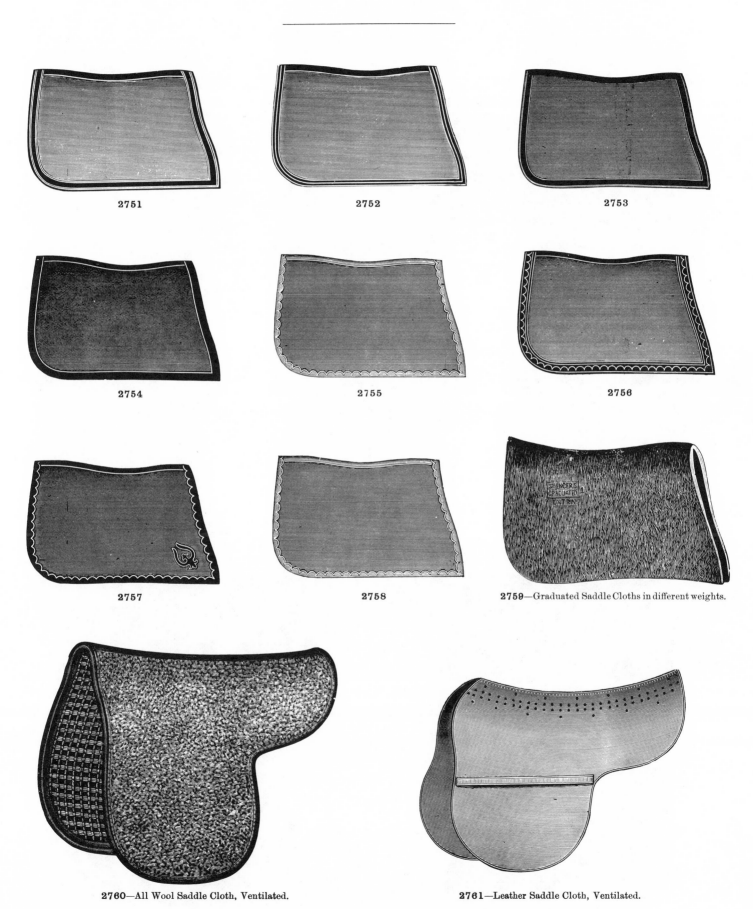

2751   2752   2753

2754   2755   2756

2757   2758   2759—Graduated Saddle Cloths in different weights.

2760—All Wool Saddle Cloth, Ventilated.   2761—Leather Saddle Cloth, Ventilated.

Military, Police and Uniform Saddle Cloths made to order.

GENTLEMEN'S SADDLE CLOTHS.

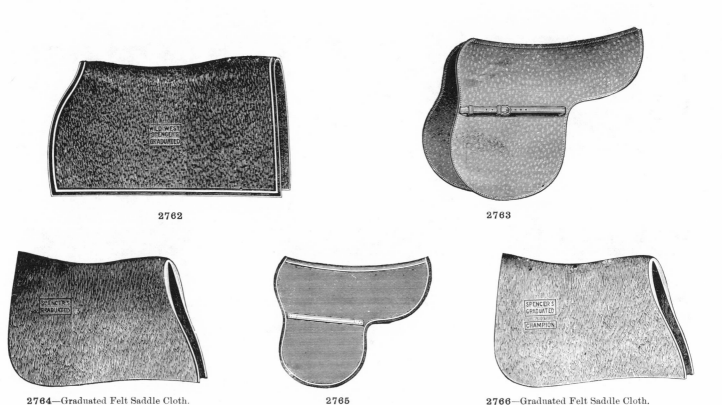

2762

2763

2764—Graduated Felt Saddle Cloth.

2765

2766—Graduated Felt Saddle Cloth.

LADIES' SADDLE CLOTHS.

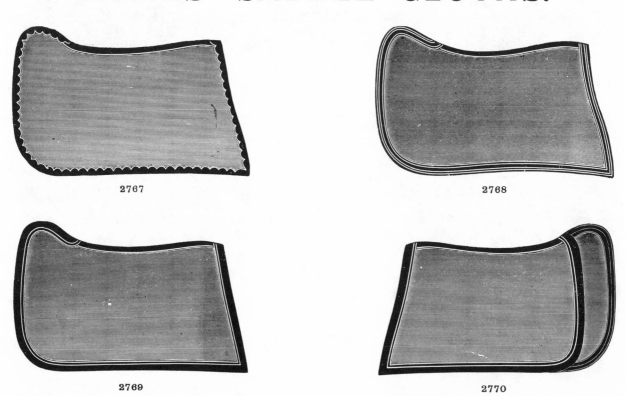

2767

2768

2769

2770

MANUFACTURING ESTABLISHMENT OF C. M. MOSEMAN & BROTHER,

WALSALL, NEAR LONDON, ENGLAND.

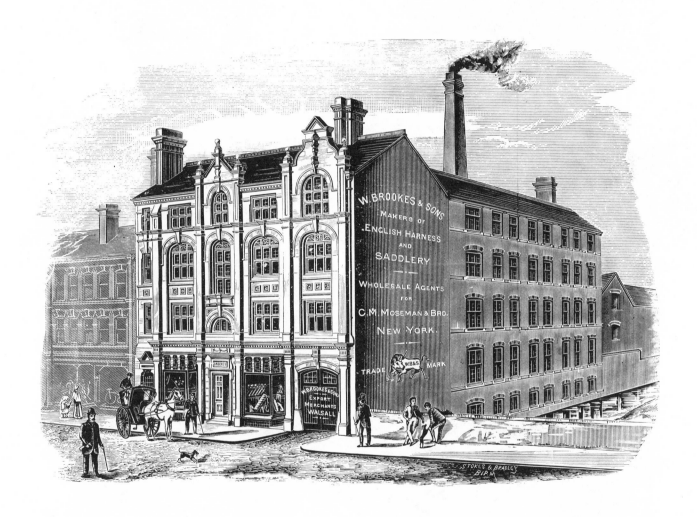

Makers of High Class Saddles, Bridles, etc. for the Hunt, the Race, Steeplechase, Polo Playing,

the Park, Road and School.

Also, Harness for Four-in-Hand, Tandem, Pair or Single Horse Traps, Broughams, Cabs, etc.

Horse Clothing, Rugs, Rollers, Muzzles, etc., and, in fact,

Everything for the Complete Equipment of a First Class Establishment.

SADDLES.

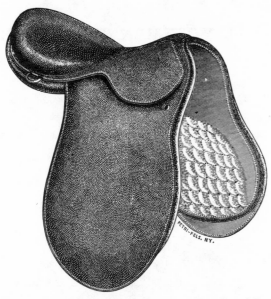

2771— All over Pigskin, Cut Back Tree, Plain Flap, French Panel, Hunting Saddle.

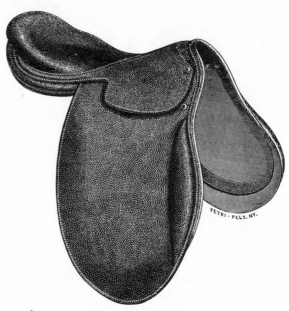

2772—All over Pigskin, Cut Back Tree, Leather inside Safe, Raised Knee Pad Hunting Saddle.

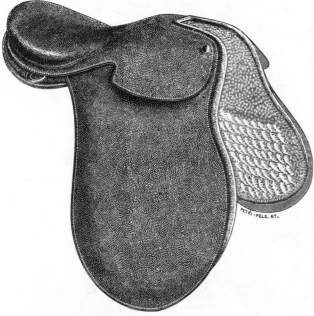

2773—Deep Cut Back Plain Solid Flap, High Class Hunting Saddle.

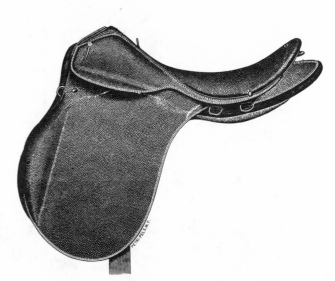

2774—Full Shaftoe Shifting Panel Tourist Saddle.

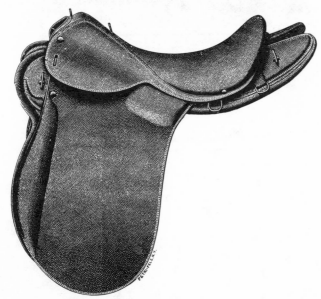

2775—Full Shaftoe Shifting Panel Tourist Saddle, with Fans and Burs.

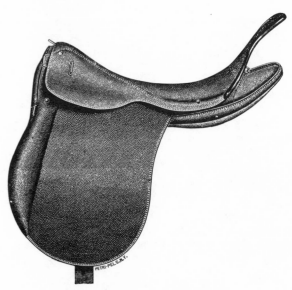

2776—Shifting Panel Military Saddle.

GENTLEMEN'S SADDLES.

Made with all the Latest Improvements at our Shops in England.

2777—Ready for a Canter.

All of our Gent's Saddles have the New Patent Spring Bar, which releases the rider in case of being thrown by the Horse.

See New and Old Style.

2778—The Old Style.

2779—The New Style.

SADDLES.

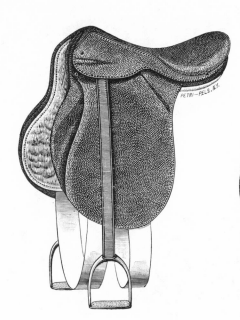

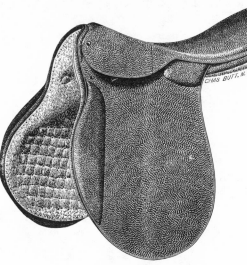

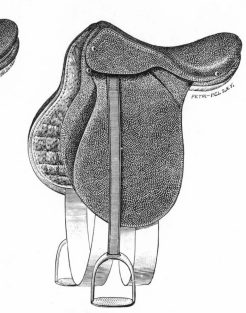

2780—Park Saddle.

7181—Hunting Saddle.

2782—Park Saddle.

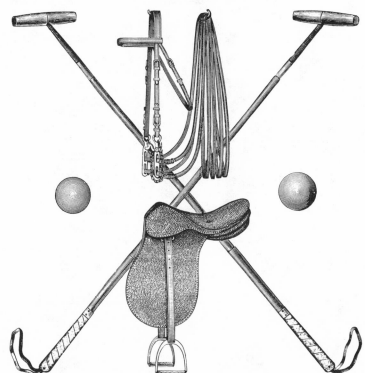

2783—Polo Saddle, Bridle, Mallets and Balls.

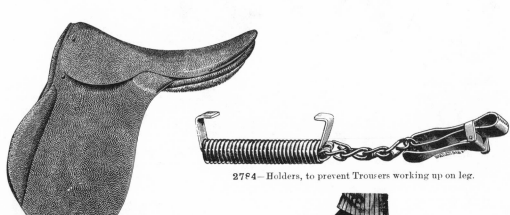

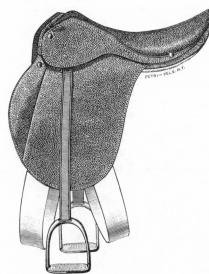

2785—Park Saddle.

2784—Holders, to prevent Trousers working up on leg.

2786—Showing Holders in use.

2787—Park Saddle.

POLO GOODS.

No. 5.—Polo Saddles, Bridles, Mallets, Balls and Belts ; also Boots to protect the Horses' Legs from the Mallet

HUNTING, RACING AND PARK SPURS.

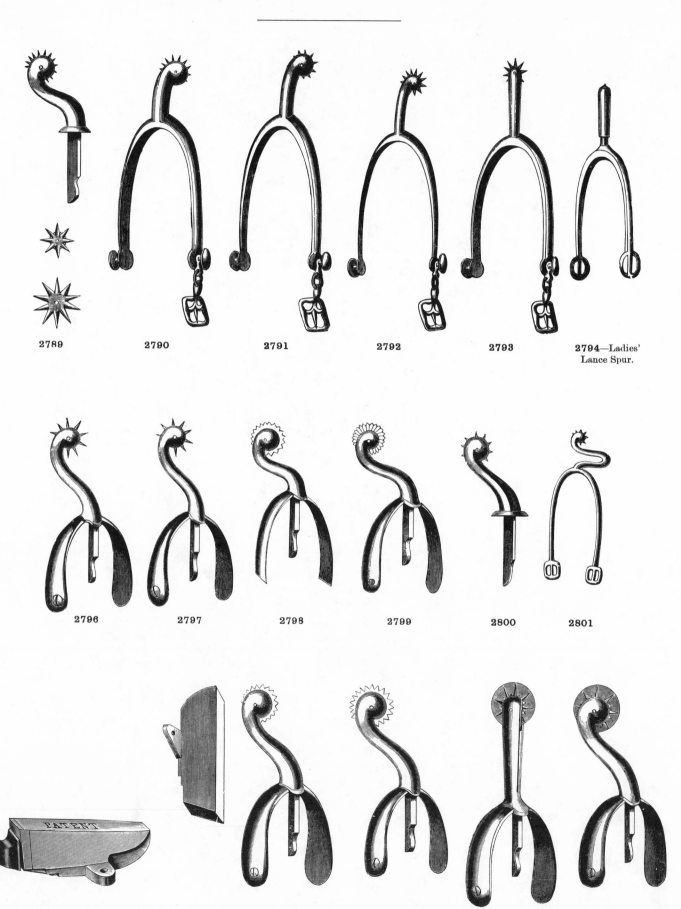

2789   2790   2791   2792   2793   2794—Ladies' Lance Spur.

2796   2797   2798   2799   2800   2801

2802—Spur Box with Trousers Protector.   2803   2804   2805   2806   2807

SPURS AND SPUR ROWELS.

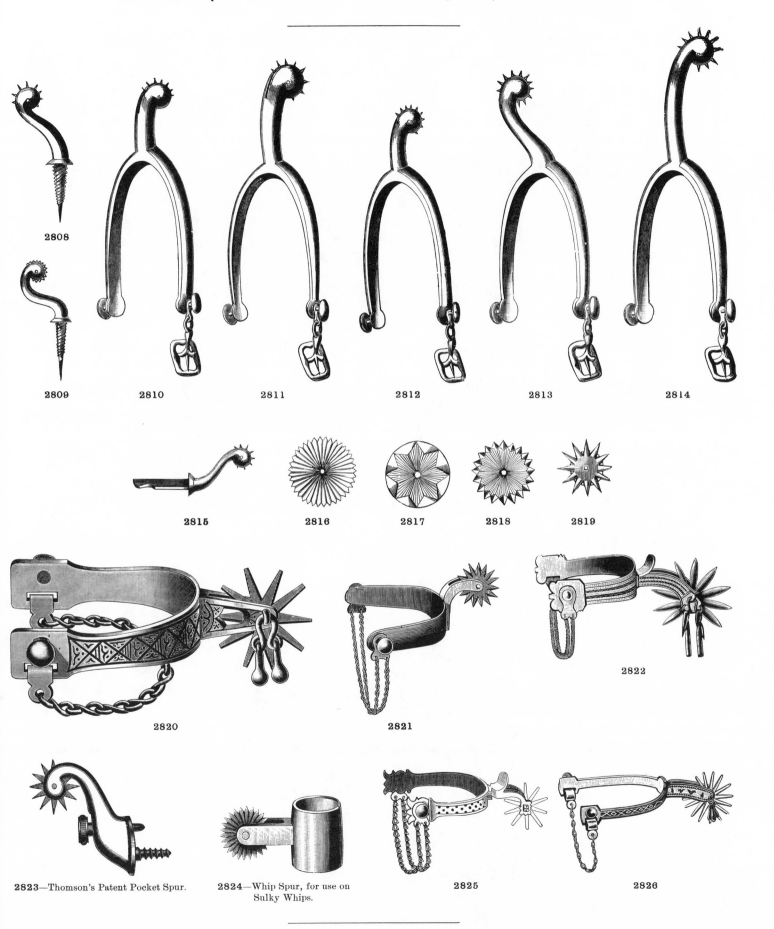

2808

2809

2810

2811

2812

2813

2814

2815   2816   2817   2818   2819

2820   2821   2822

2823—Thomson's Patent Pocket Spur.   2824—Whip Spur, for use on Sulky Whips.   2825   2826

We have a great variety of Spurs of Medium and Fine Quality, adapted to all purposes, made by many different makers; the variety being too great we cannot show them all here.

SADDLES.

2827—Adjustable Horn Full Cut Back French Tree Ladies' Saddle, with Safety Stirrup, Fitzwilliam Girth, Super Leather Bridle and Martingale complete ready for action.

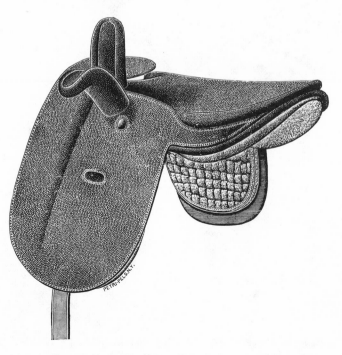

2828—Adjustable Horn Full Cut Back French Tree All over Pigskin Ladies' Saddle.

SADDLES.

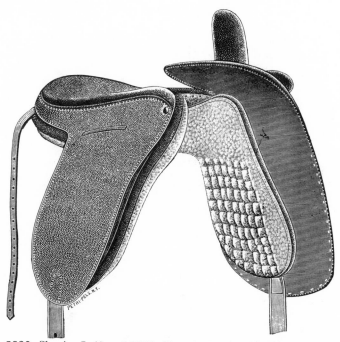

2829—Showing Front and Offside View of a French Cut Back Tree Ladies' Saddle.

2830—Showing Inside and Offside View of a French Tree Ladies' Saddle, Made for Diagonal Balance Girth.

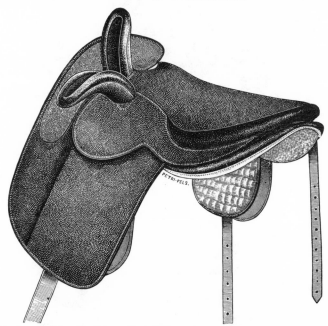

2831—Showing an Underview of a French Tree Ladies' Saddle.

2832—Inserted Doeskin Seat and Raised Eave Pigskin French Tree Ladies' Saddle.

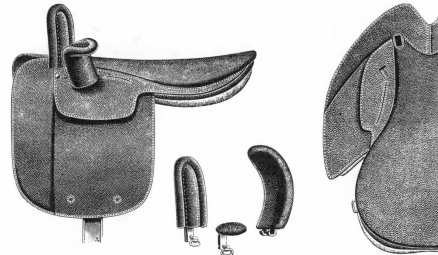

2833—Interchangeable Reversible Right or Left Hand Ladies' Saddle of different grades.

LADIES' SADDLES AND CRUPPERS.

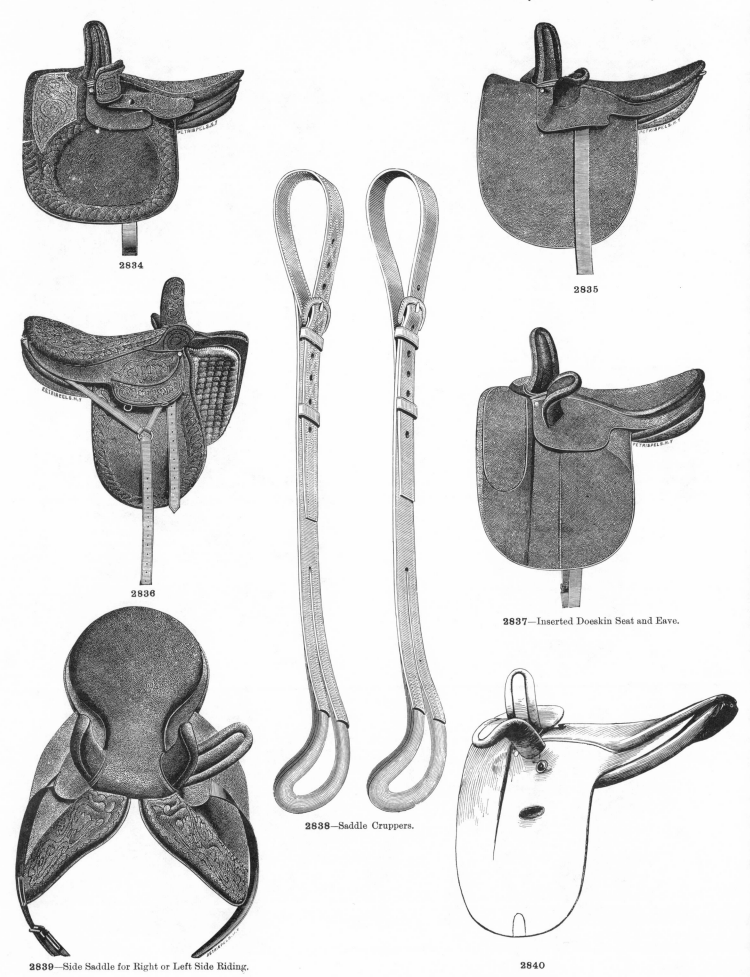

2834

2835

2836

2837—Inserted Doeskin Seat and Eave.

2838—Saddle Cruppers.

2839—Side Saddle for Right or Left Side Riding.

2840

WICKER CHAIR SADDLES
FOR CHILDREN.

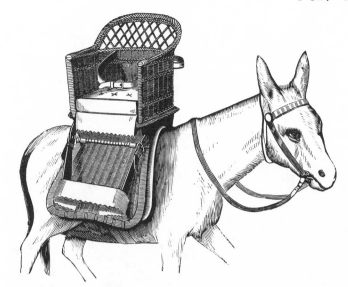

2842—Single Seat Chair Saddle.

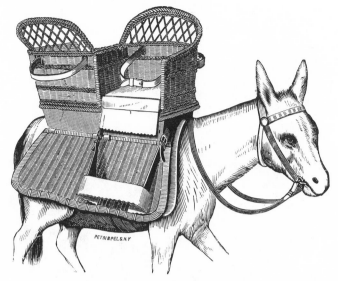

2843—Double Seat Chair Saddle.

2844

2845

2846—Pilch for Boy or Girl.
See 2848.

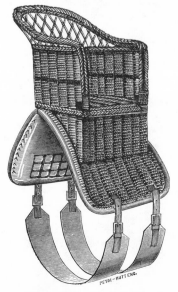

2847—Wicker Chair Saddle.

2848—Pilch for Boy or Girl,
with movable front.

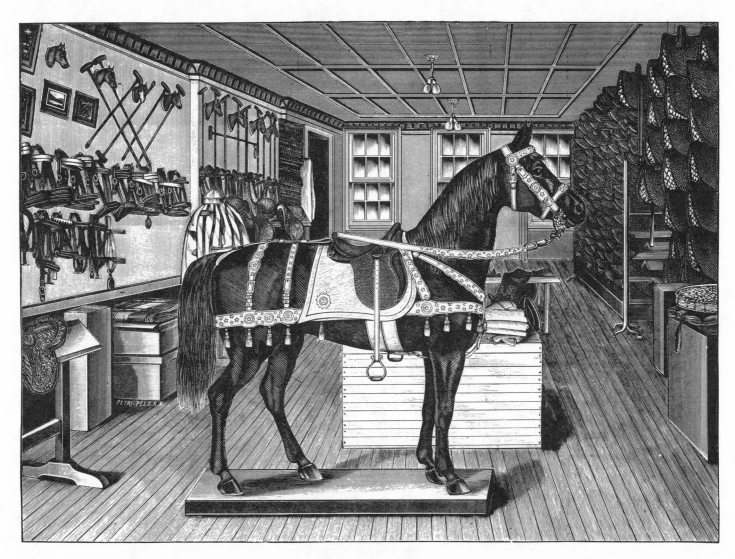

2849—Taken from a photo of a part of one of our Floors in Chambers Street, New York.

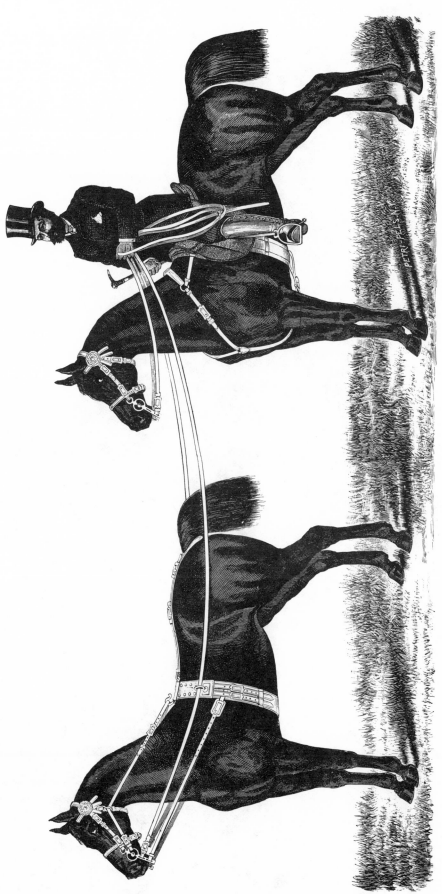

2850—White Buff Leather Tandem Riding Harness, made in all styles for the Road or Ring.

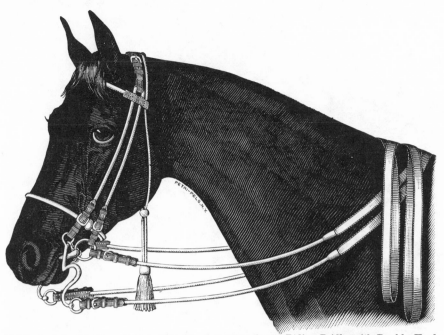

2851—Best Quality Round White Whip Cord, Leather Crown Riding Bridle, with Double Head and Double Reins, Tassel Throat, Fine Steel Bit, Bradoon and Chin Chain.

2852—Same as above, with Single Head and Double Reins, Curb Bit and Chin Chain.

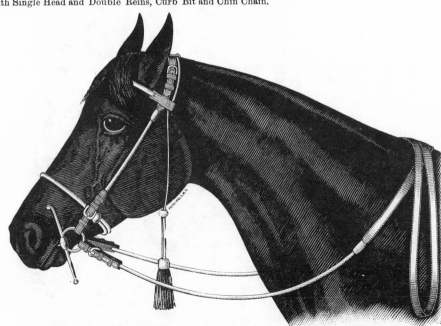

2853—Same as above, with Single Head, Single Rein and Full Cheek Snaffle Bit.

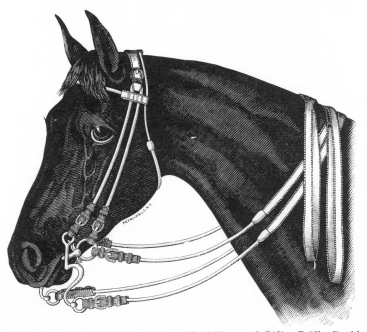

2854—Round White Whip Cord, Linen Head Weymouth Riding Bridle, Double Head and Reins, Sliding Loop Throat, Steel Port Bit and Bradoon and Chin Chain.

2855—Round White Whip Cord, Linen Head Pelham Bridle with Single Head and Double Reins, Steel Port Curb Bit and Chin Chain.

2856—Round White Whip Cord, Linen Head Snaffle Bridle, Sliding Loop Throat, Full Cheek Snaffle Bit.

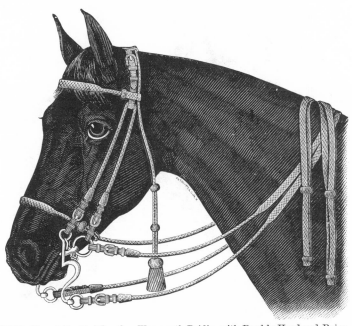

2857—Round Braided Leather Weymouth Bridle, with Double Head and Reins, Tassel Throat, Steel Port Bit and Bradoon, Chin Chain.

2858—Round Braided Leather Pelham Bridle, with Tassel Throat, Single Head and Double Reins, Steel Port Curb Bit and Chin Chain.

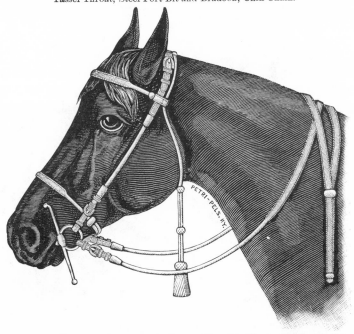

2859—Round Braided Leather Snaffle Bridle with Single Head and Rein, Tassel Throat and Full Cheek Snaffle Bit.

2860—Super Quality, Flat Cheek, Double Head and Rein Weymouth Bridle, Stitched Nose and Brow Band, all over Silver on White Metal Buckles Both Sides Finished, Fine Hard Steel Hand Forged Port Bit and Bradoon, Curb Chain and Chin Strap.

2861—Super Quality Pelham or Single Head and Double Rein Bridle, Fine Steel Hand Forged Bit, Curb Chain and Chin Strap.

2862—Super Quality Snaffle.

2863—First Quality, Flat Cheek Weymouth Bridle, Plated Buckles, Stitched Nose Band, Steel Port Bit and Bradoon, Curb Chain and Chin Strap.

2864—First Quality, Flat Cheek Pelham Bridle, Stitched Nose Band, Plated Buckles, Steel Port Bit, Curb Chain and Chin Strap.

2865—First Quality, Flat Cheek Snaffle Bridle, Stitched Nose Band, Plated Buckles, Full Cheek Snaffle Bit.

2866—Medium Quality, Flat Cheek Weymouth Bridle, Plated Buckles, Steel Port Bit and Bradoon, Curb Chain and Lip Strap.

2867—Medium Quality, Flat Cheek Pelham Bridle, Plated Buckles, Steel Port Bit, Curb Chain and Lip Strap.

2868—Medium Quality Snaffle Bridle, Full Cheek Steel Bit.

2869—Heavy Exercising Snaffle Bridle.

2870—Heavy Exercising Snaffle Bridle, Bit Looped in.

2871—Light Race Bridle, Colored Brow Band, with One or Two Reins, Egg But, Steel Jointed Mouth Bit Looped in .

BRIDLES.

2872—Stallion Bridle, with Leading Bar and Rein.

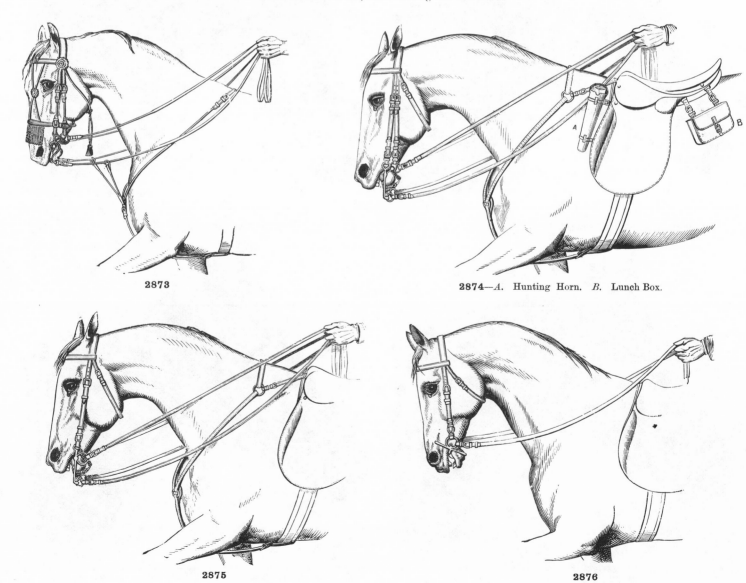

2873

2874—*A.* Hunting Horn. *B.* Lunch Box.

2875

2876

MARTINGALES AND BRIDLES.

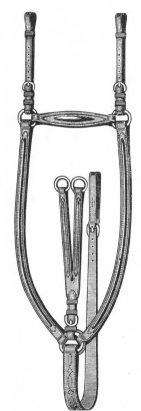
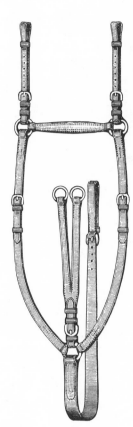
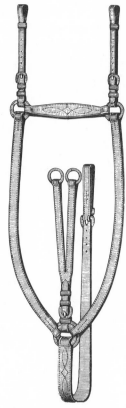
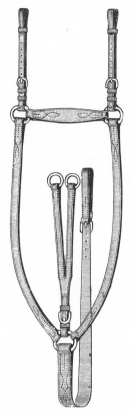
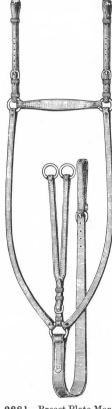

2877—Breast Plate Martingale with Raised Centre in Body and Neck, Stitched Sides.

2878—Adjustable Body Breast Plate Martingale.

2879—Lined and Stitched Body, Neck and Ring Piece, Breast Plate.

2880—Breast Plate Martingale, Figured Body and Neck.

2881—Breast Plate Martingale, Full Plain.

2882—Stallion Lead Bridle, with Plain Nose and Brow Band.

2883—Stallion Lead Bridle, with Stitched Nose and Brow Band.

LADIES' AND GENTS' STIRRUPS.

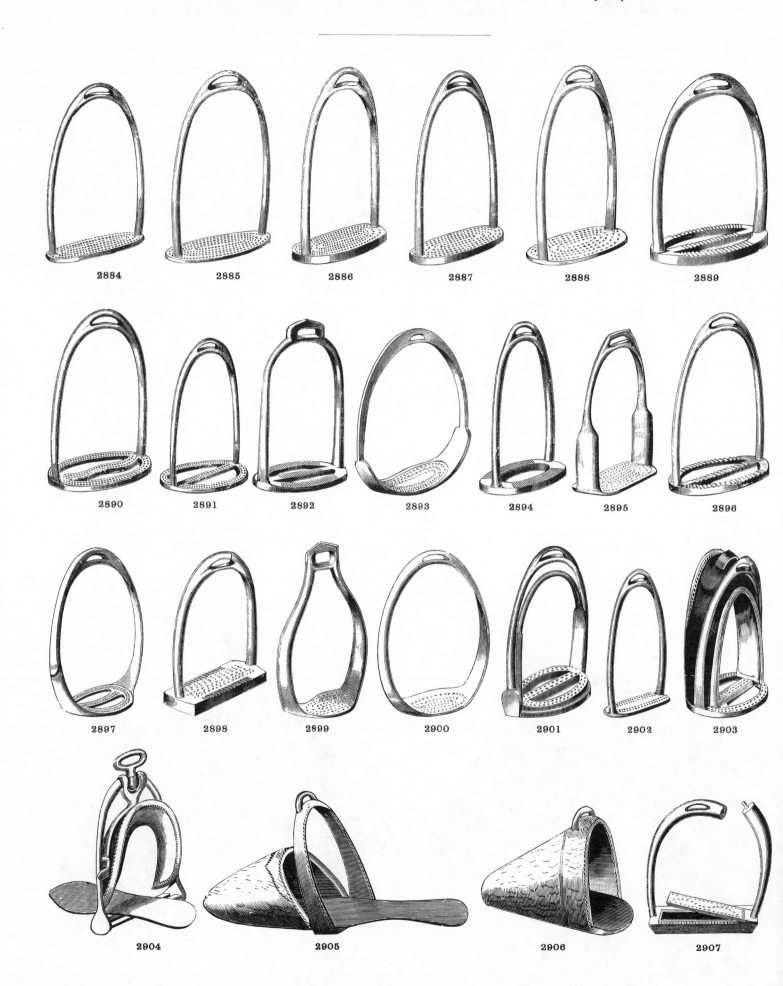

2884 2885 2886 2887 2888 2889

2890 2891 2892 2893 2894 2895 2896

2897 2898 2899 2900 2901 2902 2903

2904 2905 2906 2907

LADIES' AND GENTS' STIRRUPS.

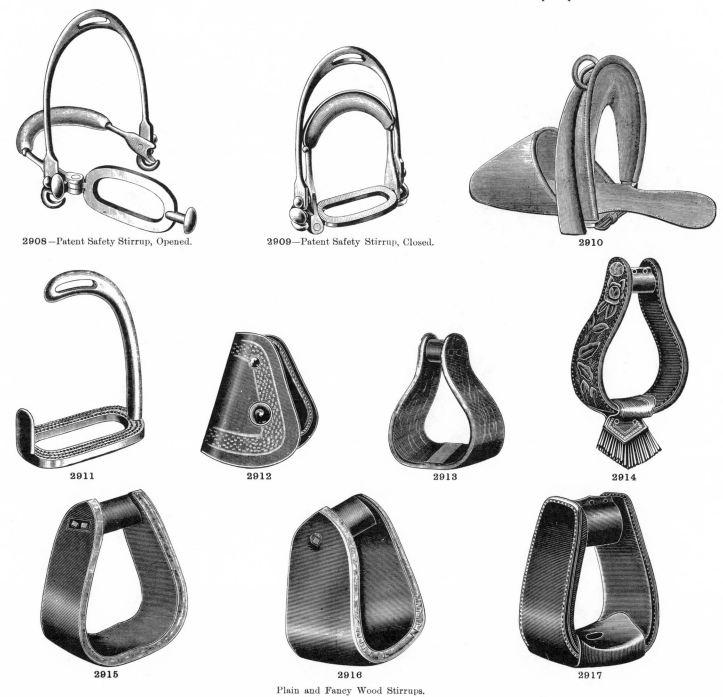

2908—Patent Safety Stirrup, Opened.

2909—Patent Safety Stirrup, Closed.

2910

2911

2912

2913

2914

2915

2916

2917

Plain and Fancy Wood Stirrups.

WALLACE'S PATENT ADJUSTABLE STIRRUP PAD.

2918—Gents' Pad.

2919—Pad Adjusted to Stirrup.

2920—Ladies' Pad.

Can be attached to any Stirrup in one minute by bending the Prongs around bottom.

SADDLE GIRTHS.

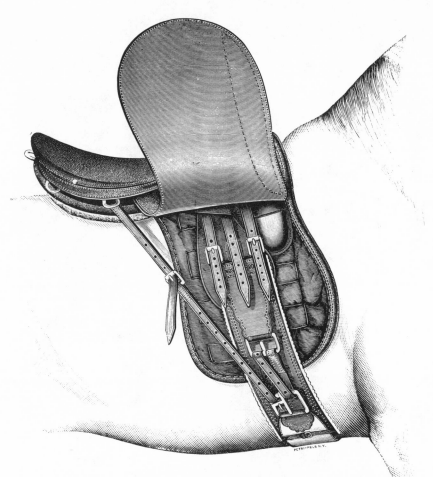

2921—Lane's Patent Adjustable Saddle Girth, shown on Gentlemen's Saddle.

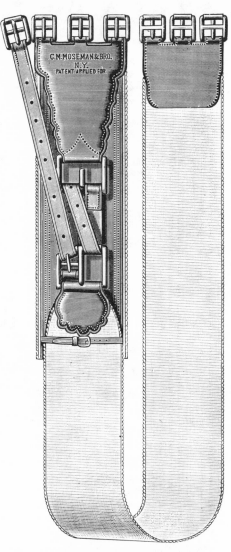

2922—Lane's Patent Adjustable Saddle Girth.

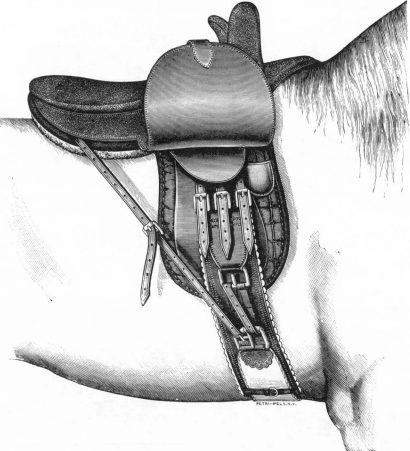

2923—Lane's Patent Adjustable Saddle Girth of White or Fawn Colored Webs, shown on Ladies' Saddle.

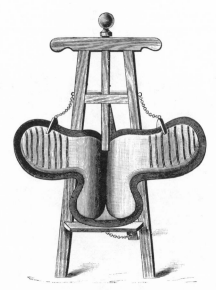

2924—Iron or Wood Rack on which to Dry Saddles.

SADDLE GIRTHS.

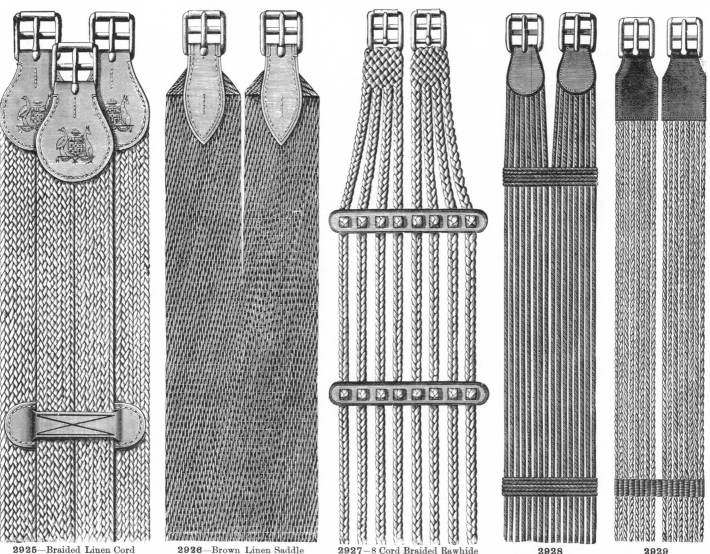

2925—Braided Linen Cord Fitzwilliam Saddle Girth.

2926—Brown Linen Saddle Girth.

2927—8 Cord Braided Rawhide Saddle Girth.

2928   **2929**
Fine Linen Corded Web Saddle Girths, Light and Strong.

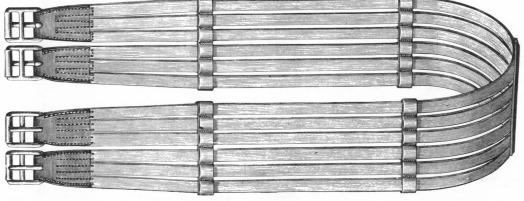

2930—Strong Linen Tubular Web Saddle Girth.

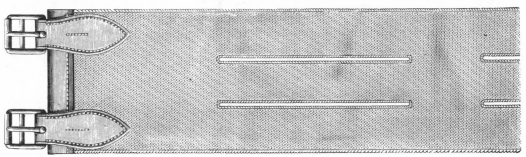

2931—Fine Linen Saddle Girth, Ventilated.

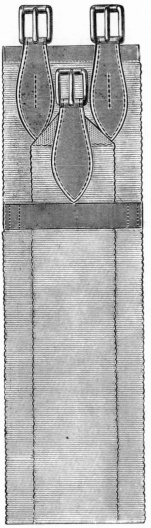

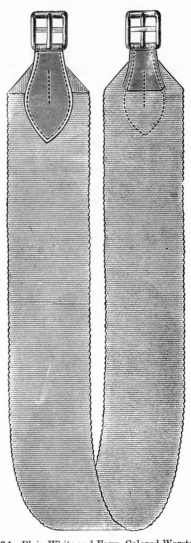

2932—Plain White and Fawn Color Worsted Fitzwilliam Saddle Girth.

2933—Plain White and Fawn Colored Worsted Saddle Girth, 2 to $3\frac{1}{4}$ inches wide.

2934—Plain White and Fawn Colored Worsted Saddle Girth, 2 to $3\frac{1}{4}$ inches wide.

2935—Fine Beveled Edge Stirrup Leathers.

2936—Medium Quality Stirrup Leathers.

2937—Linen Stirrup Holder for Race Saddles.

MISCELLANEOUS

SECTION.

All Goods shown in this Section furnished at Lowest Wholesale Prices.

LEATHER AND CANVAS LEGGINGS.

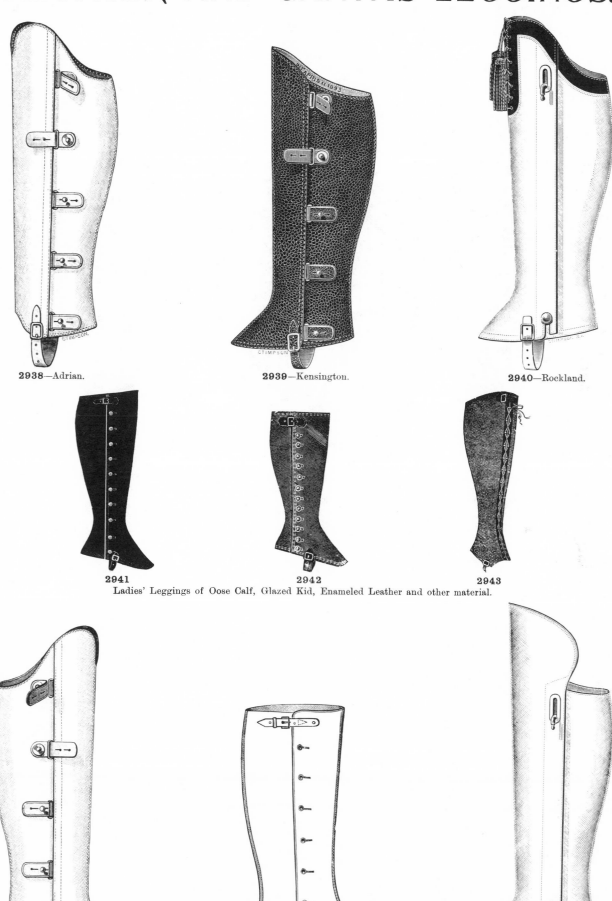

2938—Adrian.

2939—Kensington.

2940—Rockland.

2941　　　　2942　　　　2943

Ladies' Leggings of Oose Calf, Glazed Kid, Enameled Leather and other material.

2944—Regis.

2945—Derby.

2946—Havelock.

LEATHER AND CANVAS LEGGINGS.

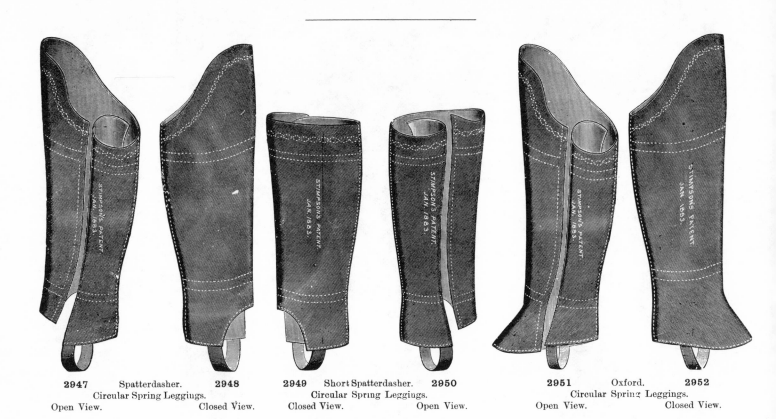

2947	Spatterdasher.	**2948**	**2949**	Short Spatterdasher.	**2950**	**2951**	Oxford.	**2952**
	Circular Spring Leggings.			Circular Spring Leggings.			Circular Spring Leggings.	
Open View.		Closed View.	Closed View.		Open View.	Open View.		Closed View.

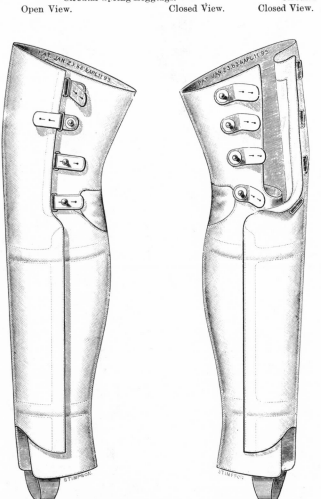
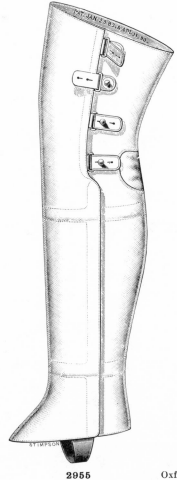
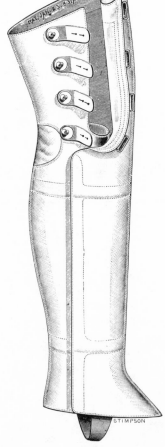

2953	Spatter Hunting.	**2954**	**2955**	Oxford Hunting.	**2956**
	Circular Spring Leggings.			Circular Spring Leggings.	
Closed View.		Open View.	Closed View.		Open View.

LEATHER AND CANVAS LEGGINGS.

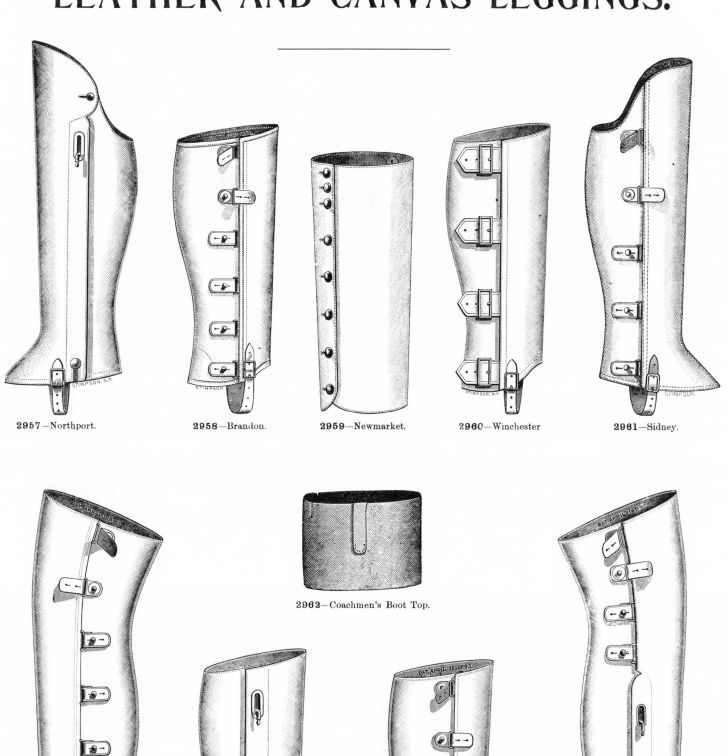

2957—Northport. **2958**—Brandon. **2959**—Newmarket. **2960**—Winchester **2961**—Sidney.

2962—Coachmen's Boot Top.

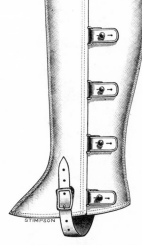
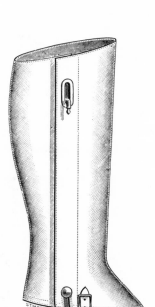
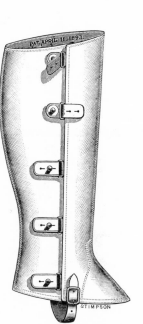
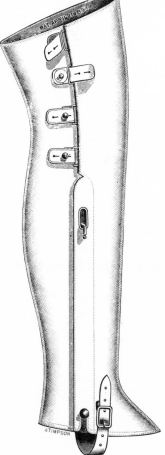

2963—Monmouth Hunting. **2964**—Hampden. **2965**—Lancelot. **2966**—York Hunting.

Hunting and Coaching Horns, Baskets, Etc.

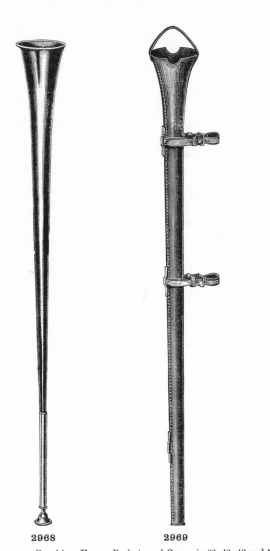

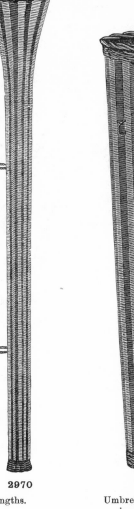

2967
Drag Horn with Valve
Attachments.

2968   **2969**
Coaching Horns, Baskets and Cases, in 36, 42, 48 and 52 inch lengths.

2970

2971
Umbrella Baskets in different
sizes, for Coaching, etc.

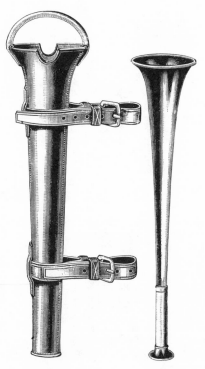

2972—Umbrella Baskets in different sizes, for Coaching, etc.

2973   **2974**
Hunting Horn and Case to Strap on Saddle.

2975   **2976**
Glass Hunting Flask and Case to Strap on Saddle.

MISCELLANEOUS.

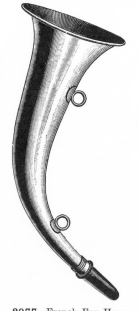

2977—French Fox Horn.

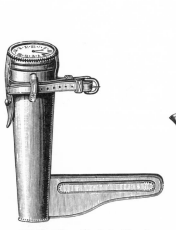

2978—Glass Flask inside of
Leather Case with Watch
in Lid, to Strap on
Hunting Saddle.

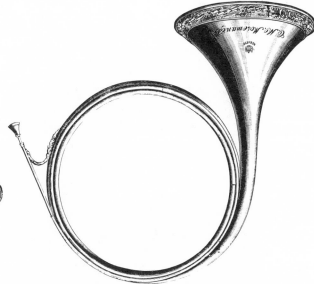

2979—French Coaching Horn

2980

2981

Hunting Lunch Box and Case to Strap on Saddle.

2982

2983

Hunting Lunch Box and Case to Strap on Saddle.

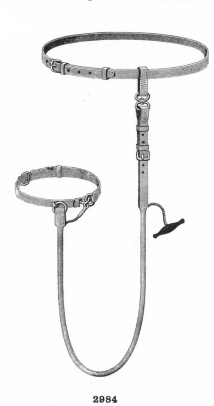

2984

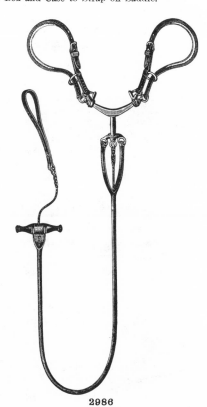

2985

2986

Dog Starters, Retrievers and Greyhound Slips.

BELTS.

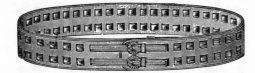

2987—Block In and Out Pattern, Brown Leather Belt.

2988—Basket Pattern Leather Belt.

2989—Lizzard, Snake, and other Skins.

2990—Fine Basket Pattern Leather Belt.

2991—Fancy Leather Belt.

2992—Celluloid Belt in two Colors.

2993—Garter.

2994—Brown Leather Belt, Beautiful Finish.

2995—Fine Colored Leather Belt.

2996—Fine Woolen Web Belt.

2997—Fine Woolen Web Belt.

2998—Fine Woolen Web Belt.

2999—Fine Woolen Web Belt.

3000—Fine Woolen Web Belt.

3001—Fine Brown Leather Belt.

MISCELLANEOUS.

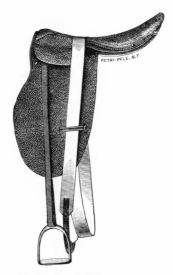

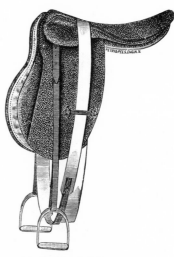

3002—Exercising Saddle.   Light Weight.

3003—Racing Saddle.

3004—Racing Saddle.

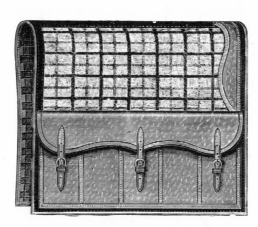

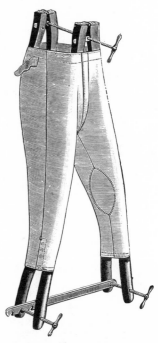

3005—Jockey's Racing Boots, all sizes.

3006—Saddle Cloth for carrying Weight under
Race Saddle.

3007—Breeches Stretcher for Drying and Cleaning
Racing Breeches.

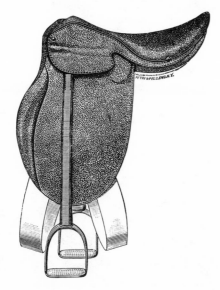

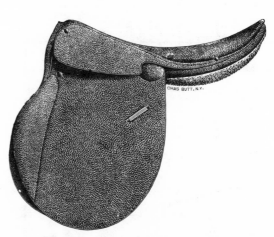

3008—Working Saddle.

3009—Exercising Saddle.   Heavy Weight.

SULKY OR TRACK WHIPS.

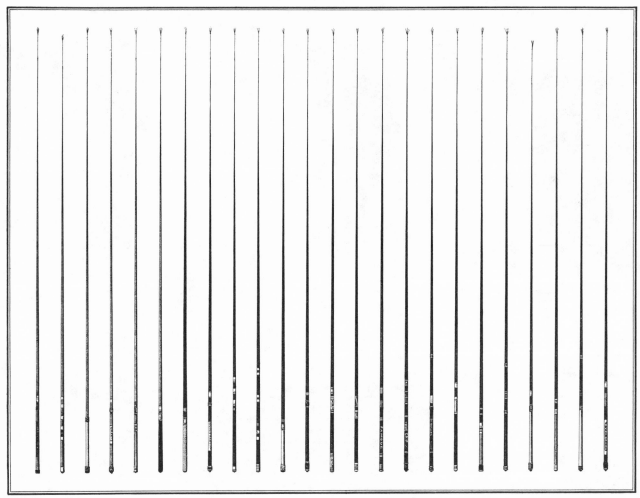

3010 3011 3012 3013 3014 3015 3016 3017 3018 3019 3020 3021 3022 3023 3024 3025 3026 3027 3028 3029 3030 3031 3032 3033

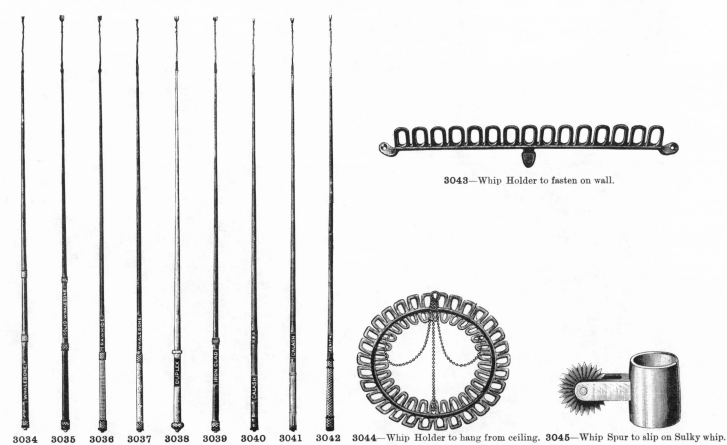

3043—Whip Holder to fasten on wall.

3034   3035   3036   3037   3038   3039   3040   3041   3042   **3044**—Whip Holder to hang from ceiling. **3045**—Whip Spur to slip on Sulky whip.

3046—The Whittaker Spreader, Sliding on a Rod on the Shaft, with Wool Covered Elastics around Leg to make a Horse Travel Wide Behind.

3047—Holder to prevent a Horse from holding the reins under his tail and to keep him from switching it.

THE ALUMINUM TAIL FASTENER

For keeping the tail up without binding the dock.

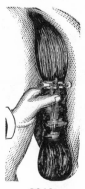 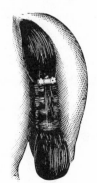

3048   3049

The cut on the left shows Fastener just before closing the clasp with separate strands around the post. The cut on the right shows Fastener as it appears in use.

GENERAL DIRECTIONS.

Divide the tail into two equal parts, twist them around each other four or five times like a rope, then fold up under the dock, lap the remaining ends around the dock until you have a few inches left, now push the long part of the Fastener down between the rolls and straight hair; open the Fastener, then draw the ends of tail over hook, as shown in left hand cut, screw both sides of clasp down, and there you are.

COSMOPOLITAN HOTEL

OPPOSITE C. M. MOSEMAN & BROTHER,

Chambers Street and West Broadway, - - - **NEW YORK, U. S. A.**

C. F. WILDEY, Proprietor.

ON THE EUROPEAN PLAN.   ROOMS, $1.00 PER DAY AND UPWARDS.

ONE OF THE BEST HOTELS FOR THE TRAVELING PUBLIC.

ACCOMMODATIONS FOR 400 GUESTS.   **PRICES POPULAR.**   THE LOCATION IS UNSURPASSED.

THIS HOTEL is located in the immediate vicinity of the largest Harness, Saddlery, Horse-Clothing, and other business houses, accessible to all places of interest and amusement, and to all railroad depots and other parts of the city, by street cars and elevated roads constantly passing its doors. It offers special inducement to those visiting the city on business or pleasure.

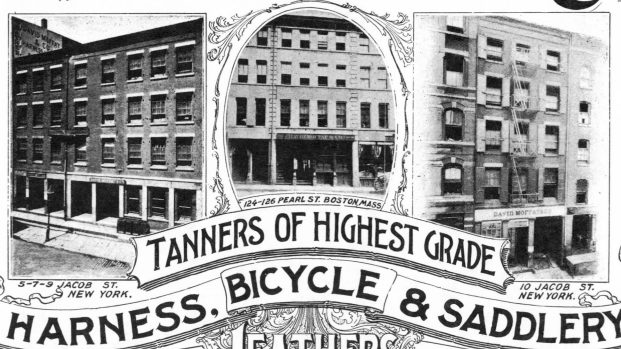

INDEX.

	PAGE.
Aprons, Waterproof	214
" Oil or Leather	214
" Carriage	214
Back Band Chains	116
Balling Irons	69
Bandages	18
Baskets, Manure	8
" Shopping	161
" Horn	294
" Coaching	294
Belts	296
Bells, Sleighing	230
Bits	121–132
" Drenching	68
Bit Holder for Polishing	20
Bitting Harness	88–89
Blackwell's Dumb Jockey	87
Blankets	193–213
Blanket Pins	217
" Giant Holder	211
" Breast	196
Boots, Horse	77–83
" Jockey	297
" Washing	21
" Shields	94
Bonner's Horse Cleaner	12
Boxes, Lunch and Case	295
Brackets, Harness	24–25
" Rein	24–25
" Saddle	24–25
" Lamp	23
" Bridle	24–25
Braid	27
Breast Collars, Double	174
" " Pads	117
" Chains	188
Breast Aprons	196
" Plate Martingales	283
Breeches Stretcher	297
Bridles, Riding	278–283
" Polo	268
" Stallion	206 & 282
" Fronts	162–167
Brooms	7, 8, 12
" Holder	25
Brushes	9–11
Button Sticks	11
" Rein	174
Buckets	21
Burnishers	20
Candles	23
Cards, Curry	13
Caps, Jockey	94
Carriage Heaters	161
Cases, Watch	160
" " with Rein Holder	160
" Lunch Box	295
Chains, Halter	186
" Rack	186
" Stall	186
" Pole	186
" Curb and Hooks	167
" Back Band	116
" Breast	188
Chamois Skins	121
Chimes, Sleighing	226–229
Chair Saddles	275
Clipping Machines	221–225
Clocks	160
Coaching Horns and Baskets	294
Coats, Waterproof, and Apron	214
" Hunting and Leggings	214
" Rubber	214
Collars	169
" Sweat	117
Collar Pads	117
Combs, Curry	13
" Mane	14
" Clipping	14
Cords	27
Covers, Horse, Oil or Rubber	214
" for Bicycle Sulky Wheels	217
" for Horses' Tails	217
Covering, Wool, for Harness	101
Cradles	68
Creepers, Ice	230
Crests and Monograms	168–169
Cruppers for Riding Saddles	274
Cushions, Sulky	94

	PAGE.
Dressings and Oils—Boston Coach Oil	22
Borsum's Pomade and Leg Polish	44
Brilliantine	45
Burnham's Leg Polish	45
Brown, E. & Sons, (London)	47–49
Clark's, (London)	56–57
Everett's Blackings, (London)	45
Evans' Saddle Paste, (London)	45
French Blacking	45
Gladding's	41
Goddard's (London)	45
Harris', (London)	46
Jamieson's, P. (Aberdeen)	42
Miller, Frank, Sons & Co	42
Propert's, (London)	50–55
Powers'	42
Richmond's, S. P. S.	44
Silicon	44
Miscellaneous	71
Dog and Greyhound Starters	295
Drenching Bits	68
Dumb Jockeys	87–88
Expanders, Hoof	82
Eye Shields	161
Fasteners, Tail	299
Feather Dusters	12
Feed Bags	117
" Boxes and Mangers	23
" Measures	21
Flasks, Hunting and Cases	294
Floats	68
Fly Nets	215–217
Foot Leveler	83
" Warmers	161
Forks	7
" Holders	25
Fox Horns and Cases	294
Frog Pads	84
Fronts	162–167
Gaiter, The Iowa	90
Gait Spreader	90
Girths for Riding Saddles	286–288
Gloves	160 & 170
Goat Harness	90
Guards, Dress or Wheel	103
Hair Shedders	13
Harness Covering, Wool	101
" Punches, Spring	19
" Housings	163
" Cleaning Racks, Movable	25
" " Closet "	25
" Brackets	25
" Double	174, 178–185
" Four-in-Hand	176–177
" Tandem Driving	108-109
" " Riding	277
" Heavy Draught	112
" Track	95
" Single	96–111
" Postillion	175
" Mule Cart	113–115
" Hoisting	117
" Goat	90
" Bitting	88–89
Halters	33–36
Halter Ties	38
" Chains	186
Hats, Cabby	161
Heaters for Carriage or Sleigh	161
Hitch Weight	36
Holders, Fork	25
" Broom	25
" Blanket	211
" Trousers	268
" Shaft	22
" Lamp	23
" Dash Lamp	23
Hoods, Rubber	214
" Woolen	94, 196
Hoof Expanders	82
" Picks	19
Hooks and Curb Chains	167
" Rein	25
" Harness Cleaning	25
Hopples	75, 80, 90
Horse Covers, Rubber or Oil	214
Horns, Drenching	68

	PAGE.
Horse Slings	69
Horns, Coaching and Basket	292
" Fox and Cases	294
Horns, Hunting and Cases	294
Hose, Carriage	21
Housings, Harness	163
Hunting Coats and Leggings	214
" Crops	152–154
" Horns and Cases	294
Ice Creepers	230
Jacks, Wagon and Carriage	22
Jockey Caps	94
" Arm Plates	94
" Boots	297
" Suits	297
" Weight Pads	297
Kicking Straps	90
Lamps	23
Lamp Holders	23
" Brackets	23
" Singeing	15 & 221
Lantern	23
Loops, Patent Trace	217
Leathers, Stirrup	288
Leggings	291–293
Lunch Box and Cases	295
Mangers	24
Mane Drags	15
Matting, Straw	26
Martingales and Breast Plates	283
Medicine Bottles	65
Medicines—Absorbine	67
Baker's	66
Bickmore's	69
Clark's, (London)	61–63
Curine	67
Caloric Vita	67
Campbell's	69
Dixon's	70
Extract Witch Hazel	69
Elliman's Son & Co. (Slough, Eng.)	71
Gombault's	66
Harvell's	70
Humphrey's	65
Kitchell's	67
Lieut. James', (London)	70
Miscellaneous	71
Naviculine	67
Oil Witch Hazel	69
Peat Moss	64, 218
Patt's	66
Pulsifer's	67
Stevens' Oint. (London)	70
Wallace's	66
Woodnutt's	70
Monograms and Crests	168–169
Nets	215–216
Odometers	101
Oil Covers, Horse	214
Oil Wagon Aprons	21
Oils and Dressings	22, 41–57, 71
Outfit, Racing	296
Pads, Breast Collar	117
" Cart Saddle	116
" Collar	117
" Saddle	117
" Rubber Stirrup	285
" Zinc Collar	117
" Frog	84
" Jockey Weight	297
Pails	21
Pillicons, Straw	26
Pillar Reins	27
Pins, Blanket	217
Pilch Saddles	275
Pole Chains	186
" Screens	174
Polo Mallets and Balls	268
" Bridles	268
Polishing Bags	20
Portable Telephone	24
Punches, Harness	19

INDEX—Continued.

	PAGE.
Plumes, Sleighing	226
Racks, Movable Harness Cleaning	25
" Boot Cleaning	22
" Harness	25
" Bridle	25
" Saddle Drying	287
" Sponge	25
Racing Saddles	297
Rein Buttons	174
" Holders, Loop	174
" " and Watch Case	160
" " Dashboard	160
" Safes	89
Remedies, Medicines	61–71, 218
Riding Saddles	234–261, 266, 267, 272–275, 297
" " Girths	286–288
" Bridles	278–283
Robes	190
Rosettes	162–164
Rollers and Surcingles	194, 195
Rowels, Spur	271
Rubbing Cloths	17
Rubber Stirrup Pads	285
" Boots	21
Rubber Horse Covers, Hoods, Wagon Aprons, Macintoshes, Coats	214
Saddles, Riding	234–261, 266, 267, 272–275, 297
" Sore Back	117
" Racing	297
" Cart	116
" Pads, Cart	116
" Cloths	263, 264, 268
" Girths	286–288
" Racks for Drying	288
Sand	20
Sandals	82
Salt Bricks	15
" " Holders	15
Seats, Folding	101
Seives	8–21
Shaft Tugs	116
" Holders	22

	PAGE.
Shaft Supporters	170
Shields for Boot	94
Shopping Basket	161
Shovels	7
Singeing Lamps	15, 221
" " Wick	15
Shoulder Knots	161
Slings	69
Sleighing Chimes and Bells	226–230
Snaps	187–189
Soaps—Frank Miller's	42
English Crown	43
Colgate's	43
Castile	43
Palm Oil	43
Saddle	43–45
Sockets, Whip	135
Spurs	270, 271
" Whip	271, 298
Spur Box	270
" Rowels	271
Springs, Draught	114
" Coil Tie	38
Sponges	21
Sponge Rack	25
" Boxes	25
Squegees	8
Stable Rubbers	17
" Dressing	26
Standards	29
Stallion Trusses	75
" Shields	75
Stirrups, Iron	284, 285
" Slippers	284
" Wooden	285
Stirrup Pads	285
" Leathers	288
Starters, Dog and Greyhound	295
Stretchers, Breeches	297
Storm Covers	214
Stall Chains	186
Straw Mattings	26
" Pillicons	26
Suits, Horse Clothing	204–206, 213

	PAGE.
Surcingles and Rollers	194, 195
Sulky Wheel Covers	217
Sweat Collars	117
" Scrapers	15, 16
Syringes	69
Tail Ties	8, 299
" Squarers	28
" Covers	217
" Fastener	299
Telephones, Portable	24
Ties, Coil Spring	38
Toe Guards	161
" Weights	76
Trace Loops, Patent Adjustable	217
Trouser Holders	268
Trusses, Stallion	75
Tubs	21
Veterinary Goods—Balling Irons	69
Cradles	68
Crib Straps	69
Drench Bits	68
" Horns	68
Floats	68
Medicine Bottles	68
Slings	69
Syringes	69
Wagon Jacks	22
Watches	160
Watch Cases	160
" " and Rein Holders	160
Wagon Aprons	214
Waterproof Coat and Apron	214
Weight Pads, Jockey	297
Whips	137–155, 298
Whip Sockets	135
" Holders	155, 298
" Stand	155
Wick for Lamps	15
Whittaker Spreaders	299
Wool, Harness Covering	101

ILLUSTRATIONS:

Use of Rubbing Cloth	17
Stable Dressed with Straw Matting	27
Squaring Horses Tail	28
Stuffing Horses Foot with Peat Moss	64
Racing Scene with Bicycle Sulkies	93
Carriage with and without Dress Guard	103
Village Cart and the late W. C. Moseman, Esq., Father of the Firm	104
Tandem Club	107

Buying Prize Winners at Tattersalls	159
On the Road behind a Pair of Trotters	173
Breaking Four-in-Hand on the Diamond Ranch, Wyoming	178
High Class and Comfortable Winter Requisites	181
One of our Horse Clothing Show Rooms	193
Burlington Blanket Show	210
Stable Showing Sanitary Bedding	216
Sioux Tribe of Indians on War Path	233

Full Equipments for Riding Parties	262
Manufacturing Establishment at Walsall, England	265
Polo Scene	269
Saddle Department	276
White Buff Tandem Riding Harness	277
Racing Outfit Complete	297
Moffat's Leather	300
Cosmopolitan Hotel	301

" PROGRESS "

IS THE WATCHWORD OF THE PRESENT ERA.

NEW IDEAS AND NEW INVENTIONS

FOR

INCREASING THE SPEED OF THE HORSE

AND

PROMOTING THE COMFORT OF THE DRIVER

ARE DEVISED AND PATENTED DAILY.

CONSEQUENTLY, there will continue to be many useful appliances introduced to the public long after this book has found its place among the lovers of the horse in all parts of the world.

THEREFORE: Should you not find here what you are looking for, do not hesitate to write us about it, and we will at once give your wants attention.

Yours for business,

C. M. MOSEMAN & BROTHER.